The Solitary Self

The Solitary Self

Individuality in the *Ancrene Wisse*

Linda Georgianna

Harvard University Press
Cambridge, Massachusetts, and London, England
1981

Publication of this book has been aided by a grant from
   the Andrew W. Mellon Foundation

Library of Congress Cataloging in Publication Data

Georgianna, Linda, 1947
   The solitary self.

      Includes bibliographical references and index.
      1. Ancren riwle.   2.   Monasticism and religious orders for
women.   3.   Monasticism and religious orders—Rules.   4.   Individuality in literature.   5.   Solitude in literature.   I.   Title.
PR1810.G4   255'.901   81-2190
ISBN 0-674-81751-6   AACR2

To Robert and Catherine

Acknowledgments

THIS study had its beginnings in a graduate seminar given in 1970 by Professor Robert Hanning of Columbia University, where I learned to read medieval literature and where I enjoyed for the first time the excitement and pleasure of an academic community functioning at its best. My warmest thanks go to two members of that seminar, Robert Stein and George Santiccioli, and particularly to its director, Robert Hanning, who, as teacher, scholar, and now a good friend as well, has been continually generous with his time, his insights, and his good humor. My aim as a teacher remains to direct now and then a seminar as rewarding for some of my students as that extraordinary seminar was for me.

Others have also contributed in numerous ways to the completion of this study. My thanks are extended to Professors C. David Benson, Joan Ferrante, Howard Schless, Siegfried Wenzel, and Elizabeth Kirk, all of whom read various versions of this book with great care and uncommon common sense. Arlene Jacobs prepared the manuscript patiently and intelligently, and a number of friends, including Mary Lamb, Maya Anyas, Jean McGarry, and Dennis Jacobs, offered advice, moral support, books, and coffee on call.

I am grateful also to the Whiting Foundation of New York and to the University of California, Irvine, for their financial support.

My warmest thanks to Robert Newsom, my husband and always my first and finest reader.

I wish especially to acknowledge the following publishers of editions and translations of medieval texts: Cistercian Publications (Kalamazoo, Michigan), for permission to quote from the *Works of Aelred of Rievaulx*, I, *Treatises and the Pastoral Prayer*, trans. Mary Paul Macpherson, 1971; the Council of the Early English Text Society, for permission to quote from *The English Text of the Ancrene Riwle: Ancrene Wisse (CCCC402)*, trans. J. R. R. Tolkien, 1962; Les Editions du Cerf, for permission to quote from *La Vie de recluse et la prière pastorale de Aelred de Rievaulx*, Sources Chretiennes, 76, ed. and trans. Charles Dumont, 1961.

Contents

Introduction
1

~ 1 ~
Self and Religious Rules
8

~ 2 ~
Self and Society: The Solitary Life
32

~ 3 ~
Self and the Sacrament of Confession
79

~ 4 ~
Self-Awareness and Sin
120

Notes
145

Index
167

Despise the world, despise nothing;
Despise yourself, despise despising yourself:
These are four good things.

—Abbess Herrad of Hohenberg,
Garden of Delights

Note on Editions and Translations

In quoting from the *Ancrene Wisse,* I have used J. R. R. Tolkien's edition of the Corpus Christi College Cambridge manuscript (CCCC 402), published by the Early English Text Society (London: Oxford University Press, 1962); of all the manuscripts, this one is the most consistent and, therefore, most readable. I have silently expanded abbreviations and have used those scribal insertions necessary for the sense of a passage without indicating the insertions, as Tolkien does, with angled brackets. I have also supplied modern punctuation to aid readability. All references are to this edition, except where otherwise noted, and are given in parentheses immediately following quotations as T plus page number.

All but a few translated passages from the *Ancrene Wisse* are taken from the excellent modern translation of M. B. Salu (London: Burns and Oates, 1955), and are given in parentheses immediately following the translation as S plus page number. Where there is no reference to a translator, the translation is my own.

Translations from modern French are mine.

Introduction

"I HAVE become a problem to myself," Augustine wrote at the end of his *Confessions*, the book that most eloquently demonstrated to the postclassical world that Christianity could provide both a reason and a method for examining one's personal history, the collection of unique though mundane experiences that make up an individual's life.[1] The seed that Augustine had planted was slow to sprout, and there is little written evidence in the early Middle Ages of individuals seeking to understand their personal histories. Not until the twelfth century did the idea take firm hold, and scholars in diverse fields have begun to recognize as the hallmark of the Twelfth-Century Renaissance the age's interest in the constellation of values that we associate with individualism, centering on the personal and private rather than the communal and public. My own study of the cultural milieu of the late twelfth and early thirteenth centuries convinces me that the period is crucial to our understanding of medieval humanism, and further, that the *Ancrene Wisse* in particular demonstrates better than any text I know the complexity with which medieval writers could examine and describe the problem of the self.

Since Charles Homer Haskins first focused attention on the Twelfth-Century Renaissance, readers have become increasingly interested in the period beginning in the late eleventh century and running through the early thirteenth century.[2] Those years saw the flowering of the vernacular languages, the rise of romance, the emergence of the first universities, the sudden expansion of town life, and the Church's growing commitment to the life of this world. It was a period marked not only by a general reawakening of intellectual activity, but particularly by an interest in the individual as he relates to himself, his God, and his world.

R. W. Southern, in his seminal essay "From Epic to Romance," locates a number of cultural shifts that indicate what he describes as "the emergence of the individual from his communal background."[3] Perhaps the most important is the remarkable shift in the image of God during this relatively brief period, away from the portrayal of God as a remote, mysteriously majestic, but vengeful Lord toward an interest in Christ, described as the God-Man whose generous Father sent Him to teach the world through His

I

suffering how to live and love. The emphasis upon Christ's human suffering gives rise, as Southern suggests, not only to a more emotional and
tender religious atmosphere, but also to an increased interest in human
feeling itself. After all, Christ's life seen as a journey through the world of
human experience, from birth to death, from hope to fear to hope again,
lent a kind of validity to the world and to human experience that it had
never had, even in the eyes of Augustine. Thus it is probably no accident
that the secular genre of romance, with its focus on the private journey of a
single knight, is born during this period. Indeed, Southern notes that
throughout the literature of the period

> we find less talk of life as an exercise in endurance, and of death in a
> hopeless cause; and we hear more of life as a seeking and a journeying.
> Men begin to order their experience more consciously in accordance
> with a plan; they think of themselves less as stationary objects of at
> tack by spiritual foes, and more as pilgrims and seekers . . . It was not
> until the twelfth century that the imagery of journeying became a
> popular expression of a spiritual quest. Then indeed, it meets us on all
> sides—in the Arthurian Romances, in allegories of love, in descrip
> tions of the ascent of the soul towards God.[4]

The interest in human experience that the new image of God and the
new literary genres suggest is more directly reflected in the rapid growth,
particularly in the late twelfth century, of the new science of moral theology, the branch of theological study that deals with the practical questions
involved in distinguishing right from wrong.[5] For moral theology, concerned with the motives and circumstances that surround the moral act, inevitably emphasizes the individuality and variety of human conduct. The
title of Peter Abelard's influential ethical study—*Scito te ipsum,* or Know
Thyself—is not merely an admonition but the most insistent demand of the
new moral science, for Abelard's systematic argument that sin is defined
not by external actions but by personal intentions shifts the burden of responsibility from the Church to the individual, who alone can recognize
and articulate the motivations and desires that define his moral life. In the
early thirteenth century Abelard's theory of intentionality combines with
the new image of a loving and generous God to produce what seems to me
moral theology's greatest contribution to medieval humanism: the sacrament of confession. With its insistence upon frequent examination of conscience and its dependence upon an image of a merciful God, who values
the sinner's self-awareness and shame enough to forgive over and over
again, the new sacrament encouraged and even demanded of every Chris-

tian the continual self-exploration and attention to minute details of everyday life first demonstrated in Augustine's *Confessions*.

Nowhere do these various but connected interests come together with more complexity than in the *Ancrene Wisse,* a well-known and lavishly praised but little studied religious work of the early thirteenth century. In spite of numerous claims of the work's importance (frequently claims to the effect that the *Ancrene Wisse* is the finest prose work written in English before the fourteenth century, or before Malory, or even before Sir Thomas More[6]), there has been no study of the work's cultural origins in the Twelfth-Century Renaissance, nor even any broad attempt to examine the work's aims and methods.[7] The *Ancrene Wisse*'s concern with the problems of the solitary life should have suggested before now that the text is central to our understanding of the period's interest in the individual. In addition, it has long been known that the *Ancrene Wisse* contains both the earliest discussion in English of "inwit," or personal conscience,[8] and one of the earliest references to a crucifix bearing the new image of the suffering Christ.[9] But these facts seem not to have sparked the interest of literary critics or intellectual historians, at least not enough to encourage closer study of a text that seems so attuned to its age's interest in personal feeling.

There are, of course, reasons for this. First of all, only recently have preliminary and essential questions about the text begun to be satisfactorily answered, questions regarding the work's date, original language, and provenance. Recent scholarship, particularly the painstaking work of E. J. Dobson, has established to most readers' satisfaction that the text was originally written in English (rather than French or Latin) by a West Midlands cleric, and was composed sometime during the first quarter of the thirteenth century (rather than a hundred years earlier).[10] An additional obstacle, however, still stands in the way of the *Ancrene Wisse* assuming its rightful place in the canon of Twelfth-Century Renaissance thought. Given the original audience of the work, it is not surprising that scholars interested in building a case for medieval humanism have overlooked the *Wisse*.[11] The work is addressed to three young anchoresses, religious recluses who were voluntarily enclosed for life within small cells attached to a local church. The impulse that led young women to become willing prisoners (for the door was bolted from the outside) was often described in the Middle Ages as the desire to become "dead to the world"; indeed, the ceremony for enclosing an anchoress in her cell was, in part at least, a burial service. Both the goal of this way of life and the close physical confinement that defined it are almost inconceivable to modern imaginations; even knowledgeable readers, who recognize that the anchoritic life was widely practiced and highly esteemed in the Middle Ages, nevertheless often feel compelled to judge the life as barbaric at worst, and at best as a movement that promoted the death of consciousness. As such, the anchoritic life stands for many readers as an acutely uncomfortable reminder of all that is considered "dark" in the Dark Ages. A work addressed to anchoresses would seem to most readers the least promising territory to search for anything we could call medieval humanism.

Yet even the most cursory glance at the *Ancrene Wisse* would indicate that its author does not share this view of the solitary life. As an example, look briefly at the most well-known—because the most frequently anthologized—excerpt from the work. The passage comes at the very end of the *Wisse*, where the author is advising the anchoresses about what he calls their exterior lives. He begins:

> ʒe, mine leoue sustren, bute ʒef neod ow driue ant ower meistre hit reade, ne schulen habbe na beast bute cat ane. (T213)

> Unless need compels you, my dear sisters, and your director advises it, you must not keep any animal except a cat. (S185)

He goes on to explain why an anchoress should avoid at all cost owning a cow:

> For þenne mot ha þenchen of þe kues foddre, of heordemonne hure, olhnin þe heiward, wearien hwen he punt hire, ant ʒelden þah þe hearmes. Ladlich þing is hit, wat crist, hwen me makeð i tune man of ancre ahte. Nu þenne ʒef eani mot nedlunge habben hit, loki þet hit namon ne eili ne ne hearmi, ne þet hire þoht ne beo nawiht þron ifestnet. (T213)

> For in such a case she has to think of the cow's fodder and the herdsman's wages, say nice things to the hayward, call him names when he impounds the cow, and yet pay damages nonetheless! It is odious, Christ knows, when there are complaints in a village about an anchoress's animals. Now if someone must needs keep one, let her see to it that it does not annoy anyone or do harm to anybody, and that her thoughts are not taken up with it. (S185)

The point, and the author as always makes it explicitly, is that an anchoress is neither a "housewife" nor a "businesswoman," and ought to have nothing that "utward drahe hire heorte," draws out her heart. That a solitary's duty is to keep her heart within is an idea to which the author returns repeatedly in his book, and, so far as it goes, it could be considered as further evidence of the world- and self-denying impulse that we assume must have led a young woman to choose this austere life. But what are we to make of the author's implicit suggestion that the anchoress consider keeping a cat? And what of the playful and highly specific descriptions of such social and peculiarly human acts as flattering and cursing the hayward by turns, or the author's amused annoyance at the double jeopardy of having to pay damages if the cow should escape as well as a fine to get the troublesome creature back? There must be more involved here than a simple distinction between the good anchoress, who remembers that she is "dead to the world," and the false anchoress who does not. For surely we cannot describe as dead to the world either the anchoress who keeps a cow or the anchoress who keeps a cat and reads of the troubles experienced by the one who keeps a cow. Indeed, we might well wonder what business the author has to begin with in writing so humorously and so deliberately of cats and cows to an audience that has been publicly and ceremonially buried.

Much of the humor of the passage, of course, turns upon the incongruous image of a buried solitary who loses her heart to her wandering cow. But at the same time, the highly specific and realistic portrayal of an anchoress's increasing entanglements with her cow suggests that, however incongruous, this is a real possibility, and one that the author has gone out of his way to bring to the anchoress's attention. Though he does it gently and with good humor, the author is insisting that the anchoress consider how easily reversible is her heart and how fragile her idealistic desire to become dead to the world. Both the tone and the subject matter of the passage, then, indicate that for the author, as well as for the anchoress who reads his book, the decision to become a solitary by no means accomplishes as radical a break with the world as we might have assumed.

It has been said that such passages—and, as we shall see, there are many of them—are atypical of the author's thought and unrelated to his larger themes. On the contrary, they are crucial, for they are the clearest illustrations of the author's organizing assumption that exterior and interior realities are inextricably bound in the solitary life, as they are in the lives of all men. The image of a cow-keeping anchoress is but the last and most humorous of the author's demonstrations of his major premise: that the world is inescapable, even for a seemingly enclosed anchoress. If the anchoress has ostensibly cut herself off from the world, it is only so that she can withdraw into herself, where she will encounter the whole moral world in miniature. If the world is her enemy, the author cautions, then the anchoress must understand that the enemy entered the anchorhold when she did.

In this book I hope to show that the *Wisse* author's interest in the mundane affairs of life is intimately related to his conception of the solitary's

most difficult task: to come to understand herself—her desires and memories, her motives and habits of mind—as a unique individual, whose relationship with God is defined not in terms of the otherworld, which is always stable, but in terms of the everyday, which is always in flux. This
interest leads him toward substantially redefining the traditional solitary
goal of becoming dead to the world, and the *Ancrene Wisse* author is unique
in transforming the traditionally self-negating solitary life into a highly
self-conscious journey through human experience. But at the same time,
the author's interest in exploring individual experience grows out of and
highlights the twelfth-century concern with individuality. Thus my aims
are twofold: to provide a reading of the *Ancrene Wisse* that will support my
view that individual experience is the work's major concern and at the
same time to place the work within a broad intellectual and cultural context within which I believe the *Ancrene Wisse* can be better understood, analyzed, and appreciated.

In each chapter except the last I have prepared the way for a detailed
reading of one or more parts of the *Ancrene Wisse* by discussion of a particular issue that developed during the Twelfth-Century Renaissance and that
will help bring into focus and define more sharply some of the *Ancrene
Wisse* author's concerns. Only rarely does this book attempt to identify specific sources of the *Ancrene Wisse* author's thought. Though a thorough
source study of the work is greatly needed, we are still a long way from an
annotated edition of the *Ancrene Wisse,* to say nothing of a full-length study
of its author's relationship to his diverse and often obscure sources.[12] Instead of searching for immediate sources, I have found it more illuminating, and I hope more useful, to attempt to establish the *Ancrene Wisse* as a
major Twelfth-Century Renaissance text by comparing it with other major
and relatively familiar landmarks of twelfth- and early thirteenth-century
thought. I hope that this broad historical approach along with close literary analysis will encourage further analysis and understanding of the *Ancrene Wisse* by a readership wider than the work's current highly specialized
audience.

My book begins where the *Ancrene Wisse* begins, with a discussion of the
idea of a religious rule. For, in the twelfth and early thirteenth centuries,
any attempt to promote individualism in the religious life ultimately had
to confront those traditional religious rules that often emphasized community over the individual and obedience to external precepts over interior
spiritual growth. The *Ancrene Wisse* author's description of most of his
book as an "inner rule" establishes his specific concern with those areas of
life that cannot be legislated by simple, prescriptive rules, and a twelfth-
and early thirteenth-century controversy over the limits of religious rules

provides the pretext for the author's rejection of traditional religious rules. Chapter 2 deals with the *Wisse* author's most original contribution to medieval thought, his redefinition of the goals of the solitary life. In parts II, III, and VII of the *Ancrene Wisse,* the author amply demonstrates that the anchoress's cell and the world outside her windows represent not a discrete external reality that can be abandoned, but a psychological reality that the solitary, by virtue of being human, always carries within her "heart." The question is not how to become dead to the world but rather how to use human desires, memories, and experiences to one's spiritual advantage.

Chapters 3 and 4 take up the important consequences of the author's view of the solitary life and deal with those subjects that, I believe, most interested him, as they did his contemporaries: temptation, sin, and confession. That one-third of the *Ancrene Wisse* is devoted to the specifics of sin and a detailed study of confession has puzzled many readers, leading some to pronounce such material "unsuitable" for anchoresses and leading others to reject these sections altogether as later additions of material originally intended for a more worldly audience. I shall argue that it is precisely these concerns that inform the *Ancrene Wisse* from beginning to end and that most clearly establish its author's connections with the Twelfth-Century Renaissance. For the author understands that if he promotes a spirituality that values human experience and habits of mind, he must also accept, and teach the anchoress to accept, the consequent recognition that the solitary, like every Christian, will inevitably fall. In the author's realistic descriptions of how and why and when, he rises to his most complex definition of the problem of self-knowledge. If the knowledge that leads man to God resides in human experience and self-reflection, then, the author argues, an anchoress cannot "hide herself away in order to escape loving" God. But if she cannot avoid human experience, neither can she avoid sin. Paradoxically, the knowledge that leads to God is identical with the knowledge that leads to sin—knowledge of the world and the flesh. The author's concern with the paradoxical effects of self-knowledge lead him inevitably toward Christianity's solution to the problem of the self: the sacrament of confession, wherein temporarily at least, self-reflection and the awareness of sin that it engenders win for the sinner God's forgiveness and a return of innocence. Both the problem and the solution are central concerns of the Twelfth-Century Renaissance and are brought together in the *Ancrene Wisse.*

ᥫ 1 ᥫ

Self and Religious Rules

OST readers, and not merely those who prefer the work's alternate title, *Ancrene Riwle,* automatically assume that the *Ancrene Wisse* is a religious rule, a genre ordinarily associated with an easily recognizable and essentially limited form: an abbreviated collection of highly specific and binding precepts governing the diet, dress, and behavior of a religious group and providing a strict timetable for prayer, work, silence, and rest. The genre was remarkably stable from the sixth century forward, largely because of the enormous influence of St. Benedict's *Regula monasteriorium* (c. 550), the archetypal religious rule.[1] St. Benedict's emphasis upon strict obedience to a fixed, written rule, as well as upon the primacy of an ordered community life withdrawn from the world, established a norm for religious rules that was rarely challenged in the early Middle Ages. So prestigious did the Benedictine model become that even those religious groups specifically excluded by Benedict from his rule—solitaries and religious groups working in the world—were in time given rules that were adaptations of the Benedictine Rule.[2]

Critics have often observed that the *Ancrene Wisse* owes little to the Rule of St. Benedict, but until recently the knowledge that the work does not derive from the archetypal religious rule has received little attention.[3] Following the lead of James Morton, the work's first modern editor and inventor of the title *Ancren Riwle,* critics have consistently treated the *Ancrene Wisse* as some form of the "usual rule."[4] Thus, while one reader defines the *Ancrene Wisse* as "a rule of life for women who were giving themselves to God," another calls it "a manual, specially composed for . . . recluses" for whom "there was no codified 'Rule.' "[5] The assumption that the work aims at supplying codified rules is also fostered by the numerous scholars who have argued for one or another date of composition by comparing the observances in the *Ancrene Wisse* with those in other religious rules that flourished during the twelfth and thirteenth centuries; thus the author's comments concerning prayer, food, dress, and hygiene are closely compared with sections of the Rule of St. Benedict, or the Rule of St. Augustine, or the Carthusian or Premonstratensian rules.[6] Such isolated comparisons give the impression that the major differences between the *Ancrene Wisse* and various religious rules concern such questions as how many baths are allowed and how many Aves said. All of these descriptions of the *Ancrene Wisse* are misleading: the few specific rules to be found in the work are pointedly set apart by the author as exceptions to his book; they are, he says "monnes fundles"—man's inventions—and as such should not overly concern the anchoresses. That they have merited so much critical concern may mean that we have missed the author's point.

Noting at the very beginning of his book that the anchoresses have frequently asked him for "a rule," the author politely replies that their request is ambiguous:

> ʒe, mine leoue sustren, habbeþ moni dei icrauet on me after riwle. Monie cunne riwlen beoð. (T5)

> You, my dear sisters, have often and earnestly asked me for a rule. There are many kinds of rules. (S1)

The kind he chooses to emphasize, what he calls an "inner rule," bears little resemblance to anything we would recognize as a religious rule and is in fact best understood as an antirule. It is descriptive rather than prescriptive, complex and discursive rather than limited, and if its message could be summarized in a sentence it would have to be that the religious life is much more *un*ruly than the young anchoresses might have at first supposed. The term "inner rule" is finally less a generic reference than a polemical term, a metaphor for an interior life that cannot be controlled by the external precepts of religious rules.

In his recent study of the origins of the *Ancrene Wisse,* E. J. Dobson has eclipsed all previous efforts to locate the point of origin of the *Ancrene Wisse* in a particular religious rule. Dobson's painstaking and thorough research puts to rest some basic misconceptions about the dating and provenance of the *Ancrene Wisse* and raises some tantalizing possibilities concerning the identity of the author. But at the same time that Dobson answers significant questions about the background of the *Wisse* author, his study raises equally important questions about the substance and structure of the author's book.

In his opening chapter, Dobson, drawing upon previous work by Derek Brewer, Vincent McNabb, and Hope Emily Allen, sets out to establish the author of the *Ancrene Wisse* as an Austin canon.[7] Central to Dobson's argument is evidence that the religious rule most closely related to the *Ancrene Wisse* is not the Rule of St. Benedict, but the so-called Rule of St. Augustine, adopted in the early twelfth century by secular canons, who in time came to be called Augustinian or Austin canons. Dobson is the first to admit that the connections he has found between the two works tell us more about the author of the *Ancrene Wisse* than about the work itself. Before beginning his study of the relationship between the Augustinian Rule and *Ancrene Wisse,* Dobson points to "the evident disproportion in the comparison" he is about to make: "the Augustinian Rule is very brief and for the most part general, *Ancrene Wisse* is long and often detailed."[8] By itself, the disproportion is not very revealing; commentaries on religious rules were often far longer and more detailed than the rules on which they were based. Yet in this case the disproportion could hardly be attributed to the *Wisse* author's efforts to provide a commentary on the Rule of St. Augustine.

Dobson, whose case for an Augustinian origin for the *Ancrene Wisse* requires that he highlight every echo of the earlier work, never claims such close interdependence between the two works. In fact, in the 70,000 words of the *Ancrene Wisse,* Dobson finds only one brief quotation from the Augustinian Rule, which the *Wisse* author attributes to St. Augustine but not to his rule.[9] Although this one borrowing in conjunction with the several other verbal echoes demonstrates, as Dobson suggests, "that the author of the later work knew . . . the earlier," the evidence would not seem to support the additional claim that "the *Ancrene Wisse* throughout shows the influence of the Augustinian Rule."[10] On the contrary, if the author was an Austin canon, and Dobson presents a convincing case that he was, it is remarkable that in writing his own guide to the religious life he should refer so rarely and so indirectly to the rule that he professed.

In addition to several verbal echoes, Dobson has found a number of formal parallels between the Augustinian Rule and the *Ancrene Wisse.* But once again he points to a crucial structural difference that calls into question the influence of the earlier work upon the later. Having already noted that a number of verbal resemblances do "not extend in detail," Dobson adds that the structural parallels to the Rule of St. Augustine are restricted to parts I and VIII of the *Ancrene Wisse,* two parts "separated, in the English book, by the whole length of the Inner Rule, enclosed within the Outer Rule by a deliberate structural device, a piece of formal symbolism."[11] The author explicitly divides his book into two unequal parts: a brief outer rule that encloses a lengthy inner rule.[12] Parts I and VIII form the outer rule, a term the author uses to define both the nature of the rules discussed in these sections, which concern external behavior, and their position *outside* the main concerns of his book, which he says will be taken up in parts II through VII, the inner rule.

So, apart from one direct quotation, the parallels Dobson has found between the Augustinian Rule and the *Ancrene Wisse* are restricted to those brief sections at the beginning and end of the *Ancrene Wisse* that the author explicitly defines as tangential to his main concerns. Thus the verbal and formal parallels that Dobson has uncovered, while sufficient to establish the author's familiarity with the Augustinian Rule, occur so rarely and are so oblique as to suggest that the author was unwilling to emphasize or even acknowledge his indebtedness to this religious rule. Taken by itself, such evidence tells us little about the structure or aims of the *Ancrene Wisse.*

If Dobson's study of the *Wisse* author's Augustinian connections does not explain the form of the *Ancrene Wisse,* it does shed some light, albeit indirectly, upon the work's relationship to the genre of religious rules. The point of origin of the *Ancrene Wisse* is not a particular religious rule, but rather a widespread controversy over the restrictions that all religious rules impose upon the religious life, a controversy originating in the twelfth century with the Austin canons and their unusual rule. The Augustinian Rule, developed as a religious rule about a hundred years before the *Ancrene Wisse* was written, is the first influential rule to challenge the archetypal Benedictine rule model, and the new rule paves the way for a more pervasive reconsideration of the whole notion of a religious rule. Arguing along lines established by his early thirteenth-century contemporaries and immediate predecessors, the *Ancrene Wisse* author questions the authority of manmade rules in his introduction and suggests that such rules dilute the force of the gospel's singular demand for a personal and individual response to Christ's message of love. Because the *Wisse* author defines the aims of his work in polemical terms, we can better understand his argument after we have reviewed briefly the stages of the controversy to which he is responding.

Long before the twelfth century, questions concerning the limits and scope of religious rules had been raised by monastic writers. For the earliest monastic legislators the term "rule" referred to a body of tradition, primarily scriptural, collected by individual abbots. St. Benedict (or the so-called Master upon whose work his rule is based) was the first monastic legislator to define the religious life in terms of obedience to a written, fixed, and binding rule.[13] But at the same time that he limits previous definitions of a religious rule, Benedict recognizes the existence of another rule. At the end of his treatise he calls his a "minimum rule for beginners" and suggests that there is a higher rule reserved for those seeking "the summit of perfection":

Ceterum ad perfectionem conversationis qui festinet, sunt doctrinae sanctorum Patrum, quarum observatio perducat hominem ad celsi-

tudinem perfectionis. Quae enim pagina, aut qui sermo divinae auc-
toritatis Veteris ac Novi Testamenti, non est rectissima norma vitae
humanae? ... quid aliud sunt nisi bene viventium et obedientium
monachorum instrumenta virtutum?

But, for him who would hasten to the perfection of the monastic life,
there are the teachings of the holy Fathers, by observing which a man
is led to the summit of perfection. For what page or what utterance of
the divinely-inspired books of the Old and New Testament is not a
most unerring rule for human life ... what else are they but tools of
virtue for good-living and obedient monks?   (chapter 73)

But this more perfect and more amorphous rule of the Scriptures, Benedict
continues, is a source of "shame and confusion" for most monks, who
should therefore remain in the monastery, living in strict accordance with
the written rule, until death.[14] Benedict, who had himself been a hermit,
thus ultimately rejects the eremitic goal of personal perfection in favor of
community life strictly ordered by obedience to a common rule. Obedience
to a manmade rule is not, in Benedict's view, the only path to salvation,
but "sinking the individual in the community" by means of a strictly en-
forced common rule is, for Benedict, the surest path.[15]

Although Benedict's emphasis upon the primacy of community life prevailed in the centuries following his death, his insistence upon strict obedience to the precepts of his rule was largely ignored as religious groups
sought to accommodate the rule to changing circumstances.[16] But the particularity and prescriptiveness of the Benedictine Rule was, in effect, redis-
covered in the early twelfth century by the new "white" Cistercian monks,
who explicitly defined their differences with traditional "black" Benedictines in terms of the Cistercian demand for strict fidelity to St. Benedict's
Rule. R. W. Southern says of the Cistercians that "they were the last generation of medieval men to believe that it was good for all men to be
monks."[17] The reason they were the last may well be that they were the
first generation of medieval men, since the time of St. Benedict, to insist
that the monastic life be strictly defined by the Rule of St. Benedict, read
literally and observed "ad apicem literae," to the last dot.[18]

The Benedictine-Cistercian quarrel over how to read the Rule of St.
Benedict had immediate consequences outside the monastery. Nonmonastic religious groups who could claim no allegiance to a fixed, written rule
came under fire from both the black and the white monks, who were
caught up in a legalistic debate over which order was more faithful to St.
Benedict's Rule. In the past such groups had responded to calls for reform
by adopting some form of the Benedictine Rule. However, the Benedic-

tine-Cistercian quarrel, in drawing attention to the particularity and to the exclusiveness of St. Benedict's Rule, seems to have encouraged these groups, most notably the canons, to seek for the first time an alternative to the model of the Benedictine Rule.

J. C. Dickinson, in tracing the early history of the canons, indicates that calls for canonical reform were by no means new in the twelfth century.[19] Canons, secular clergy who served as clerks in large churches and dioceses, had since the early days of the Church claimed the apostolic life as their model, but in fact canons often departed from what was called "the rule of the apostles," which consisted of one rule, the common ownership of property. Previous attempts at reform had not succeeded in regularizing the canons' religious lives, in part because such reform movements usually resulted in the adoption of religious rules that were essentially monastic and Benedictine and therefore were impractical guides for the secular canons. Under pressure once again in the late eleventh and early twelfth centuries to return to their "rule," various groups of canons responded by renouncing private property and giving themselves a new title, *canonicus regularis*.[20] The term was widely contested at first, with resistance coming mainly, and not surprisingly, from the original *regulares,* the black and white monks. For if there was anything on which Benedictines and Cistercians could agree, it was that a rule as vague and imprecise as the "rule of the apostles" was not a legitimate claim to the title *regularis*. The term only won acceptance sometime in the mid–twelfth century, after a document now known as the Rule of St. Augustine had somewhat mysteriously become attached to the canons.[21] The document in question was not known as a religious rule before the canons appropriated it, and with good reason. It is, in a sense, the first antirule, developed a hundred years before the *Ancrene Wisse* was written.

The rule is more brief by far than the Rule of St. Benedict and consists of two parts. The first part, of unknown origin and called, for textual reasons, *Regula secunda,* lists in briefest possible form (about four hundred words) precepts governing daily prayer, work, silence, and discipline. This prescriptive section, and the only section that resembles other religious rules, rapidly dropped out of usage after a house of canons complained to Pope Gelasius in 1118 that many of its precepts were impractical.[22] In later versions of the rule, the *Regula secunda* does not appear, and the second half of the document is left to stand by itself. This half, known as *Regula tertia,* is a slightly modified version of a letter written by St. Augustine (c. 423) to a house of wayward nuns. It can best be described as a general, discursive summary of basic Christian beliefs. It never refers to the terms "rule" or "order" and seems intended to serve primarily as a reminder to its audience of the importance of a harmonious community life.

The rule concentrates upon outlining the proper attitudes of members of a religious house toward themselves, each other, and their superior. Obedience to authority is discussed but takes a far inferior place to the necessity of love. Charity should reign in a religious house, Augustine counsels, not envy, or anger, or pride. All should be done for the common good, and spiritual unity in love should be the constant guiding principle of the religious life. Prescriptions in the treatise usually take the form of general, spiritual advice reminiscent of that found in Scripture:

> Orationibus instate ... Carnem vestram domate ... quantum valetudo permittit ... Non sit notabilis habitus vester.

> Be instant in prayer ... Subdue your flesh ... as far as your health allows ... Let your garb be inconspicuous.[23]

Even such rules as these are encouraged not for their own sake, but as preventive measures against discord, which Augustine sees as the most serious threat to the common life. Augustine calls his treatise not a rule but a *libellus,* a little book, and he urges his readers to look at themselves in this book "as in a mirror." He ends by entreating them to observe all that he has set down "non sicut serv[ae] sub lege, sed sicut liber[ae] sub gratia constituti" ("not as bondswomen under the law, but as free women established under grace").[24]

"The great beauty" of this rule, R. W. Southern shrewdly notes, "was that it left so much to the imagination."[25] It could easily be adapted to the widely differing circumstances of the many houses of canons, while at the same time allowing the canons to present themselves as united under one rule. Benedictine and Cistercian monks, on the other hand, and even some canons, had reason to question whether the treatise was a legitimate religious rule at all, for it was neither "sure, fixed, or adequate."[26] Yet the prestige of St. Augustine's name in time overcame all doubts; by the middle of the twelfth century St. Augustine is listed alongside St. Benedict as one of the two great monastic legislators, and by the end of the century thousands of religious houses had adopted the Augustinian Rule. The flexibility of the new rule allowed some religious groups to fortify it with strict customs borrowed from the Cistercians and become all but indistinguishable from monastic orders. Other religious groups, most notably the Dominican friars whose founder was an Austin canon in the early thirteenth century, took their rule, with its emphasis upon inner values rather than external conditions, out into the world to preach the gospel's message in towns all over Europe.[27]

It should already be apparent that the invention of a new religious rule did more than solve the practical and political needs of one religious group. That Augustine's *libellus* came to be accepted as a religious rule marks the most dramatic change in the genre of religious rules since the sixth century. The extraordinary popularity of the Augustinian Rule suggests that a more flexible and more inclusive alternative to the Benedictine Rule was needed, particularly at a time when the Cistercian monks were arguing so persuasively that the Rule of St. Benedict, with its emphasis on withdrawal from the world and strict obedience to its written precepts, could no longer be all things to all men. Yet arguments for the redefinition of a religious rule based upon spiritual rather than practical or political grounds seem lacking during this period. The canons did not, after all, set out to design an antirule, nor did they, as a group, reject on moral grounds the notion that the religious life depends for its legitimacy upon adherence to a specific religious rule. Instead, they discovered a document wholly different from the Benedictine Rule, whose prestige more than its substance met the technical objections against their order. Moral arguments on behalf of flexibility and individualism in the observance of religious rules were certainly made during the first half of the twelfth century, but the legalistic spirit prevailed.[28] Not until the late twelfth and early thirteenth centuries can reaction against the legalism inherent in the debate over specific religious rules be clearly heard. The reaction comes, not surprisingly, from nonmonastic and even antimonastic quarters, primarily from the university, from preachers, and from friars. The *Ancrene Wisse,* written between 1215 and 1222, forms a significant part of this reaction.

The larger, spiritual questions implicitly raised by Augustine's distinction between fixed laws and free grace are first made prominent in the late twelfth century by schoolmen interested not in the legitimacy of any specific religious rule, but rather in defining what M. D. Chenu has called the "theology of law."[29] Peter the Chanter, master of theology at the University of Paris, opposes the binding precepts of religious rules to the "liberty of the gospel" in his influential *Verbum abbreviatum* (c. 1191–1192), a work from which the *Ancrene Wisse* author borrows frequently.[30] In a chapter titled "Against the Burdensome Host of Traditions," Peter argues that excessive attention to specific rules can obstruct an individual's personal response to the higher rule of the gospel:

> Sunt et aliae (traditiones) licitae, nullumque offendiculum mandatis divinis parientes, et tamen prae multitudine sua gravant constituentes, et inobedientes illis transgressores; nisi in parcitate et paucitate, et nonnisi pro manifestissima causa et utili instituendae essent, obicem videntur praebere divinis praeceptis. Hae evacuant evangelicam libertatem . . .

Vide Apostolum nonnisi paucas traditiones honestas et mysticas
instituisse ... Antonius etiam eremita quibusdam religiosis quaeren-
tibus ab eo regulam et formam religiose vivendi, tradidit eis codicem
Evangelii . . .

Multitudine etiam inventorum praegravamur, cum dicat auctoritas,
quia etiam de utilibus aliqua post ponenda sunt, ne multitudine uti-
lium gravemur ... Non reliquas spiritum litterae vivificantem,
propter traditionem, determinationem, vel remotam alicujus exposi-
tionem.

There are other traditions that are allowable, even inoffensive in any
way to God's commandments. And yet when they are numerous they
weigh heavily upon those who uphold them and upon those who
transgress them; unless such traditions are kept brief and few and
have been instituted for the most obvious and useful reasons, they
become an obstacle to obeying divine precepts. They restrict the liberty of the gospel ...

Note that the Apostle had no traditions except a few venerable and
mystical ones. Also when certain religious came to the hermit Anthony seeking a rule and model for the religious life, he gave them a
copy of the gospel ...

We are oppressively burdened with a multitude of contrived practices, although authority speaks, because even some useful things
have to be tossed aside or we get borne down by them ... Do not
abandon the vital spirit of the letter in favor of anybody's tradition or
refinement or obscure explanation.[31]

In the early thirteenth century, Jacques de Vitry, a contemporary of the
Ancrene Wisse author who was a well-known preacher and student of Peter
the Chanter, takes the argument against exclusive and specialized religious
rules one step further in his *Historia occidentalis* (1218–1221).[32] Like his
teacher, Jacques is opposed to the accumulation of restrictive rules and
customs that obscure the gospel's simple commands. As a preacher he is
also concerned that lay Christians living and working in the world understand that they need not retire to a monastery or profess a particular religious rule to legitimize their spiritual lives. Instead, he argues, all faithful
Christians deserve to be called *regulares,* united under the single "rule" of
the gospel:

Non solum eos qui seculo renunciant et transeunt ad religionem, regulares judicamus, sed et omnes Christi fideles sub evangelica regula
Domino famulantes, et ordinate sub uno summo Abbate viventes,
possumus dicere regulares.

In my judgment it is not only those who renounce the world and go
into religion who are *regulares,* but all the faithful of Christ who serve
under the gospel's rule and live by the orders of the single greatest
Abbot or Father of all.[33]

Finally, the argument that the religious life need not derive its authority
from any manmade rule is expressed most dramatically by another of the
Ancrene Wisse author's contemporaries, Francis of Assisi, himself a layman.
While St. Dominic was content to organize his order of preaching friars
under the flexible Rule of St. Augustine, Francis rejects the formalism of
all religious rules. He comes before Pope Innocent III in 1209 to defend
the legitimacy of his new order of friars without benefit of an elaborate
rule: "I do not come here with a new rule," he claims; "my only rule is the
gospel."[34] Francis's argument is more than a clever maneuver to evade a recent papal decree that no new religious orders be founded. His belief in the
gospel as a sufficient rule for the religious life is complete and absolute. As
M. D. Chenu points out in his important discussion of the "rule of the gospel," Francis insists that the rule of Scripture be read *"sine glossa;* that is,
without any of those explanations which dilute the meaning in order to
accommodate it to passing conditions."[35] When Cardinal Ugolino urged
Francis and his followers to return to one of the established rules—either
that of Benedict or of Augustine—Francis is reported by his biographer to
have answered:

> Fratres mei, fratres mei, Deus vocavit me per viam simplicitatis et
> humilitatis, et hanc viam ostendit mihi in veritate pro me et pro illis
> qui volunt mihi credere et me imitari. Et ideo nolo quod nominetis
> mihi aliquam regulam, neque sancti Benedicti, neque sancti Augus-
> tini, neque sancti Bernardi.

> My brothers, my brothers, God has called me by the way of simplicity
> and of humility, and he has pointed out this way as being the true
> way, both for me and for those who wish to believe me and imitate
> me. So don't talk to me about some rule or other, neither that of St.
> Benedict, nor of St. Augustine, nor of St. Bernard.[36]

These three writers have in common a suspicion of the special claims of
religious rules. The ruled life, they argue, depends not upon withdrawal
from the world to follow the special path dictated by formal religious rules,
but upon an individual's direct and personal response to the gospel. The
binding precepts of religious rules, these writers suggest, not only exclude
many Christians from the religious life, but may be harmful to those who
overvalue them, in that such manmade rules may dilute the force of the

gospel, diminishing the power of an individual's personal response to God's personal message of love. Peter the Chanter, Jacques de Vitry, and St. Francis refuse to accept the monastic argument, to which the Austin canons had cleverly responded in the preceding century, that the legitimacy of the religious life could only be established by profession of a fixed religious rule. The ruled life is the moral life, the later writers argue, which depends upon the interior disposition of an individual, not upon the external conditions of a religious order.

Such strong, even radical, reactions against religious rules had far more widespread effects upon the growing evangelical movement that Chenu has traced than upon religious orders themselves.[37] Just as the Austin canons eventually attached precepts and customs to their rule, so too the Franciscan friars, as their numbers grew, saw the necessity of a somewhat more organized life, guided by a written code.[38] But before the opposition to the formalism of religious rules had run its course, it was to receive its fullest and most self-conscious treatment in the *Ancrene Wisse,* to which we turn.

"Ant ȝe, mine leoue sustren, habbeþ moni dei icrauet on me after riwle" ("And you, my dear sisters, have often and earnestly asked me for a rule" [T5; S1]). The anchoresses have obviously asked the author, their friend and perhaps their current spiritual adviser, for a religious rule, and they no doubt expected to receive some version of either the Rule of St. Benedict or the Augustinian Rule.[39] Although religious groups, including solitaries, often requested rules to reform or regularize their religious lives, such motives are unlikely in this case. The *Ancrene Wisse* author repeatedly congratulates his three charges on the orderly life they lead and in fact suggests several times that the devout, young anchoresses have been overly hard on themselves in matters of food, drink, and discipline.[40] A surprising number of the external rules the author provides at the end of his book concern comforts that the anchoress should permit herself, rather than those to be denied.[41]

If it is true that the anchoresses already lead a "ruled" life, we must wonder why they have so often asked the author for a rule. Later in his introduction the author indicates that local churchmen have been exerting pressure upon the anchoresses to identify themselves with some bona fide religious order, apparently either the Benedictines or the Cistercians, since the author, in discussing this question, refers exclusively to the black and white monks. It seems then that the anchoresses, like the Austin canons a century before, are being asked to demonstrate the legitimacy of their order.[42] The author, particularly if he is an Austin canon, could have responded most easily to the anchoresses' request by providing some version of the Augustinian Rule (which he would certainly name, because the name alone would bring the assurances that outsiders sought). But he does not. Instead the author sets about the delicate task of teaching his educated audience that their request for a religious rule is naive. In substance his argument has much in common with Peter the Chanter's "On the Burdensome Host of Traditions" and with St. Francis's response to a similar request to join an established order.[43] In tone, however, the author's argument varies considerably. When he addresses those "ignorant people" who would have the anchoresses join an established order, he speaks more vehemently than either Peter the Chanter or St. Francis. When he addresses the anchoresses, on the other hand, whom he has known for some time and holds in the highest regard, he assumes the gentle tone of a friend and teacher.

The author opens his book with a brief and learned discussion in Latin of the term *regula* before addressing his audience in English:

Recti diligunt te. In Canticis, sponsa ad sponsum. Est rectum gramaticum, rectum geometricum, rectum theologicum. Et sunt differencie totidem regularum. De recto theologico sermo nobis est, cuius regule due sunt. Una circa cordis directionem, altera uersatur circa exteriorum rectificationem. Recti diligunt te. "Lauerd," seið godes spuse to hire deorewerðe spus, "þe rihte luuieð þe." Þeo beoð rihte þe luuieð efter riwle. Ant ʒe, mine leoue sustren, habbeþ moni dei icrauet on me after riwle. Monie cunne riwlen beoð, ah twa beoð bimong alle þet ich chulle speoken of, þurh ower bone, wið godes grace. (T5)

"The righteous love Thee," says the bride to her Spouse in the Canticle of Canticles. *We can speak of what is "right" in Grammar, or "right" in Geometry, or "right" in Theology, and each of these studies has its own rules. Here we are concerned with what is theologically "right" and the rules of this pursuit are two.*

The first is concerned with the right directing of the heart, the second with the right ordering of exterior things. "The righteous love Thee, Lord," says God's bride to her beloved Spouse. The righteous are those who live according to rule, and you, my dear sisters, have often and earnestly asked me for a rule. There are many kinds of rules, but I shall speak here of two out of all of them, because of your request, and with the help of God's grace. (S1)

By playing upon the etymology of the word *regula,* connecting it with *rectum,* the right, the author quickly establishes that there is only one "right" way, the way of love described in the Canticle of Canticles (1:3). Using the

same etymological trick, the author then broadens his readers' frame of reference for the term "rule" beyond the narrow genre of religious rules, re-
minding them that "there are many kinds of rules," including the rules of
geometry and grammar.[44] Finally, he defines as his subject the rules concerning what is "theologically right," a broad and fundamental topic that
both appeals to his audience's learning and dismisses as irrelevant the technical question of which religious rule the anchoresses ought to profess.

Having thus already suggested that the anchoresses' request for a rule is
ambiguous, the author moves on to the two kinds of rules that will concern him in his book, repeatedly emphasizing his distrust of rules invented
by men. The first rule and the author's primary concern involves "the right
directing of the heart":

> Þe an riwleð þe heorte ant makeð efne ant smeðe wiðute cnost ant
> dolc of woh inwit ant of wreiȝende þe segge: "Her þu sunegest,"
> oþer: "Þis nis nawt ibet ȝet ase wel as hit ahte." Þeos riwle is eauer
> inwið ant rihteð þe heorte. Et hec est caritas quam describit Apos-
> tolus, de corde puro et consciencia bona et fide non ficta. Þeos riwle is
> chearite of schir heorte ant cleane inwit ant treowe bileaue . . . De qua
> Augustinus: Nichil petendum preter regulam magisterii. Et Apos-
> tolus: Omnes in eadem regula permaneamus. (T5)

> [The one rules the heart and makes it even and smooth, without knot
> or wound of an injured, accusing conscience which says]:[45] "In this
> matter you are committing sin," or: "That is not yet amended as well
> as it ought to be." This rule is always interior, guiding the heart. *It is
> the charity of which the Apostle speaks, which comes from a pure heart, and
> a good conscience, and true faith . . . Of this Augustine says: "Nothing must
> be sought contrary to the rule of the supreme authority": and the Apostle:
> "Let us all continue in the same rule."* (S1)

This interior rule is not reserved for the spiritual elite, or for those who
belong to a religious order. The heart's rule applies equally to all men and
is the concern of "all religion" because it was invented by God, not man:

> Rihten . . . ant smeðin [the heart] is of euch religiun ant of euch
> ordre þe goð ant al þe strengðe. Þeos riwle is imaket nawt of monnes
> fundles, ah is of godes heaste; forþi ha is eauer ant an wiðute chan-
> gunge, ant alle ahen hire in an eauer to halden. (T7)

> [To straighten and smooth (the heart) is the virtue of every religion
> and every religious order. This rule is not made up of man's inven-
> tions], but is part of what God commands; therefore it remains al-

ways the same, without changing, and all are bound to follow it always and unchangingly.   (S2)

The author does not, as do Peter the Chanter and St. Francis, call his inner rule the rule of the gospel, but he clearly has Scripture in mind when he opposes God's commands to rules invented by men. His most detailed definition of the inner rule is a summary of the gospel's commands in brief:

Luue ant eadmodnesse ant þolemodnesse, treoweschipe ant haldunge of þe alde ten hestes, Schrift ant penitence: þeos ant þulliche oþre, þe beoð summe of þe alde lahe, summe of þe neowe, ne beoð nawt monnes fundles ne riwle þet mon stalde, ah beoð godes heastes. Ant forþi euch mon mot ham nede halden, ant ȝe ouer alle, for þeos riwleð þe heorte; of hire riwlunge is al meast þet ich write, bute i þe frumðe of þis boc ant i þe leaste ende.   (T8)

Love, humility and patience, fidelity and the keeping of the ancient commandments, Confession and penance, and other such matters, some belonging to the Old Law, some to the New: these are not the invention of man, nor a rule laid down by man. They are the commands of God; and for that reason everyone is under an obligation to keep them, and you most especially, because they govern the heart, and it is of the governance of the heart that I am chiefly writing in this book, except at the beginning and at the very end.   (S3)

Those exceptions, of course, refer to what the author calls the outer rule, which like religious rules is manmade and can be explicitly and simply defined:

Þe oþer riwle is al wiðuten ant riwleð þe licome ant licomliche deden, þe teacheð al hu me schal beoren him wiðuten: hu eoten, drinken, werien, singen, slepen, wakien. Et hec est exercitio corporis que iuxta apostolum modicum ualet.   (T6)

The other [rule] is completely external, and governs the body and its actions. It gives directions about all outward behavior, about eating and drinking, dress, singing, sleep and vigil. *This is "bodily exercise" which according to the Apostle, "is profitable to little."*   (S2)

This outer rule has received much critical attention from readers eager to demonstrate the *Ancrene Wisse*'s dependence upon some established religious rule. And yet the author clearly marks the material of the outer rule as the exception to his book, emphasizing its relative unimportance in a number of ways. First of all, the length of the outer rule is insignificant by comparison with that of the extensive inner rule. Second, he places the two parts of the outer rule, one dealing with daily devotions, the other with rules governing diet, dress, and the like, at the other edges of his book. Furthermore, as in the passage just cited, the author takes every opportunity in outlining the outer rule to remind the anchoresses that these rules, in comparison with the inner rule of love, "are of small importance" (S182). Finally, he emphasizes the subordinate relationship of the outer rule to the inner by means of two recurring analogies, one chosen from the *artes,* the other from the language of aristocratic households. The latter is particularly appropriate to his well-born charges, who have renounced their futures as ladies of great households:

> Hec . . . est quasi regula recti mechanici quod geometrio recto continetur. Ant þeos riwle nis nawt bute forte serui þe oþer: þe oþer is as leafdi, þeos as hire þuften, for al þet me eauer deð of þe oþer wiðuten nis bute forte riwlin þe heorte wiðinnen. (T6-7)

> *It* [the outer rule] *is much like a rule of the science of mechanics, which serves the science of geometry.*
> So this rule exists merely to serve the other. The other is the lady, this her handmaid, for all those actions which belong to the outer rule serve only to govern the heart within.   (S2)

The inner rule governing the heart and the subordinate outer rule closely resemble the two rules St. Benedict treats in his *Regula monasteriorum.* While Benedict never calls his primary rule an external rule, he does call it a "minimum rule for beginners," and most of his precepts concern external behavior. The higher rule that Benedict hesitatingly mentions at the very end of his treatise, and that is to be found in "the divinely-inspired books of the Old and New Testament," is roughly synonymous with the *Wisse* author's definition of his inner rule. The difference between the two rules for Benedict is one of accessibility: the higher rule is available only to those few religious men seeking the "summit of perfection" and even then is accessible only through and after long probation under the external rule of obedience.

For the *Ancrene Wisse* author, on the other hand, both the accessibility and the priority of the two rules are exactly reversed. As his opening quotation from the Canticle of Canticles implies, the interior and individual rule of love is central, not as a remote possibility reserved for the elite few, but as an ever-present necessity required of all Christians. The external rule, while not altogether expendable, is of little value ("modicum valet") without the prior existence of the inner rule, always the author's first concern and the subject of most of his book. More closely resembling an evangelist than the writer of a religious rule, the author argues that salvation for solitaries, as for all men, depends upon a personal, self-conscious response to the gospel's message of love, rather than upon making or keeping arbitrary, external rules, no matter how helpful or how comforting such rules might be. Furthermore, the *Wisse* author follows through on his belief by undermining the authority of his own modest, external rules even before he presents them.

Given the author's definitions of the inner and outer rules, it is not difficult to see why obedience is hardly relevant to either. In keeping the inner rule, the problem is not so much obedience as it is understanding or awareness ("weote" [T7]), for God's commands are not as easily understood and applied as men's. The author assumes that the anchoress wants to obey God's laws, but the question is, how can she best do so in the subtle atmosphere of the anchorhold. The inner life, in the *Ancrene Wisse*, is complex, and so too must the inner rule be. Both God and the devil proceed in the anchorhold by cunning ("wið liste" [T113], or "unwrench," [T138]), and the inner rule attempts to teach the anchoress the various strategies of both. As the inner rule comes to be understood by the anchoress, the response called for is never passive obedience, but rather active, even aggressive, love.

The question of obedience, as we saw earlier, is central to the notion of a religious rule. St. Benedict defines explicitly the quality of obedience required by those who profess his Rule:

> Haec ipsa obedientia tunc acceptabilis erit Deo et dulcis hominibus, si quod jubetur non trepide, non tarde, non tepide, aut cum murmurio, vel cum responso nolentis efficiatur.

> This obedience itself will then be acceptable to God and pleasing to men, if what is commanded be not done timorously, or tardily, or tepidly, nor with murmuring or the raising of objections.   (Chapter 5)

The Augustinian Rule, as the only religious rule not dependent upon the Benedictine model, puts much less emphasis upon obedience to specific precepts but nevertheless requires obedience to superiors, and each house of canons, anxious to prove the legitimacy of the order, added its own precepts and customs to the more general rule. In the *Ancrene Wisse* author's discussion of obedience, his preference for the moderate approach exemplified in St. Augustine's letter is clear. But even so, the author's distrust of all external rules is far more explicit and self-conscious than that of the canons as a group. His fear that the anchoresses, who are already somewhat overly fastidious in keeping prescriptive rules, will allow attention to the outer rule to subvert their understanding of the inner rule of love leads him to question the value of obedience both to superiors and to the written rule itself.

Like members of other religious groups, the anchoresses are asked to take a vow of obedience. But whereas *regulares* vow obedience specifically to their superiors and to their rules, the object of the anchoress's obedience is kept purposely unspecific. She is told to obey any formal commands of her bishop, though presumably such commands would govern extreme cases only, such as the removal of the anchoress from her cell (T8; S3). In less extreme cases, such as a visit from the bishop, the author is more cautious about the type of obedience required:

> ȝef bischp kimeð to seon ow, hihið sone towart him. Ah sweteliche bisecheð him, ȝef he bit to seon ow, þet ȝe moten þer onont halden ow towart him as ȝe habbeð idon ant doð to alle oþre. ȝef he wule allegate habben a sihðe, lokið þet hit beo ful scheort; þe ueil anan adun, ant draheð ow behinden.   (T34)

> If the bishop comes to see you go to him at once; but if he asks to see your face then humbly beg that in this matter you may behave to him as you have done and do to everyone else. If he insists, see to it that it is for a very short time; drop your veil very soon and draw back.   (S27–28)

This self-conscious, hesitant obedience, which is almost pacification, contrasts sharply with the immediate and unhesitating obedience required by St. Benedict. Here the emphasis is upon the anchoress's self-awareness and her responsibility to protect herself, not upon the bishop's authority.[46]

If the author is dubious about the allegiance owed to the bishop, he is downright suspicious of all lesser authority. Concerning the choice of a spiritual director or confessor, he advises extreme caution:

> To sum gastelich mon þet ȝe beoð trusti upon (as ȝe mahe beon o lut), god is þet ȝe easki read ant salue þet he teache ow toȝeines fondunges, ant i schrift schawið him, ȝef he wule iheren, ower greaste ant ower ladlukeste sunnen, forþi þet him areowe ow, ant þurh þe areownesse inwardluker crie Crist mearci for ow, ant habbe ow in his bonen. Set multi ueniunt ad uos in uestimentis ouium intrinsecus autem sunt lupi rapaces. "Ah witeð ow ant beoð warre," he seið, ure lauerd," for monie cumeð to ow ischrud mid lombes fleos ant beoð

wedde wulues." Worltliche leueð lut, religiuse ȝet leas; ne wilni ȝe
nawt to muchel hare cuððunge. (T36)

It is good to seek counsel and healing from some spiritual man whom
you trust (and there are few whom you can) in order that he may instruct you against temptations, and in Confession tell him, if he will
hear them, your greatest and most hateful sins, so that he may take
pity on you, and because of his pity, inwardly cry to Christ for mercy
for you, and remember you in his prayers. "But guard yourselves and
be cautious," Our Lord has said, "for many come to you clothed in
lambs' fleece who are raging wolves." Do not put much trust in people of the world; trust religious even less; and do not wish too much
for their acquaintance. (S29)

Given the author's particular suspicion of supposedly religious men, it is
easy to see why he rarely emphasizes obedience to one's spiritual adviser.
He does, early in his introduction, advise that

euch ancre habben þe uttre riwle efter hire schriftes read ant hwet se
he bit ant hat hire in obedience, þe cnaweð hire manere ant wat hire
strengðe. (T8)

each anchoress shall keep the exterior rule according to the advice of
her confessor and perform in obedience whatever he asks or demands
of her, since he knows her circumstances and her ability. (S3)

However, both in his introduction and in his final chapter ("External
Rules"), the author makes clear that the responsibility to modify or eliminate parts of the external rule lies mainly with the anchoress herself:

Of mete, of drunch, flesch forgan oðer fisch, alle oþer swucche
þinges, of werunge, of liggunge, of ures, of oþre beoden, segge swa
monie oðer o swucche wise: þeos ant þulliche oþre beoð alle ifreo
wil, to don oðer to leten hwil me wule ant hwen me wule. (T8)

Matters of eating and drinking, for example, or abstaining from meat
or fish, and all other things of the kind, clothing, rest, saying one's
hours and other prayers, the number of them and the manner in
which they are said—these things and others like them are all left to
one's own choice. One may do them while one wants to and stop
when one wants to. (S3)[47]

Even in confession, where one would expect the authority and advice of
the confessor to dominate absolutely, the author urges the anchoress to

consider her motives and the possible consequences of confessing some sins to some priests. Furthermore, the anchoress herself assumes most of the confessor's duties, leaving him with little about which to question or advise her.

The *Wisse* author departs even more radically from traditional religious rules on the question of obedience to the written rule itself. If he is ambivalent about persons to whom the anchoress owes obedience, he is unambiguous in his counsel that she *not* vow obedience to the outer rule, either as he himself has written it, or as the anchoress, in conjunction with her confessor, has altered it. For the author's external rule, like all religious rules, is finally only "monnes fundles." To vow to keep it would be to attach too much authority to it. Furthermore, the author is wary of the effects of such a vow upon the inner life, always his first concern. Echoing the opinion of Peter the Chanter that even well-meaning rules "weigh heavily upon those who uphold them and upon those who transgress them," the *Wisse* author argues that if the anchoress were to vow to keep the outer rule, she might fall into the dangerous sin of presumption if she kept her vow well, or despair if she did not. The author's favorite targets of reproach are those religious who presume salvation because they keep the external rules of their order to the letter:

> Hercne Michee, . . . godes prophete. "Ich chulle schawi þe soðliche hwet is godd ant hwuch religiun ant hwuch ordre, hwuch halinesse godd easkeð of þe. . . . Do wel ant dem wac eauer þe seoluen, ant wið dred ant wið luue ga mid godd ti lauerd." Þeras þeose þinges beoð, þer is riht religiun, þer is soð ordre; *ant do al þet oðer ant lete þis nis bute trichunge ant a fals gile. Ve uobis scribe ant pharisei ypocrite.* (T11; my emphasis)

> This is what God's prophet Micah says, . . . "I will show you truly what good is, what religion and 'order' are, and what holiness God asks of you. Do good; walk with God who is your Lord, in fear and love, always remembering that you yourself are weak." Where these things are, there is true religion and true "order"; *and to do all the rest and neglect this is mere deceit and hypocrisy: Woe to you, scribes and Pharisees, hypocrites.* (S5; my emphasis)

Presumption deadens conscience, and, as the author has made clear in his opening remarks, only a strong, active conscience can keep the inner rule alive. On the other hand, an overly sensitive conscience can lead the heart into despair, a state diametrically opposed to what the author calls "þe goð ant al þe strengðe" of the inner rule and of all religion—that it keeps the heart "even and smooth" by teaching one how to deal with the awareness ("weote" [T7]) of sin. A vow to keep manmade rules may overstimulate a conscience already sensitized by the complex demands of the inner rule:

> Nulle ich nawt þet ȝe bihaten [external rules] as heaste to halden; for as ofte as ȝe þrefter breken eni of ham, hit walde to swiðe hurten ower heorte ant makien ow swa offearet þet ȝe mahten sone (þet godd forbeode ow) fallen i desesperance, þet is, in an unhope ant an unbileaue forte beon iborhen. (T9)

> I do not want you to promise solemnly to obey [external rules] as if they were commandments, for if you departed from any of them afterwards, it would cause too much pain to your hearts and make you so much afraid, that you might soon (and may God preserve you from this) fall into despair, that is, into a state without hope or faith in your salvation. (S3-4)

In sum, the *Ancrene Wisse* author explicitly questions the value of unhesitating obedience, whether to superiors or to the external rule itself. The effect of simple obedience, notes Walter Ullmann, is to relieve "the individual of making critical assessments and of forming his own judgment."[48] But it is precisely the process by which an individual makes critical assessments that concerns the author of the *Ancrene Wisse*, both in his discussion of the outer rule, and in that of the inner rule. Thus, although influenced enough by traditional religious rules to require a vow of obedience, the author insists throughout that the quality of that obedience be hesitant, cautious, and self-conscious. In fact, he encourages precisely the kind of obedience condemned by St. Bernard and the Cistercians as a betrayal of one's religious rule, obedience examined "in astu cordis," in the cunning of one's heart.[49]

The *Wisse* author reserves his harshest judgments for those who practice another kind of cunning, the petty legalism of those who have repeatedly asked the anchoresses to which "order" they belong. Having insisted that the anchoresses not attach undue authority to their own or any other literal and external rule, the author devotes the end of his introduction to a stinging attack upon those whose preoccupation with the precepts of religious rules have allowed them to lose sight of the spiritual meaning of "order" and "rule," and it is here that the author's antipathy toward traditional religious rules and orders is most explicit:

> ȝef ei unweote easkeð ow of hwet ordre ȝe beon, as summe doð þe telleð me (þe siheð þe gneat ant swolheð þe flehe), ondswerieð of

sein Iames . . . ȝef him þuncheð wunder ant sullich of swuch ondswere, easkið him hwet beo ordre, ant hwer he funde in hali writ religiun openlukest descriueþ ant isutelet þen is i sein Iames canonial
epistel. He seiþ what is religiun, hwuch is riht ordre. Religio munda
et immaculata apud deum et patrem hec est: visitare pup[illos] et
viduas in nec[essitate] sua, et immaculatum se custodire ab hoc seculo. (T9)

If any ignorant person should ask you to which Order you belong, as
you tell me some people do (straining the liquid to get rid of a gnat
and yet swallowing a fly), say that you belong to the Order of St.
James . . . If such an answer astonishes him, ask him what constitutes
"order" and where in Holy Writ he might find religion more clearly
and plainly described than it is in St. James's canonical epistle. There
he describes religion and true "order"; *Religion clean and undefiled be-*
fore God and the Father is this: to visit the fatherless and widows in their
tribulation and to keep oneself unspotted from this world. (S4)

The author, for his part, will not allow the legitimacy of the anchoresses'
"order" to derive from any manmade order or rule, but rather from Scripture, in this case a definition of religion from St. James's Epistle, which was
used by several twelfth-century writers to undermine the legalistic claims of
both Benedictines and Cistercians.[50]
   The author's ironic reference to the "Order of St. James" is not his only
reference to the Benedictine-Cistercian quarrel. He specifically identifies the
black and white monks, or at least their defenders, with those "ignorant
people" who have swallowed the "fly" of legalism:

Þus þe apostle sein Iame þe descriueð religiun, nowðer hwit ne blac
ne nempneð he in his ordre. Ah moni siheð þe gneat ant swolheð þe
flehe, þet is, makeð muche strengðe þer as is þe leaste. (T10)

So St. James the apostle, when he is describing what religion is, says
nothing about "white" or "black" in his "order." But there are many
who strain out the gnat and swallow the fly, that is, they go to great
lengths where there is the least need. (S4–5)

Although the author concedes that large religious groups require some
uniformity in dress and other external matters, he reminds his readers that
such uniformity is useful only as the sign of a group's "inward unity of . . .
love." In overvaluing the sign, religious orders (and the author seems to
include all religious orders in this category except the new orders of friars)

have neglected the thing itself and deserve the wrath that Christ (Matthew 23:25, 27) reserved for hypocrites:

> Ve uobis scribe et pharisei, ypocrite, qui mundatis quod deforis est calicis et parapsidis; intus autem pleni estis omni spursicia similes sepulcris dealbatis. (T11)

> Woe to you, scribes and Pharisees, hypocrites; because you make clean the outside of the cup and of the dish, but within you are full of uncleanness, like to whited sepulchres. (S5)

Obviously, such a vehement attack is not directed specifically to the anchoresses, though it is meant as a warning to them, prompted by their request for a religious rule. The author here speaks directly to those religious groups, particularly the monastic groups, involved in the contemporary controversy over religious rules. His vehemence, as well as his refusal to endorse even a rule as flexible and moderate as the Augustinian Rule, indicates just how suspicious he is of the motives and assumptions of those who have urged the anchoresses to identify themselves with some established order and rule. After all, he argues, following once more the logic of Peter the Chanter, devout men and women led exemplary religious lives long before the first religious rule was invented:

> Pawel þe earste ancre, Antonie ant Arsenie, Makarie ant te oþre, neren ha religiuse ant of sein Iames ordre? Alswa seinte Sare ant seinte Sicleclice ant monie oþre swucc hewepmen ba ant wummen, wið hare greate matten ant hare hearde heren, neren ha of god ordre? Ant hweðer hwite oðer blake as unwise ow easkið, þe weneð þet ordre sitte i þe curtel. (T10)

> Were not Paul, the first hermit, Antony and Arsenius, Macharius and the others, religious of the Order of St. James? And SS. Sarah and Syncletica and many other similar people, both men and women, with their coarse sleeping-mats and their harsh hair-shirts, were not they of a good "order"? And what matter whether it was white or black as those foolish people ask you, who think that "order" lies in the habit? (S5)

Order in the religious life is, for the *Wisse* author, a matter of self-awareness, which can only be taught by an interior rule. Overattention to a fixed and seemingly authoritative religious rule can as easily deaden self-awareness as promote it.

In his offer of an inner "theological rule" based upon Scripture instead of a religious rule, in his refusal to allow the anchoresses to attach undue authority to any manmade rule, and especially in his castigation of those who think that religion can be defined by simple obedience to fixed, external rules, the *Ancrene Wisse* author makes clear that his book, instead of promoting a particular religious rule, attempts to move its original readers beyond the prescriptiveness of religious rules altogether and toward a more self-conscious awareness of their interior lives. The *Ancrene Wisse*, then, does not derive from a particular rule, even the moderate Rule of St. Augustine. Instead, the book is written in opposition to those who would demand a fixed and particular set of external precepts as the only legitimate definition of an individual's spiritual goals. That opposition can be said to have been prepared for by the development of the Augustinian Rule a hundred years earlier, but it owes more of its force and its substance to the more radical opposition to all religious rules that developed in the late twelfth and early thirteenth centuries.

The Rule of St. Augustine was the first widely accepted religious rule to challenge St. Benedict's notion that a specific and binding religious rule is the best measure of the spiritual life. The monastic ideal, especially as reinforced by the Cistercians, was to create "supernatural order in the midst of flux."[51] In practice this meant substituting the monastery and religious community for the world, and, to some extent at least, substituting obedience for love. The canons' objections to this ideal were largely practical; already working in the world, they needed a rule flexible enough to complement their religious lives, and prestigious enough to thwart attacks on the legitimacy of their order. Their success in having the Augustinian Rule recognized as a legitimate religious rule paved the way for a more self-conscious reconsideration of the whole notion of an exclusive, manmade religious rule. In the late twelfth and early thirteenth centuries a solution to the problem of legitimacy in the religious life much bolder and more uncompromising than the canons' solution was formed in diverse quarters. There is only one legitimate rule of life, say Peter the Chanter, Jacques de Vitry, St. Francis, and the *Ancrene Wisse* author—the inner rule of the gospel, which, because it does not depend upon the special circumstances of religious orders and religious rules, applies equally to all Christians. Men's inventions or approximations should not be substituted for God's commands. The rule of the gospel is the rule of charity, these writers argue, and the command to love, unlike the command to obey external rules, requires a personal, interior, spiritual response that cannot be measured by adherence to even the strictest and most exclusive religious rules.

In one sense, the *Ancrene Wisse* makes a strange companion to these new rules, for the Augustinian Rule as well as the "rule of the gospel" promoted by Peter the Chanter and St. Francis both focus primarily upon the active life, the religious life of Christians who live and work in the world, rather than in monasteries. The *Wisse* author, writing for narrowly enclosed, contemplative recluses, faces none of the practical problems that had to be considered by those interested in rules for canons, friars, and laymen. In fact, given the extreme physical circumstances of the anchoresses, one might logically expect the author to compose as exclusive and otherworldly a rule as he could imagine, incorporating all of the strictest Cistercian precepts. Yet the author decidedly chooses an inclusive and highly individualized rule guided by the one inner and personalized rule of love. Indeed, most of the six-part inner rule is as applicable to devout Christians living in the world as it is to anchoresses, a fact that has puzzled a number of critics.[52] Partly, the *Ancrene Wisse* author's choice to write an antirule indicates that the new desire for individuality and flexibility in the religious life had moved beyond practical and political concerns. But in part the author's choice of the more flexible and "worldly" rule is an implicit denial of the monastic belief that one can, by ordering the exterior life, escape the flux of the world. In fact the inner rule of the *Ancrene Wisse* is designed to show just how "unruly" the world is, even for a solitary, seemingly enclosed anchoress.

~ 2 ~

Self and Society: The Solitary Life

S OLITARIES, by definition, are those religious who have most radically withdrawn from the world. That the anchoresses addressed in the *Ancrene Wisse* have more in common, by way of a religious rule, with canons and friars than with cloistered monks seems, therefore, incongruous. Viewed historically, the solitary ideal is marked by the desire to become "dead to the world." Severely ascetic and obviously antisocial, this goal implies an absolute denial of self and the world that extends beyond the renunciation of all physical pleasure to include the renunciation of even the most common of human and social desires—concern for family, friends, and one's own well-being. Many scholars have found the *Ancrene Wisse* exceptional in this regard for its "moderation" and "good sense."[1] But it seems to me that the author moves beyond simply moderating the severities traditionally associated with the solitary life. While it cannot be denied that the *Ancrene Wisse* is, by our standards at least, an ascetic work, it is also an uncommonly worldly book.

It is curious that a book written for recluses should be so dense with reminders of every conceivable aspect of medieval town life—the market, mill and barnyard, the parlor, battlefield and tournament, the manners of knights, ladies, servants, soap peddlers, cloth merchants, wrestlers, and thieves. Janet Grayson's recent study of the imagery of the *Ancrene Wisse* suggests that the author finds references to the outer world useful as analogies to the interior world of the anchoress's heart.[2] Grayson amply demonstrates that the inner-outer dichotomy, first established by the author in his characterization of religious rules, sets the pattern for his imagery throughout the work: he will draw an image from the outer world, probe it for its spiritual significance, then (and often unexpectedly) return to its literal meaning. I would suggest, however, that the author's interest in the external world extends far beyond his sensitivity to "the allegorical potential of an idea or image."[3] One of his central aims is to convince the solitary that she *cannot* finally escape her awareness of the world just outside her window by allegorically transforming it into spirit. The author sets out to demonstrate that the anchoress's attraction to the world originates within her own heart; therefore, her inner, spiritual life and outer, worldly circum-

32

stances are inextricably bound, not by analogy, but in fact. One is not a symbol for the other, nor can one replace the other. The anchoress's quest for spiritual communion with Christ must be a journey *into* the world of human desire, not away from it.

The *Ancrene Wisse* was written at the historical moment when some important distinctions between laymen and religious were breaking down. The work of the friars in the towns and cities of medieval Europe typifies a growing feeling that salvation, even sanctity, is possible in the world. Furthermore, the new spirituality of the age emphasized the potential of human and worldly desires to lead men to an intimate and sensuous love of God. The portrayal of Christ as a man living among men captured the imagination of laymen and religious alike. In the light of these cultural developments, the traditional solitary goal of otherworldliness might be seen as suspect or anachronistic. At least it can be said that with the increasing value being accorded to life in the world, the status and function of solitaries had to be reexamined. In the increasingly nonmonastic view of the world, solitaries became difficult to account for. For example, they provided a problem for twelfth- and thirteenth-century canonists, intent on categorizing Christians in terms of the status and privileges of the three estates—monastic, clerical, and secular:

> Such diverse truths left canonists undecided about the status of hermits. They were decidedly not monks. But they escaped the reproach of acephalism; these faithful, subordinated to the Church hierarchy, could not be taken for gadabouts, living without a fixed rule . . . the common tendency was . . . to identify hermits with clerks because of their connection with secular life, and to consider them the most humble aspirants toward spiritual perfection.[4]

Although solitaries had always been somewhat difficult to classify, their dramatic withdrawal to the remote wildernesses of Europe and the Near East had ensured their place as the most elite religious group from the fourth century forward. But in the twelfth century both the Church's increasing commitment to life in the world and the fact that solitaries now lived more often in or near town than in the wilderness made the solitary life more difficult than ever to explain. The new solitaries seemed to participate in two realms at once: the ideal and traditional sphere of absolute withdrawal from the world and the practical sphere of involvement in it. The physical arrangement of the anchorhold, which the *Ancrene Wisse* author describes early in his work, testifies to the precarious position of solitaries vis-à-vis the world. The anchoress is locked in a small cell attached to the side of a local church, but she is not enclosed or protected by it; she

looks through one small window into the church and through another out
onto the world. The inner rule of the *Ancrene Wisse* can be described as the
author's attempt to reconcile these two worlds, and these two windows.

Solitude as a spiritual goal has its roots in the desert tradition of the
fourth century.[5] No sooner had the new Christian Church emerged from
its catacomb existence than a small minority of Christians began to retreat
from the now legal and therefore "safe" world of the established Church to
the untamed and uncompromising world of the remote Egyptian desert.
While the Church was entering upon a new period of accommodation to
the world, the desert stood as an adequate symbol, as well as a fact, signify-
ing a few men's unaccommodating desire to win salvation by experiencing
the extreme spiritual and physical dangers of life alone. The impulse to
withdraw was twofold. On the one hand, the retreat to the desert was a
protest against the softness of a Christian life unhampered by persecution
and protected by the increasingly powerful Church hierarchy. In this respect the desert fathers actively sought to become "dead to the world"
through self-surrender and extreme self-denial. But on the other hand, the
movement was from the very beginning strongly individualistic, marked
by a demand for a more personal contact with spiritual forces than the
Church could provide.[6] The desert fathers may have desired the anonymity
of inner peace and contemplation, but what they more often describe are
individual, heroic battles with legions of devils.

There had been misgivings about a life outside the Church's structure as
early as the time of St. Benedict. But the great monastic legislator himself
had never denied or even questioned the high status of the solitary life: if it
was not the safest way to heaven, it was still the highest way. Though always a life chosen by only a few, until the High Middle Ages the solitary
life—whether eremitic or anchoritic—was esteemed as the very pinnacle of
spiritual progress. St. Simeon living atop his sixty-foot pillar serves as a vis-
ual representation of the exalted position of solitaries over all other Christians, and the crowds that came to observe him attest to the reverence paid
to what we now consider a bizarre example of holiness.

Ample proof of such reverence for the solitary ideal can be found in the
number of solitaries who figure in the Church's earliest literature. When
the persecutions ceased in the fourth century, the heroic tales of martyrs
were quickly replaced by the no less heroic and vivid battles of desert fathers with devils in all guises. Saints' lives for nearly the next one thousand
years were more or less carefully modeled on Athanasius's *Life of St. Anthony,* the greatest of the desert hermits.[7] So powerful was the desert example that even hagiographers of what are usually considered very "public"
saints—bishops and abbots—felt obliged to cast their heroes in the desert

mold in one way or another: either at the beginning of the Life, as the place from which the saint was reluctantly drawn, or else at the end of the Life, as the saint's chosen place of retirement. It is not enough for the hagiographer that St. Cuthbert, for example, was hospitable, just, discreet, and kind; nor is it enough that as a bishop he performed every conceivable public act of mercy:

> Curam pauperum gerens, esurientes pascens, nudos uestiens, peregrinos suscipiens, captiuos redimens, uiduas et pupillos tuens, ut mercedem uitae aeternae inter choros angelorum cum Domino nostro Iesu Christo accipere mereatur.

> He cared for the poor, fed the hungry, clothed the naked, took in strangers, redeemed captives and protected widows and orphans, that he might merit the reward of eternal life amid the choirs of angels in the presence of our Lord Jesus Christ.[8]

What is more important for the biographer (and therefore, presumably, for his audience) is that Bishop Cuthbert began and ended his life with glorious solitary combat on the Isle of Farne,

> undique in medio mari fluctibus circumcinctam, . . . Ubi prius pene nullus potuit solus propter uarias demonum fantasias aliquod spatium manere.

> which is in the midst of the sea and surrounded on every side by water, a place where, before this, almost no one could remain alone for any length of time on account of various illusions caused by devils.[9]

Though Cuthbert's work in the world was important, it is primarily for his "anachoritae uirtutem" that his biographer wants him to be remembered.[10]

Largely because it had been more or less codified in such popular saints' lives as Cuthbert's and Anthony's, the desert ideal remained intact throughout the Benedictine centuries, though in practice the number of desert solitaries shrank considerably as monasticism caught hold. In the late eleventh century the desert language returned as a response to conditions similar to those that had prompted the first desert fathers to withdraw. Once again the Church was ready to enter a period of accommodation to the world, this time in the guise of the Gregorian Reform; simultaneously, the urge to withdraw completely from the world led an elite few to self-styled "desert-wildernesses" in Europe. Yet this time the impact of the eremitic movement seems muted.

There are a variety of reasons why the eleventh-century eremitic revival was short-lived; two of them, it seems to me, were bound to change the character and status of the solitary life. First, the leaders of the Gregorian Reform were less accommodating than aggressive in their assault upon the secular world. Unlike conditions after the persecutions, when unexpectedly and quite abruptly the Church's power in the world increased almost in spite of itself, the Gregorian leaders of the eleventh century actively sought political power. As an institution the Church had become far more efficient and organized than the struggling Church of the fourth century. During the course of the lay investiture controversy the Church had emphatically committed itself to the affairs of the world. Indeed, the vigor of Church leaders who confidently dictated to emperors, kings, and princes bespeaks a supreme optimism that the Church not only could thrive outside the cloister, but could effectively rule the world.[11] Such a powerful and confident Church hierarchy could certainly control, regulate, and quickly assimilate the small new eremitic groups. And while the Gregorian movement failed in its more obvious goal of divesting secular authority of its power, it did succeed in ensuring a powerful position for the Church in the world. The Church was never again destined to go underground, either to the catacombs, to the desert, or behind the walls of monasteries.

Second, simultaneous with the growth of ecclesiastical structure, which could be said to have doomed the desert revival from the start, had come a much more mundane but equally serious problem. The enormous expansion of society in the eleventh and twelfth centuries and the resulting myriad of new towns all over Europe made the practical requirements of remoteness difficult to achieve. In England especially, where one historian notes that by the twelfth century no spot in the country was more than half a day's walk from the nearest village or town,[12] the desert cry of the new breed of solitaries seems somewhat futile. Indeed, though the solitary ideal is not yet questioned, there is a good deal of nostalgia or romantic idealism evident in the eremitic revival. For though the new monasteries were self-consciously called deserts,[13] physical solitude was in fact rare. And in one of the few places in England where it was actually created—Revesby—it was, as one historian wryly notes, "at the expense of destroying three small towns."[14]

Short of the destruction of villages however, people could do little to ensure or even create solitude in the twelfth century except express a wish for it. Yet the wish is forcefully expressed, and, ironically enough, by two of the most politically prominent of twelfth-century saints, Peter the Venerable and Bernard of Clairvaux, men not only embroiled in public debate with each other, but also involved in virtually every international, political, and religious dispute of their day. Though the most public of saints, both professed a particular devotion to the Carthusian Order, the only new religious order arising from the eremitic reform to remain at least semieremitic.[15] Furthermore, Peter the Venerable, in his widely read letter to the hermit Giselbertus writes:

> Nam inclusionis et solitudinis tuae recordatus, me mundo expositum medullitus ingemui, et te ei morientem ne dicam mortuum gratulans intellexi.[16]

> When I was reminded of your confinement and solitude, I sighed inwardly for myself, exposed to the world, and I understood your willing dying or death to the world.

St. Bernard also was perpetually embarrassed over his conflicting desires, for solitude on the one hand and for leadership in the Cistercian Order on the other. Continually traveling, speaking, and writing, he would from time to time renew his solitary desire in letters to Carthusians, to whom he confessed himself as a "sort of contemporary chimaera," tormented by conflicting goals.[17] That St. Bernard could be so overwrought by the split between his own religious life and that of the desert fathers is proof enough that the desert ideal was still powerful. But it is not long before even the wish for solitude loses some of its force. The Church's new interest in the world, together with the rise of new towns throughout Western Europe, forces what seems to me to be a crisis in the status and interpretation of the solitary life.

Not surprisingly, the clearest signs of the crisis appear in twelfth-century works written for and about solitaries. Two representative works, both written in England within a few years of St. Bernard's death, indicate a novel desire to reconcile the traditional otherworldliness of the solitary life with the new spiritual and practical conditions of twelfth-century Europe. At the same time, the extreme and somewhat awkward solutions presented in these works highlight the later achievement of the *Ancrene Wisse* author, who creates a carefully balanced tension between the solitary's participation in the world and her withdrawal from it.

The *Life of Christina of Markyate* depicts what might be called the socialization of the solitary ideal. Christina's anonymous biographer not only takes for granted a continuous interplay between the solitary and the world, but even goes so far as to present the traditional requirements of the solitary life—withdrawal from the world and severe asceticism—as goals that serve primarily worldly ends: physical protection from hostile pursuers, political power, and even financial success. At the other extreme stands Aelred of Rievaulx's *De vita eremitica*, which seems in most respects a reactionary treatise. Its author insists that a solitary must render herself abso-

lutely "dead to the world" by practicing the most severe forms of asceticism. But at the very end of the work Aelred suddenly changes course and,
without warning or preparation, offers a series of meditations that turn
upon all of the solitary's most human and worldly desires. That these two
works offer such different characterizations of the solitary life is in itself an
important sign of a breakdown in tradition. More important, however, is
that neither author seems willing or able to connect what he implies is the
solitary's rich, expansive, interior life with her stringent physical circumstances. The *Ancrene Wisse* author alone concentrates on this connection
and successfully redesigns the solitary life to meet the new spiritual and
practical needs of his day.

The *Life of Christina of Markyate* is a peculiar work in many respects, but
especially when viewed as the life of a solitary.[18] For though Christina's
birth, marked by clear signs from heaven of the child's future holiness, is
traditional, what follows bears little more than a remote resemblance to the
usual life of a solitary.[19] For one thing, the author makes no attempt to
justify the solitary life on any traditional grounds. It is not, as with St.
Benedict, the ultimate spiritual test, undertaken after long trial in the
monastery; nor is it, as seen by Cuthbert's biographer, an early choice that
typifies the saint's degree of perfection before he is unwillingly called back
to serve in the world. For Christina the solitary life is not a choice at all,
but rather a necessity imposed upon her by unusual circumstances. Christina desires, quite simply and rather unheroically, to enter a convent, hardly
a unique goal for an Anglo-Saxon noblewoman in twelfth-century England.[20] What makes this rather commonplace desire so extraordinary is that
all who surround Christina, from her increasingly determined parents to
Ralph, the "justiciar of the whole of England," seem bent on frustrating
her desire to enter the convent.

When Christina finally does escape the numerous and ingenious traps
designed to trick her into marriage,[21] she is forced to take refuge in a solitary's cell rather than in the monastery only because she fears for her life,
rather than for her soul, and deems the narrow confinement of the cell the
best hiding place available. Here the dangers of the world that force the
holy into seclusion, a traditional motif of desert literature, are not spiritual
but physical. The various cells that Christina occupies are described in
graphic detail, and all are described primarily as good hiding places:

> Carcer erat iuxta oratorium senis. et domo illi contiguus qui cum illo
> fecit angulum coniunctione sua. Is antepositam habens unam tabu-
> lam poterat ita celari. ut de foris aspicienti nullum interius haberi
> persuaderet. ubi tamen amplitudo plus palmo semis inesset. In hoc

ergo carcere Rogerus ovantem sociam posuit. et ligni robur pro hostio conveniens admovit. Et hov eciam tanti ponderis erat. quod ab inclusa nullatenus admoveri sive removeri poterat. Hic igitur ancilla Christi coartata supra durum petram sedit usque ad obitum Rogeri. id est .iiii. annis, et eo amplius. Latens illos quoque qui cum Rogero simul habitabant.   (p. 102)

Near the chapel of the old man and joined to his cell was a room which made an angle where it joined. This had a plank of wood placed before it and was so concealed that to anyone looking from outside it would seem that no one was present within, since the space was not bigger than a span and a half. In this prison, therefore, Roger placed his happy companion. In front of the door he rolled a heavy log of wood, the weight of which was actually so great that it could not be put in its place or taken away by the recluse. And so, thus confined, the handmaid of Christ sat on a hard stone until Roger's death, that is four years and more, concealed even from those who dwelt together with Roger.   (p. 103)

Another cell is "in secretissimam amarissimamque cameram vix illi pre angustia sufficientem detrusa" ("[h]idden out of sight in a very dark chamber hardly large enough, on account of its size, to house her"), where she could easily remain "occultata" (pp. 92–93).

It is especially noticeable in an otherwise highly dramatic and vividly descriptive work that so little is said about what Christina *does* in her cell, except that she finds "delect[ationem] pro Christi." Some of her trials within the cell are described, but few of these are the traditional solitary's bouts with devils sent by God to test the maiden's strength or virginity.[22] She suffers hardships, but rather than being self-imposed exercises in asceticism, these trials are quite literally pressed upon her by the necessity of her close confinement. One dwelling is so small that it "non admittebat necessarium tegumentum algenti" ("would not allow her to wear even the necessary [covering] when she was cold" [pp. 102–103]). Her lack of warm clothing, her severe fasting, even her inability to leave her cell to fulfill the demands of nature ("necessaria que natura postulabat"), are necessary for physical, not spiritual, survival:

Itaque necesse fuit immobiliter eam in loco sedere. torqueri et tacere. Quia si Rogerum habere voluerat voce vel pulsu vocari eum oportebat. Sed qualiter hoc faceret abscondita que nec ausa fuit semisuspiria? Metuebat namque ne quis preter Rogerum adesset. qui vel anelitu spirantis audito latebras suas deprehenderet.   (p. 104)

So it was necessary for her to sit quite still in the place, to suffer tor-
ments, and to keep quiet, because if she wished Roger to come to her,
she had to summon him either by calling or knocking. But how
could she do this from her hiding-place when she dared hardly
breathe? For she was afraid that someone else besides Roger might be
near, and hearing her breathing, would disclose her hiding-place.   (p.
105)

This passage is especially interesting in that the biographer self-consciously alludes to a well-known summary of the desert ideals: "Tu sede, tu
tace, tu sustine," counsel the fathers. But in Christina's case the quiet sitting serves the purpose not of allowing her to hear God, but of preventing
her from being heard and discovered by her persecutors.

Finally, after a series of dramatic adventures interspersed with heavenly
consolations, Christina does fulfill her original and only wish: "in [St.
Alban's] monasterio professionem suam facere" (p. 126). Though sought
after by the heads of monasteries all over England and Europe, Christina
prefers to take her vows at St. Alban's, the monastery of her choice since
she had been a child. She does remain in a hermitage close to the monastery rather than within the abbey itself, but again no particular desire for
the solitary life is given as the reason; it is quite possible that Christina was
required to live in the hermitage only because the monastery had no facili-
ties for women. Only once does Christina express a fleeting desire to retire
to some "remotas terras" where she could live "incognita" (p. 146). However, since by this time being hidden from the world is no longer a security
requirement, friends persuade Christina to stay among them. Besides, she
has by now become very important to the monastery. Through her connections the hermitage, which had been declining, is generously endowed
with wealth.[23] She makes friends and advisees of priests, abbots, and politi-
cians and becomes involved in disputes ranging from papal mandates to
King Stephen's troubles with the barons and clergy. In fact it is rumored
by some unworthies that she is more businesswoman than saint: "secu-
larium agendorum prudentem procuratricem appellabant" (p. 172). Her
hermitage becomes much like the enclosure of one of her dreams:

In oracionibus . . . constituta vidi ambitum quemdam de lignis candi-
dissimis. et hiis perspicuis circumseptum ostio fenestrisque carentem
ad modum claustri.   (p. 164)

When I was at prayer I saw a kind of enclosure surrounded by high
fences which were transparent: it resembled a cloister without doors
or windows.   (p. 165)

Though they enclose and protect Christina from harm, the walls are never-theless quite transparent; Christina can therefore be a visible participant in local affairs and can be drawn out of her cell and her contemplation when-ever the divine will needs her services in the world. And that is remarkably often.

The last section of the *Life,* a full third of the manuscript, concerns Christina's directing the affairs of one Abbot Geoffrey, a wealthy monk who is introduced in the text as a solution to the most worldly of prob-lems, Christina's financial difficulties.[24] In return for Geoffrey's generosity Christina becomes his adviser, counseling the well-connected abbot some-times in spiritual matters but more often in his intricate political affairs. Three times Christina prevents Geoffrey from setting off for Rome, not be-cause the missions might harm Geoffrey's soul, but because she foresees that they would be politically disastrous for the abbot, whose wealth and position depend upon his maintaining a friendly relationship with the iras-cible King Stephen.[25] Indeed, it is no wonder that Christina is famed for her business sense. When the text breaks off (the rest of the manuscript is lost) Christina is pursuing the traditional ascetic tactics of fasting and keeping vigil for the most untraditional and worldly ends of protecting Geoffrey's interests:

> Familiaris et amici abbatis .G. . . . Christina die ac nocte memor erat, et circa eum quod illi expediret probe satagebat ieiunando, vigilando deum exorando, angelos et alios sanctos in celo et in terra supplicando misericordiam Dei super illum precibus et obsequiis, que minus recte videbatur gerere sapienter increpando: sa——— (p. 192)

> Christina's thoughts were with her dear friend Abbot Geoffrey . . . night and day, and she busied herself with his interests by fasting, watching, calling upon God, the angels, and other holy folk in heaven and on earth, asking for the mercy of God with humble prayers, sensibly reproving him when his actions were not quite right. (p. 193)

Thus Christina, who never did want to become a solitary, never does be-come one, at least not in any traditional sense. Her biographer has created a fascinating and skillful narrative to which the forgoing analysis hardly does justice. But in addition to portraying vividly a distinct individual whose particular motivations and goals shape every phase of her life, he has also portrayed a solitary who is, to use St. Bernard's phrase, a contemporary chimera. The intervals that Christina spends as a solitary in her cell seem incidental to her life. Unlike St. Bernard, however, neither Christina nor her biographer anguish over her lack of solitude, except when external circumstances require physical protection. Her inner life—whether psychological or spiritual—is neither defined nor determined by her withdrawal from the world.

The biography suggests, I believe, a shift in interest during the twelfth century away from the solitary's traditional triumph of becoming passively "dead to the world" and toward more active and worldly virtues, in this case prudence, cunning, and determination. Christina does not achieve perfection or renown by passive endurance of supernatural trials, as did earlier desert solitaries. Her trials are in fact exceedingly natural: conflicts with parents, fear of discovery, and concern for the well-being of friends. The biographer's interest in Christina's spiritual accomplishments begins with his admiration for her clever and prudent manipulation of people and circumstances. Christina's sanctity, then, is achieved almost in spite of, and certainly not because of, her solitary life.

If the *Life of Christina of Markyate* were the only evidence available concerning twelfth-century attitudes toward the solitary life, we would have to conclude that the solitary ideal lost both its significance and appeal during this period in which Christianity was turning its attention toward the spiritual possibilities of life in the world, rather than apart from it. We know, of course, that that is not true; the number of solitaries in England and Europe did not significantly decline until the very end of the Middle Ages.[26] Literary and cultural historians who have attempted to characterize the solitary ideal in the High Middle Ages rarely mention the *Life of Christina of Markyate*, probably because it is so easy while following Christina's adventures to forget that she is, in fact, a solitary. But they never fail to mention Aelred of Rievaulx's *De vita eremitica,* a rule for solitaries that influenced the *Ancrene Wisse* directly and that amply demonstrates that the solitary tradition was by no means lost in the twelfth century. Nevertheless, it has not been sufficiently recognized that Aelred's work, like Christina's biography, shows clear signs of tension between the otherworldly ideal of the solitary tradition and the new twelfth-century interest in a more worldly spirituality.

Moving from Christina's exciting and dramatic world to Aelred's quiet Cistercian cloister may seem a long step. When Aelred first came to Rievaulx, he announced that he had finally arrived at the "desert," having come from the "kitchens" of the world.[27] Here at least, it would seem, the traditional desert goals could be wholeheartedly embraced. Yet Aelred is as ill at ease in describing the solitary ideal as Christina's biographer, though his reaction takes a different form. Aelred is alarmed by the lack of supervision in the solitary life. In his *De vita eremitica,* written for his sister who had long been a solitary, Aelred seeks not so much to extoll the traditional solitary life as to regulate and stabilize it.[28] A recent biography of Abbot Aelred notes that in most of his works Aelred

> displays no enthusiasm for those who withdraw "on their own initiative to some wood . . ." and "eat when they like, sleep when they like, work and rest when they like." He prefers the common life under rule not only because it involves the intimate sacrifice of one's own will, but also because it provides the objective assurance of a balance which is appropriate to man's present situation.[29]

In fact, both because of personality and Cistercian ideology, Aelred is unwaveringly committed to the community life. On the rewards of friendship, a great twelfth-century theme that bespeaks the age's interest in human as well as divine love, no one could write more movingly than Aelred, except perhaps Cicero, whose treatise *De amicitia* Aelred adapted.[30] Aelred's interest in the affairs of the world by no means approaches that of Christina's biographer. But his commitment to a spiritual life grounded in human love and friendship certainly separates him from the solitary tradition. "In his eyes," notes one religious historian, "the interior life *is* a social one, a communion among monks."[31]

Because he believes that the spiritual life depends for its nourishment upon close ties with a community of monks, Aelred is at somewhat of a loss when asked by his sister to describe and provide a rule for the solitary life. Thus, he begins his address:

> Utinam a sapientiore id peteres, et impetrares, qui non coniectura qualibet sed experientia didicisset, quod alios doceret. (*DVE*, 42)

> How I wish you had sought and obtained [a rule for the solitary life] from someone wiser than myself, someone whose teaching was based not on mere conjecture but on personal experience. (*LR*, 43)

Aelred is not merely being modest here; his confusion concerning the benefits of the solitary life is evident both in his introduction and in the curiously disjointed structure of his work as a whole.

Aelred's introduction to his rule betrays a marked ambivalence toward the solitary life as a religious ideal. He begins with a standard tribute to the desert fathers, but at the same time he seems bewildered by the reasons those venerable men chose the solitary life. Only belatedly does he suggest that some chose to live alone for positive, rather than negative reasons:

> Primum igitur oportet te scire que causa, quave ratione huiusmodi vita ab antiquis vel instituta sit vel usurpata. Sunt quidam, quibus

inter multos vivere perniciosum est. Sunt et alii quibus et si non perniciosum, est tamen dispendiosum. Sunt et nonnulli quibus nihil
horum timendum est, sed secretius habitare magis aestimant fructuo-
sum. Itaque antiqui vel ut vitarent periculum, vel ne paterentur dis-
pendium, vel ut liberius ad Christi anhelarent et suspirarent am-
plexum, singulariter vivere delegerunt.   (*DVE,* 42, 44)

You must first understand the reasons that motivated the monks of
old when they instituted and adopted this form of life. Living in a
crowd means ruin for some people; for others it will mean, if not
ruin, at least injury, others again, unmoved by an apprehension, simply considered living in solitude to be more fruitful. The monks of
old then chose to live as solitaries for several reasons: to avoid ruin, to
escape injury, to enjoy greater freedom in expressing their ardent
longing for Christ's embrace.   (*LR,* 45)

This "greater freedom" is never again referred to in Aelred's rule. In fact,
immediately after conceding it as a possible motive for solitaries, Aelred
qualifies the concession considerably by suggesting that while some desert
fathers might have sought spiritual freedom, others feared it:

Hinc est quod plures in heremo soli sedebant, vitam manuum suarum
opere sustenantes. Illi vero qui nec hoc sibi securum, propter solitu-
dinis libertatem et vagandi potestatem, arbitrabantur, includi potius
et infra cellulam obstruso exitu contineri tutius aestimabant.
(*DVE,* 44)

Some lived alone in the desert, supporting themselves by the work of
their hands; but there were others whose confidence was undermined
by the very freedom inherent in the solitary life and the opportunity
it affords for aimless wandering. They judged it more prudent to be
completely enclosed in a cell with the entrance walled up.   (*LR,* 45)

Thus ends Aelred's tribute to the desert tradition. Its vague and ambivalent
praise contrasts sharply with, for example, St. Jerome's famous homage to
the desert ideal:

O desertum, Christi floribus vernans . . . Quamdiu te tectorum ubrae
praemunt? Crede mihi, nescio quid plus lucis aspicio.[32]

O desert blooming with the flowers of Christ . . . How long will you
remain in the shadows of city roofs? Believe me, I see here more of
the light.

But if Aelred would consider the desert ideal bewildering even at its purest, as it was during St. Jerome's time, he finds it almost impossible to sympathize with the contemporary recluse, who lives not in the desert at all, but in busy towns, bustling with merchants in markets, gossips and schoolchildren. After only one brief paragraph of muted homage to the solitary life, Aelred lashes out at the typical recluse, "ignorant," "dissolute," "distracted," "idle," "shameful," and sometimes even pregnant.[33]

In the rule itself Aelred's first purpose is to stabilize and regulate the contemporary recluse's life. He teaches what he knows best, strict Cistercian rules of conduct, based largely upon the Rule of St. Benedict, but here narrowed to one purpose: the preservation of chastity. A. Squire may judge the *De vita eremitica* harshly, but no more so, I believe, than Abbot Aelred judged the purpose of the solitary life: "Fundamentally Aelred's work . . . is an ascetic letter on the preservation of virginity, which incorporates a Benedictine timetable and dietary, together with some . . . advice on how to meditate."[34] It is interesting that Squire makes no distinction here between the two parts of Aelred's rule. Aelred's closing remarks make clear that he intends his work to be divided into an "inner" and an "outer" rule:

> Habes nunc sicut petisti: corporales institutiones, quibus inclusa exterioris hominis mores componat; habes formam praescriptam qua interiorem hominem vel purges a vitiis, vel virtutibus ornes. (*DVE*, 168)

> You have now what you asked for: rules for bodily observances by which a recluse may govern the behavior of the outward man; directions for cleansing the inner man from vices and adorning him with virtues. (*LR*, 102)

But in fact Squire is correct in overlooking Aelred's divisions, for the two kinds of rules, so carefully separated in the *Ancrene Wisse*, are virtually indistinguishable in the *De vita eremitica*.

Both parts of Aelred's treatise deal primarily with virginity as the most important goal of the solitary life. The outer rule relies upon the precision of St. Benedict's Rule as an aid in the solitary's battle to keep her thoughts pure; Aelred's discussion of food and drink, for example, centers upon which foods the recluse should avoid, "lest they poison her purity" (*LR*, 59–60). The inner rule merely amplifies the same point, beginning with a more general discussion of virginity:

> Ita proinde in virginitatis suae custodiam totum animum tendat, cogitationes expendat. (*DVE*, 84)

Let the whole object then of her striving and of her thoughts be the preservation of her virginity.   (*LR*, 64)

Aelred then repeats his earlier injunctions regarding food and drink and suggests a number of ascetic practices even more severe than those outlined in the outer rule. The goal of the inner rule is virtually identical with that of the outer rule: to eliminate threats to the solitary's chastity by eliminating all sensual desire. Thus the solitary is counseled to consume what food she must "with pain and shame, at times with tears" (*LR*, 64). When carnal temptation is strong, the solitary should fast even more strictly, "for when the flesh is sorely afflicted there can be little or no pleasure" (*LR*, 66). In one of the harshest passages of the inner rule, Aelred advises the recluse not to worry that overly severe fasting might bring on illness:

> Quid enim interest utrum abstinentia an languore caro superbiens comprimatur, castitas conservetur? Sed remissio, inquit, cavenda est, ne forte occasione infirmitatis, incurramus illecebras voluptatis. Certe si languet, si egrotat, si torquentur viscera, arescit stomachus, quaelibet deliciae oneri magis erunt quam delectationi.   (*DVE*, 94)

> What difference does it make whether it be by fasting or by sickness that the pride of the flesh be tamed and chastity preserved? "But we must be on our guard against relaxation," it will be said, "lest perhaps on the grounds of infirmity we may be led astray by the attractions of pleasure." But you may be sure that the man who feels weak, who is ill, whose bowels are wrung, whose stomach is dried up, will find any pleasure more of a burden than a delight.   (*LR*, 69)

Such vigorous asceticism was not unusual, of course, in the lives of the desert fathers; what is unusual is that Aelred's inner rule places so little emphasis upon the compensatory spiritual freedom that he mentions in his introduction as a goal of the solitary life. With one major exception, Aelred seems to argue that the interior life of a solitary, like her exterior life, must center upon denying altogether the world of physical desire.

The exception, of course, is the section composed of three meditations that ends Aelred's treatise on the solitary life. The meditations, on the past (the life of Christ), the present life in the world, and the future life of death and judgment, have been justly praised for their beauty and closely studied for their originality and influence upon later meditative literature.[35] Indeed, the meditations lived on long after the rule itself had been set aside as an anachronism, and their importance to the history of spirituality cannot be denied. But the meditations are rarely studied as a part of a larger work, and so the tension between the subject matter of the meditations and that of the work as a whole has not been recognized.

That Aelred was aware of the gap between the meditations and the rest of his rule is evident. In his closing summary of the *De vita eremitica* he places the meditations in a category by themselves, apart from both the outer and the inner rules (*DVE*, 168). Furthermore, there is no mention of the meditations in his introduction, or in the inner rule itself. Instead, the meditations begin abruptly, introduced as "a few words added on the love of God" ("de dilectione Dei pauca subiungam" [*DVE*, 116]). Even the most cursory reading of the meditations makes the reasons for Aelred's abrupt transition clear: they are based upon entirely different spiritual assumptions from those of the rule itself.

When we turn to the first meditation, on the life of Christ, it is as though we have entered a new world. Gone is Aelred's pessimism which, in the more ascetic passages of the rule, borders on a loathing of humanity. Absolute self-denial and the elimination of all sensual desire is replaced by a warm love and tender passion for the humanity of Christ. The recluse is urged to recall every human and homey detail of Christ's life, to follow its events as though she had lived them. The details of the life, and the joys the recluse may expect from meditating on them are powerfully, sensually, and minutely described:

Sed iam surgentes, eamus hinc. Quo? inquis. Certe ut insidentem asello coeli terraeque Dominum comiteris, tantaque fieri pro te obstupescens, puerorum laudibus tuas inseras, clamans et dicens: Hosanna Filio David, benedictus qui venit in nomine Domini.

Iam nunc ascende cum eo in coenaculum grande stratum, et salutaris coenae interesse deliciis gratulare. Vincat verecundiam amor, timorem excludat affectus, ut saltem de micis mensae illius eleemosynam praebeat mendicanti. Vel a longe sta et quasi pauper intendens in divitem, ut aliquid accipias extende manum, famem lacrymis prode.

Cum autem surgens a coena, linteo se praecinxerit, posueritque aquam in pelvim, cogita quae maiestas hominum pedes abluit et extergit, quae benignitas proditoris vestigia sacris manibus tangit. Specta et expecta, et ultima omnium tuos ei pedes praebe abluendos, quia quem ipse non laverit non habebit partem cum eo.

Quid modo festinas exire? Sustine paululum, Vides ne? Quisnam ille est, rogo te, qui supra pectus eius recumbit, et in sinu eius caput reclinat? Felix quicumque ille est. O, ecce video: Ioannes est nomen eius. O Ioannes, quid ibi dulcedinis, quid gratiae et suavitatis, quid luminis et devotionis ab illo haurias fonte edicito. (*DVE*, 130, 132)

But we must rise and go hence. Where to? you ask. To be sure, to accompany the Lord of heaven and earth as he rides on an ass; to marvel at the great things which are done on your behalf and mingle your praise with that of the children, crying out: "Hosanna to the Son of David, blessed is he who comes in the name of the Lord." Now then go up with him into the larger upper room, furnished for supper, and rejoice to share the delights of the meal which brings us salvation. Let love overcome shyness, affection drive out fear, so that he may at least give you an alms from the crumbs of that table when you beg for something. Or stand at a distance and, like a poor man looking to a rich man, stretch out your hand to receive something, let your tears declare your hunger. But when he rises from the table, girds himself with the towel and pours water into the basin, consider what majesty it is that is washing and drying the feet of men, what graciousness it is that touches with his sacred hands the feet of the traitor. Look and wait and, last of all, give him your own feet to wash, because the man whom he does not wash will have no part with him.

Why are you in such a hurry to go out now? Wait a little while. Do you see? Who is that, I ask, who is reclining on his breast and bends back his head to lay it in his bosom? Happy is he, whoever he may be. O, I see: his name is John. O John, tell us what sweetness, what grace and tenderness, what light and devotion you are imbibing from that fountain.   (*LR,* 86)

Obviously, the sensuality of this meditative participation is meant as a kind of compensation to the recluse for the self-denial of her own life.

The meditations are evidence that Aelred does not altogether deny the power and influence of human desires on the spiritual life, and in this feeling he has much in common with the *Ancrene Wisse* author. The quality of spirituality for which both aim is not "otherworldly," or of the desert; it is a warm passion for Christ as a man in the world. But Aelred, who could succeed so well in analyzing the progress of such spirituality in the context of community life, where the love shared by monks was seen as an intermediate step toward an intimate love of Christ, could not, it seems to me, understand how such love could result from the solitary life. The meditations are tacked onto the rule almost as an afterthought. They are neither prepared for nor defined by the limits of the rule. Though Aelred claims in his preface that he will write "spiritualia corporalibus, ubi utile visum fuerit, interserens," (blending the spiritual with the corporal wherever it seems useful [*DVE,* 42]), there is almost no blending of the two at all. Aelred's prescriptions for the "interiorem hominem," are in fact a continuation of his concern for the exterior man, specifically a continuation of his discussion of chastity, which is presented throughout the work as its *own* reward until, abruptly, we arrive at the meditations. Aelred does describe the rule and the meditations as the "two elements in the love of God," but he does not establish any real connection—either psychological or dogmatic—between them.[36] He does at least imply a time relationship between the two elements, advising solitaries to meditate on the life of Christ only after they have perfected the rule:

> Cum igitur mens tua ab omni fuerit cogitationum sorde virtutum exercitatione purgata, iam oculos defaecatos ad posteriora retorque. (*DVE*, 116)

> When your mind has been cleansed by the practice of the virtues from all the thoughts which clogged it, cast your eyes back, purified as they are now, to the past. (*LR*, 80)

But how the solitary moves from the austere rule to the "sweet love" of the meditations is nowhere explained. The recluse who has successfully deadened herself to the world and to her own emotions is suddenly and unexpectedly brought back to life in the meditations, with all her senses and desires intact. If such a sensual love of Christ is the result of Aelred's rule, he, like St. Benedict before him, cannot explain how.

Thus Aelred seems caught between the traditional ascetic and antisocial goals of the solitary tradition, and a twelfth-century religious concern with human love. Although in his other (and, I might add, his more typical) works, written for monks, Aelred dwells upon the latter concern, in the *De vita eremitica* he feels compelled to endorse the former, insisting that the solitary must be "dead" to human love and all other worldly emotions. If the solitary does arrive at the same goal of love as monks, it is not by way of human friendship or any other worldly way that Aelred can describe.

These two works, then, provide two extreme responses to a peculiarly twelfth-century problem: how to reconcile esteemed and traditional solitary goals with a new interest in the ordinary affairs and desires of people living in the world. In the *Life of Christina of Markyate* the solitary ideal is all but dismissed by a biographer interested in describing Christina's extra-ordinary interactions with the political, social, and ecclesiastical world. In the *De vita eremitica* Aelred focuses directly on the desert ideal but does not sympathize with it and finally sets it aside in favor of meditations that emphasize human relationships and the homey details of everyday life. Both works exemplify the new twelfth-century interest in life in the world, but neither can reconcile this interest with the otherworldly solitary tradition.

If both writers assume that a special love for Christ can result from the solitary life, neither focuses upon the process of arriving at that love. It results more or less automatically.

The *Ancrene Wisse* author, in defining the role of the world in the solitary life, faces squarely the problem that both Aelred and Christina's biographer avoid: how to create a fruitful interrelationship between the outer world and the inner life of a recluse. Both Christina's biographer and Aelred posit an interior life essentially unaffected by the outside world. The *Ancrene Wisse* author, on the other hand, cannot conceive of an inner life that has no objective correlative in the outer world. The world of people, objects, relationships, and desires cannot be ignored, the *Wisse* author implies, for the attractions of the world are powerful and not altogether evil. The anchoress cannot shut out the world altogether without also shutting out the possibility of loving Christ, who was, after all, a man. Of course, "dallying" with the world, as the author puts it, can as easily result in disaster—sin— as it can result in love. But sin is a risk that all Christians run in their search for salvation, and the author's faith in the power of confession to revitalize the spirit permits him a freedom that neither Aelred nor Christina's biographer can afford. That freedom allows the author to create for the anchoress a unique sphere of experience wherein inner and outer realities, spiritual and carnal desires, desert ideals and both physical and psychological necessities, all combine in a dynamic process that defines the anchoress's spirituality.

The traditional, otherworldly desert ideals expressed in the *Ancrene Wisse* are continually undercut and transformed by the author's awareness that an anchoress, like all other Christians, lives and dies in the world. The world is a vehicle for sin, but it is also the only vehicle for spiritual progress toward love of God; in either case, it is her relationship with the world that defines and legitimizes the anchoress's solitary life. The *Ancrene Wisse* author is unique in his exploration of the solitary's problematic relationship with the world, and the ways in which she can effectively use the world to her spiritual advantage.

Ostensibly, the anchoresses have embarked upon the traditional, elite journey of the desert solitary. The *Ancrene Wisse* author notes in his introduction that his charges have entered their cells so that they "ouer oþre religiuse" might keep themselves "unwemmet," unspotted from the world (T10). The author emphasizes that their renunciation of the world should ideally be absolute; he reminds the anchoresses that they have been "smiret" and "biburiet" (anointed and buried [T58; S47]), apparently referring to the special Mass for the Dead and mock burial that usually

formed part of the elaborate ceremony for enclosing new anchoresses in
their cells.[37]

As if the ceremony itself were not enough to impress upon the anchoress
that she has renounced the world once for all, the author several times reminds her that her anchorhold is her "burinesse," her grave, and that she
should consider herself one of the dead. Not only is the anchorhold a symbolic grave, but the author asks the anchoress to make the identification
literal by digging herself a real grave within her cell:

> Ha schulden schrapien euche dei þe eorðe up of hare put þet ha
> schulien rotien in. Godd hit wat þet put deð muche god moni
> ancre. (T62)

> They should scrape up earth every day out of the grave in which they
> shall rot. God knows, the sight of her grave near her does many an
> anchoress much good. (S51)

This advice connects the anchoress with such earlier solitaries as St. Guthlac, who literally lived in the grave he dug out.[38] Furthermore, the author
specifically identifies the solitary life with the desert tradition. Like Aelred,
he reminds those who distrust the solitary life of its very respectable roots,
though unlike Aelred he is careful to add women—Saints Sarah and Syn-
cletica—to the traditional list of desert solitaries.

In part III, "The Regulation of Inward Feelings," the author deals most
fully with the "order" of anchoresses, and he also plays most frequently
upon traditional desert themes here. The biblical Judith, traditionally the
patroness of anchoresses,[39] is here held up as a model of this austere life:

> Iudith bitund inne, as hit teleð in hire boc, leadde swiðe heard lif,
> feaste ant werede here. Iudith bitund inne bitacneð bitund ancre, þe
> ah to leaden heard lif as dude þe leafdi Iudith. (T67)

> Judith, shut up in her chamber, as we are told in her Book, led a very
> hard life. She fasted all the days of her life . . . and wore haircloth. Ju-
> dith, who was shut up in her chamber, represents the enclosed ancho-
> ress, who ought to lead a hard life as the lady Judith did. (S57)

Like Judith, and like the pelican who dwells alone in the wilderness (T63;
S53), the anchoress should lead a hard, lean life alone, apart from the
world. Like Esther, whose name in the author's etymology means "ihud,"
hidden (T88; S74), and like the night raven (T75; S63), the anchoress
should keep herself and her good works hidden and private.

Though apparently invisible or hidden, the anchoress is also told she is a

visible model of sanctity to all Christians and a reliable and steady support
for the whole Church. The author points out that unlike the other birds
who live alone, the anchoress lives not in the wilderness, but "under the
eaves of the Church":

> Þe nihtfuhel i þe euesunges bitacneð recluses þe wunieð forþi under
> chirche euesunges þet ha understonden þet ha ahen to beon of se hali
> lif þet al hali chirche, þet is, cristene folc, leonie ant wreoðie up on
> ham, ant heo halden hire up wið hare lif halinesse ant hare eadie
> bonen. (T74)

> The night-raven under the eaves symbolizes recluses who live under
> the eaves of the church because they know that they ought to be so
> holy in their lives that all Holy Church, that is, Christian people, may
> lean upon them, while they hold her up with the holiness of their
> lives and their blessed prayers. (S63)

So stable and unwavering should her holiness be that she should be able to
steady the whole Church.

The author, following popular etymology, notes that the name "anchoress" comes from "anchor":

> Forþi is ancre ancre icleopet, ant under chirche iancret as ancre under
> schipes bord, forte halden þet schip, þet uþen ant stormes hit ne
> ouerwarpen. Alswa al hali chirche, þet is schip icleopet, schal ancrin o
> þe ancre, þet heo hit swa halde, þet te deofles puffes, þet beo tempta-
> tiuns, ne hit ouerwarpen. (T74-75)

> It is for this reason that an anchoress is called an anchoress, and an-
> chored under a church like an anchor under the side of a ship, to hold
> it, so that the waves and storms do not pitch it over. So all Holy
> Church, which is called a ship, shall be anchored to the anchoress, and
> she shall hold it secure so that the puffing and blowing of the devil,
> that is, temptations, do not pitch it over. (S63)

Though she herself lives the most private of lives, her name and the position of her anchorhold proclaim a sort of public contract to support the
Church:

> Euch ancre haueð þis o foreward, be þurh nome of ancre, ant þurh
> þet ha wuneð under þe chirche to understiprin hire ȝef ha walde
> fallen. (T75)

Every anchoress has bound herself to this agreement, both by her name "anchoress," and by living at the side of a church so that her house forms a sort of buttress to it. (S63)

So safe and sure seems this agreement that her dwelling place and her name proclaim her status and relationship to the world "ʒet hwen ha slepeð," ("even while she sleeps" [T75; S63]). Even though she is "hidden" and in the "desert," she is also "i folc ihehet" ("raised up among the people" [T90; S76]), for Esther's name paradoxically means both hidden from the world and esteemed by it.

The anchoress in the desert, "hidden," "dead," "anchored," "secure,"— this static image of the anchorhold as a grave often arouses the ire of twentieth-century critics such as Francis Darwin, who finds these three anchoresses "reduced to a position resembling rather too closely that of praying automata mechanically performing certain ritualistic acts" in secret.[40] And if this were the whole or even the greater part of the *Ancrene Wisse* author's treatment of the experience of the solitary life, I would have to agree. But in fact the author is as suspicious of static ideals and mechanical performances as ever Mr. Darwin could wish. Recall his own suspicion of the outer rule, which he aptly describes as "quasi regula recti mechanici," ("much like the rule of the science of mechanics" [T6; S2]). The mechanics of how an already hidden, secure, model anchoress attains the rarified heights of perfection are not of primary concern to the author. Rather, more often than not, he dwells upon the incongruous experience, and the tension that that incongruity produces, of a very lively "corpse," buried in a supposed "grave" with three open windows.

The romantic nostalgia that led the eremitic reformers of the previous century to "create" deserts is all but absent in the *Ancrene Wisse*. The desert goal presented in part III is ideal but self-consciously imaginary; the author refers to the desert tradition not as an ultimatum but as a "comfort" to console the anchoress in times of stress:

Understondeð, leofliche mine leoue sustren, þet ich write of anlich lif forte frourin ancren, ant ow ouer alle. (T80)

Understand, my dear sisters, that I write of the solitary life to comfort anchoresses, and you above all.

The anchoress needs comfort because stress will be the rule, rather than the exception in her life. A hard realist, the author cannot forget, nor does he allow the anchoress to forget, that the anchorhold is *not*, after all, either a desert or a grave, nor can it ever be. When all is said and done this anchorhold is a small cell attached to what was probably the center of town—the local parish church. Desertlike seclusion can never, therefore, be taken for granted; indeed, it can hardly be attained at all. Furthermore, and more to the point, the anchoress is not a corpse whose senses are deadened, but very much a living woman, struggling with herself as well as the outer world. Her sanctity must arise, like that of all other Christians, out of her struggle.

Throughout the work the author emphasizes the tension between traditional solitary ideals and physical or emotional realities. Though ideally the anchoress has retreated to a cell to remain "unspotted by the world," every page of the *Ancrene Wisse* gives evidence of the extremely socialized world in which the anchoress lives and which she cannot ignore, because that world exists not only outside of her but also within her own heart and memory.

At the height of the eremitic reform, the anonymous hagiographer of the *Life of St. Alexis* could imagine a spiritual life so otherworldly that it allowed the holy man to live for seventeen years in his parents' own house, unrecognized by, and unmoved by, family and friends alike.[41] In the case of St. Alexis, the commitment to holiness quite literally transformed his appearance as well as his soul. At the same time, the lack of that commitment made Alexis's parents, wife, and friends unable to recognize him, and therefore unable to tempt him. But for the *Ancrene Wisse* author, neither the world nor one's own history can be so conveniently ignored. The anchoress's vocation—to become a solitary—renders her neither invisible nor blind. She is not an otherworldly saint but a mere mortal, striving to become holy. Her struggle to become "hidden" is constant; when she is not at war with the world outside herself, she is fighting inner desires to reach out for companionship, love and comforts, for husband, children, family, and friends. She is never allowed to confuse what she strives toward with what she is.

The *Wisse* author continually points out that every otherworldly ideal toward which the anchoress moves has its underside that emphasizes her vulnerability and humanity. For example, the anchoress's model and patron is Judith, who remained apparently untouched by the world, secure in her chamber. But the author no sooner mentions this desert ideal of solitude as a protection than he points out that Judith's name has another association, seemingly unrelated to sainthood. Her name, the author says, means "schrift," or confession (T72; S61), which sacrament, he points out, belongs not to otherworldly saints, but to human sinners.

The author's tendency continually to undercut desert ideals is most evident in part III, which he vaguely describes in his introduction as being

about certain birds whose natures resemble those of anchoresses (T12).
The first bird to which he compares the anchoress is the pelican. He opens
the chapter by stating the ideal and probably traditional association between the solitary and the pelican: both live "in the wilderness." But the
author immediately deflates the ideal association by setting side by side
with it a far more mundane characteristic of pelicans, that they are prone to
anger, as though to suggest that something about solitude makes the pelican angry. Such anger in a supposedly saintly anchoress might seem incongruous, but the author considers it a very real possibility, and one that can
negate the value of solitude altogether:

> Similis factus sum pellicano solitudinis, et cetera. "Ich am," [David]
> seið, "as pellican þe wuneð bi him ane." Pellican is a fuhel se wea-
> mod ant se wreaðful þet hit sleað ofte o grome his ahne briddes hwen
> ha doð him teone; ant þenne sone þrefter hit wurð swiðe sari, ant
> makeð swiðe muche man, ant smit him seolf wið his bile þet he sloh
> ear his briddes wið, ant draheð blod of his breoste, ant wið þet blod
> acwikeð eft his briddes isleine. Þis fuhel, pellican, is þe weamode
> ancre. Hire briddes beoð hire gode werkes, þet ha sleað ofte wið bile
> of scharp wreððe. Ah hwen ha swa haueð idon, do as deð þe pellican:
> ofþunche hit swiðe sone, ant wið hire ahne bile beaki hire breoste,
> þet is, wið scrift of hire muð þet ha sunegede wið ant sloh hire gode
> werkes, drahe þet blod of sunne ut of hire breoste, þet is of þe heorte,
> þet sawle lif is inne. Ant swa schulen eft acwikien hire isleine briddes,
> þet beoð hire gode werkes.   (T63–64)

> *I am become like to a pelican of the wilderness,* etc. "I am like a pelican,"
> [David] says "which lives in solitude." The pelican is a bird which is
> so prone to anger that it often kills its own young when they have
> provoked it; and then soon afterwards it becomes very repentant, and
> makes great lamentation, and strikes itself with its bill, with which it
> has slain its young, and draws blood from its own breast, and with
> that blood it brings to life again the young which have been killed.
> This bird, the pelican, is the anchoress who is prone to anger. Her
> young are her good works, which she often kills with the bill of her
> sharp anger. But when she has done this, let her then do as the peli-
> can does, be sorry for it at once, and with her own bill strike her
> breast, that is through confession by her mouth, with which she has
> sinned, and so killed her good works, let her draw the blood of sin
> out of her breast, that is, out of the heart, in which is the life of the
> soul, and thus her slain young will come alive again, that is, her good
> works.   (S53)

It is interesting that the author not only transforms the ideal solitary into an angry anchoress, but also considers the possibility of anger real enough to provide immediately both an outlet for it and a remedy, confession.[42]

Part III ends with a discussion of another bird having rather contradictory characteristics. The sparrow like the pelican, the author notes, represents the ideal anchoress because it lives alone, but it

> haueð ȝet a cunde þet is biheue ancre, þah me hit heatie: þet is þe
> fallinde uuel. For muche neod is þet ancre of hali lif ant of heh habbe
> fallinde uuel; þet uuel ne segge ich nawt þet me swa nempneð, ah
> fallinde uuel ich cleopie licomes secnesse oðer temptatiuns of flesches
> fondunges, hwer þurh hire þunche þet ha falle duneward of hali heh-
> nesse. Ha walde awilgin elles oðer to wel leoten of, ant swa to noht
> iwurðen. (T91)

> has another characteristic which is becoming to an anchoress, though
> it is generally unpopular, and that is the falling sickness. For there is
> great need that an anchoress whose life is holy and exalted should
> have the falling sickness; I do not mean the actual disease which is
> so-called; I am giving the name "falling sickness" to a disease of the
> body, temptations of the flesh by which she feels as though she were
> falling down from a height of holiness. Otherwise she would grow
> overconfident and think too highly of herself and so come to noth-
> ing. (S76–77)

This is not merely a contrived transitional paragraph, bridging the gap between parts III and IV ("On Temptations"), nor is it simply an exhortation on the necessity of humility. Instead the author is describing what he sees as the very texture of the solitary life—a constant shifting from ideal to real, or from inner to outer, as the author would put it. The various birds the author uses in part III to describe the solitary life are apt images not so much because their flight represents the anchoress's freedom from the world, but because birds belong to *two* worlds at once:

> Treowe ancres beoð ariht briddes of heouene, þe fleoð on heh ant
> sitteð singinde murie o þe grene bohes, þet is, þencheð uppart of þe
> blisse of heouene þe neauer ne faleweð ah is aa grene, ant sitteð o þis
> grene singinde murie, þet is, resteð ham i þulli þoht, ant ase þeo þe
> singeð, habbeð murhðe of heorte. Brid tah oðerhwile forte sechen
> his mete, for þe flesches neode, lihteð to þer eorðe. Ah hwil hit sit on
> eorðe, hit nis neauer siker, ah biwent him ofte ant bilokeð him aa
> ȝeornliche abuten. Alswa þe gode ancre, ne fleo ha neauer se hehe, ha

mot lihten oðerhwiles dun to þer eorðe of hire bodi—eoten, drinken, slepen, wurchen, speoken, heren of þet hire neodeð to of eorðliche þinges. Ah þenne, as þe brid deð, ha mot wel biseon hire, bilokin hire on euch half, þet ha nohwer ne misneome, leste ha beo . . . ihurt summes weis þe hwil ha sit se lahe.   (T70)

True anchoresses are indeed birds of heaven, flying high up, or sitting and singing in happiness on the green boughs, that is, lifting up their minds to the happiness of heaven, which never fades but is always green, and sitting in this greenness, singing happily, that is, remaining in such thoughts with gladness of heart, like people singing. A bird, however, sometimes comes down to the ground to look for food, because of the needs of the body; but as long as it is on the ground it does not feel safe, and it keeps turning and looking about it all the time. So it is with the good anchoress. However high she flies, she must sometimes come down to the ground because of her body, in order to eat, drink, sleep, work, talk, and hear about earthly affairs in so far as they concern her; but then, like the bird, she must look well about her, and look out all around herself, not growing unwary, lest she should be . . . harmed in some way, while she is so low.   (S59)

Thus the anchoress, unlike the early desert fathers who could all but dismiss the real world, must participate in the world even as she seeks to flee it.

Given her paradoxical position, the anchoress cannot simply will herself blind or dead to the world. To reach her ideal goal, a certain kind of blindness, the anchoress must paradoxically be quite clear-sighted, like the bird who is especially watchful while on the ground. She is asked to develop an "inre sihðe," which entails not the negation or deadening of her ability to see, but rather a specialized way of seeing that makes her constantly aware of the potential sinfulness of the world and at the same time able to transform her inescapable desire for contact with the world into a humanly satisfying love of Christ that is spiritual but sensual.

One important indication of the author's interest in the interrelationship between the anchoress's inner and outer life is demonstrated by Janet Grayson in her recent stylistic analysis of what she calls the "inner-outer pattern of images" in the *Ancrene Wisse*.[43] Her analysis of an image like that of the anchoress's hands in part II is a typical example of the pattern that Grayson sees at work throughout the *Ancrene Wisse:*

The anchoress is warned to keep her hands inside the window to avoid physical contact with male visitors:

Hwen se ȝe moten to eani mon eawiht biteachen, þe hond ne cume
nawt ut, ne ower ut, ne his in. [T34]

This simple caution is a regulation of the outer Rule in the sense of
its directness. It is repeated later in stronger terms when she is told
to shut the window on a man who reaches for the curtain: "ȝef
ei wurðeð swa awed þet he warpe hond forð toward te þurl clað,
swiftliche ananriht schutteð al þet þuel to ant leote him
iwurðen" [T51]. The outstretched hand that reaches after flesh (a
literal, or outer figure) becomes transformed radically into the nailed
hands of Christ in the concluding section of the chapter, in a meditation on the passion. The movement of images has been inward from
the physical-literal outer image of the hands of the anchoress and the
male to the spiritual-tropological inner figure of Christ's hands:

> Godes honden weren ineilet o rode. þurh þe ilke neiles ich halsi
> ow ancres, nawt ow, ah do oþre, for hit nis na neod, mine leoue
> sustren: haldeð ower hondon inwið ower þurles. [T62]

> God's hands were nailed to the cross. By those nails, I adjure you
> anchoresses—(not you, my dear sisters, for there is no need)—but
> you others: keep your hands inside your windows.

Regulations bring the Rule outward as the author continues his
warning that touching with the hands brings trouble, entices the
man, leads to sin and, what is worse, angers God . . . The mingling of
levels belonging to the inner and outer life reinforces the need for
careful scrutiny of the sense of touch, and the reinforcement is
stronger than had the author relied only on a rule governing 'han-
dling.'[44]

Here and elsewhere in her study, Grayson amply demonstrates that this
"mingling of the levels of world and spirit" typifies the *Ancrene Wisse* author's art. This point alone sets the *Wisse* author's achievement apart from
that of Aelred of Rievaulx, who does not follow through on his promise to
"blend the spiritual with the corporal."

But Grayson's study, because it focuses primarily on the imagery of the
Ancrene Wisse, misses a crucial point. The interpenetration of inner and
outer realities is not merely an imagistic pattern; it typifies the anchoress's
experience. It is not just the author who, as Grayson puts it, "bridges" inner
and outer experience "as if all of life were refractions of a single design."[45]
The author's point is that it is the anchoress *herself* whose unavoidable
contact with the world demands that she constantly assess the effect of the

outer world upon her inner life. If images like that of the hands or that of Judith reverse themselves in meaning, so also does the anchoress's perception of the things of this world, and her reaction to them. If she cannot leave the world behind, she can at least learn to manipulate it to her own spiritual advantage. And this manipulation is the source of both the density of the *Ancrene Wisse* and the extraordinary dynamics that take place in this grave-cell.

The seeming paradox of perceiving and manipulating the world while supposedly being dead to it is most fully explicated by the author in the opening chapter of the inner rule, "Custody of the Senses." As Salu's title implies, the chapter concerns the role of sensual perception in the anchoress's life. One would think, given both the anchoress's physical circumstances—narrowly enclosed in a small cell—and the desert tradition that rendered solitaries impervious to worldly desires, that she need have little fear of the sensual world intruding upon her spiritual exercises. This impression is heightened by the chapter on devotions that immediately precedes "Custody of the Senses." The devotions calmly accompany the anchoress from rising in the morning, through her hours, the Mass, meals, and on to bed at night. The impression is of an anchoress, unaffected by the world or time, and safe in her cell from all disruptive intrusions.

The opening chapter of the inner rule immediately shatters this illusion. The author's focus here is not on the walls of the anchorhold, which protect the anchoress and effectively cut her off from the world, but instead upon the three windows of the anchorhold, which serve to *connect* the solitary with the world. The author's concentration upon the three windows—facing the parlor, the church, and the street—is the clearest evidence that, in the author's view, an anchoress is not dead, nor is an anchorhold a grave.

In a complex opening paragraph, the author prepares for an extended discussion of those windows by showing the anchoress that life within the anchorhold is neither calm, quiet, nor "dead." The young solitary cannot appreciate the dangers inherent in her windows until she realizes that the attraction of the world originates in her own heart:

Omni custodia serua cor tuum quia ex ipso uita procedit. Wið alles cunnes warde, dohter, seið Salomon, wite wel þin heorte, for sawle lif is in hire ʒef ha is wel iloket. Þe heorte wardeins beoð þe fif wittes: sihðe ant herunge, smecchunge ant meallunge, ant euch limes felunge. Ant we schulen speoken of alle, for hwa se wit þeose wel, he deð Salomones bode; he wit wel his heorte ant his sawle heale. Þe heorte is a ful wilde beast ant makeð moni liht lupe, as seint Gregoire seið: Nichil corde fugatius. Na þing ne etflid mon sonre þen his ahne

heorte. Dauið, godes prophete, meande i sum time þet ha wes et-
steart him: Cor meum dereliquit me, þet is, "Min heorte is edflohe
me." Ant eft he blisseð him ant seið þet ha wes icumen ham: Inuenit
seruus tuus cor suum. "Lauerd," he seið, "min heorte is icumen aȝein
eft; ich hire habbe ifunden." Hwen se hali mon ant se wis ant se war
lette hire edstearten, sare mei an oðer of hire fluht carien. Ant hwer
edbrec ha ut from Dauið, þe hali king, godes prophete? Hwer? Godd
wat, ed his ehþurl, þurh a sihðe þet he seh, þurh a bihaldunge, as ȝe
schulen efter iheren.   (T29-30)

With all watchfulness keep thy heart, because life issueth out from it. "With
watchfulness of every kind, O daughter, guard thy heart well," says
Solomon, "for, if it is well guarded, in it is the life of the soul." The
guardians of the heart are the five senses: sight and hearing, taste and
smell, and touch, or the feeling that is in every part of the body; and
we shall speak of all of these, for whoever guards these well, carries
out Solomon's command; he guards his heart and the health of his
soul well. The heart is a very wild animal and often leaps lightly out
as St. Gregory says: *Nothing is more apt to escape than the heart.* "Nothing escapes from a man's control so easily as his own heart." David,
God's prophet, lamented once that his heart had escaped from him:
"My heart has fled from me"; and later he rejoiced and said that it had
come home again: "Lord," he said, "Thy servant has found his heart
again; it has come back." If a man so holy, so wise, and so watchful
allowed his heart to escape, others may very well fear that theirs may
escape too. And where did it break away from the holy king David,
God's prophet? Where? God knows, at the window of his eye;
through a sight that he saw, through something at which he looked,
as you shall later hear.   (S21)[46]

This passage and those that immediately follow it are dense and deserve
close analysis. Solomon's words, literally translated, read: "With all watchfulness guard your heart because the life proceeds out of it." The author at
first ignores the active verb "procedit" and instead translates the admonition in the most idealistic and hopeful fashion, saying that *if* the anchoress
guards her heart, her soul-life will remain intact: "For sawle lif is in hire ȝef
ha is wel iloket." But he will not allow the passive and static "is in hire" to
rest for long. Abruptly the heart is not standing still at all, as it ideally
should, and as we would expect in the narrowly enclosed anchorhold, but
is instead leaping lightly about like a "ful wilde beast." The image may
seem startling, even grotesque, but it serves as a pointed reminder that we
are no longer in the desert, where the saint stands firm as wild beasts assault him from without. In this spiritual landscape, the wild beast lives in

the anchoress's own heart, and disruptive action is initiated from within, by the anchoress herself. And action is the key to this opening paragraph: static verbs of keeping, guarding, and being are quickly replaced by images of leaping, escaping, and flying out, on the one hand, and returning, or coming home, on the other. And all this action results from a seemingly passive "bihaldunge."

Throughout part II the author will not write mainly about the leap into sin, but will concentrate on how the anchoress can "keep" her heart at home in the first place and thus become an ideal solitary. Yet so difficult is this task that the author finds it necessary to provide what could be called a psychological safety valve for his charges from the very start: if the heart of "so holy" and "so wise" and "so wary" a man as David can leap out, then the anchoress must expect her own heart to escape her control and leap into sin as well. Furthermore, the author assures the anchoress that the heart that escapes can be retrieved. How often the heart will in fact escape, and how it can be made to return, will be the subjects of parts IV and V, "On Temptations" and "Confession." But the sacrament of confession can only comfort the recluse after she has learned how deceptively easy sin can be, even for a solitary, into whose heart sin can enter so quietly, with a "liht lupe" (light leap).

To avoid sin, the anchoress must learn through how many channels the heart can escape. The most obvious and visible avenues of escape are the anchorhold windows, because they form the most obvious connection between the anchoress's inner life and the outside world. If the anchorhold *walls* are the most evident signs that the anchoress has renounced the world, her *windows* are evidence to the contrary, evidence that the world is inescapable. But the windows of the anchorhold, in turn, suggest another set of windows, the anchoress's own eyes, more dangerous avenues of escape because they are nearer to her heart, the symbolic center of her inner life. At the end of the passage just quoted, the author points out that David's heart leapt out through his eyes:

Ant hwer edbrec [his heart] ut from Dauið, þe hali king, godes prophete? Hwer? Godd wat, ed his ehþurl, þurh a sihðe þet he seh, þurh
a bihaldunge, as ʒe schulen efter iheren.

   Forþi, mine leoue sustren, þe leaste þet ʒe eauer mahen luuieð
ower þurles. Alle beon ha lutle, þe parlurs least ant neare-
west. (T30)

And where did [his heart] break away from the holy king David,
God's prophet? Where? God knows, at the window of his eye;

through a sight that he saw, through something at which he looked,
as you shall later hear.

  Therefore, my dear sisters, be as little fond of your windows as possible. Let them all be small, those of the parlour smallest and nar-
rowest. (S21)

The author's own imaginative leap here, from David's "eye-windows" to
the windows of the anchorhold is, as Grayson points out, both abrupt and
typical of the author's imagistic method.[47] The association is not merely a
literary trick. As the author will soon demonstrate, the windows of the anchorhold would pose no problem for the ideal anchoress, one who was
truly blind or indifferent to the world. But the anchoresses for whom he is
writing are not blind, and windows *are* for looking.

  The author, having jumped from David's eyes to the windows of the anchorhold, takes time out to describe the physical qualities of the anchorhold windows: they should be small and well covered. But he quickly returns to his major theme: no matter how small, or how carefully covered,
windows need only be as large as an anchoress's eyes to connect her with
the whole bustling, social, chaotic world outside the anchorhold. Furthermore, the author contends that the anchoress, because she is not a saint but
a mere mortal, is not indifferent to that world. She sees through her window not as through a glass darkly, but as through a magnifying glass, because whatever she sees is magnified by her inner desire to see it.

  Having introduced the images of the leaping heart, the anchorhold windows, and the corresponding "eye-windows" of the anchoress herself, the
author now sets out to show how inseparable these are, not just imagis-
ticlly, but in fact. He proves his point with a carefully designed retelling of
the story of Eve's fall, pointing out that the first sin was not one obvious
"leap" into hell, but was instead a series of tiny leaps that nevertheless resulted in the fall of all mankind:

  Of Eue, ure alde moder, is iwriten on alre earst in hire sunne inʒong
  of hire ehsihðe ... Eue biheold o þe forboden eappel, ant seh hine
  feier ant feng to delitin iþe bihaldunge, ant toc hire lust þer toward,
  ant nom ant et þrof, ant ʒef hire lauerd. Low hu hali writ spekeð, ant
  hu inwardliche hit teleð hu sunne bigon; þus eode sunne biuoren ant
  makede wei to uuel lust, ant com þe dede þrefter þet al moncun
  ifeleð. (T31)

  Of Eve, our first mother, it is recorded that at the very beginning of
  her sin its entry was through her eyes ... Eve looked upon the forbidden apple and saw that it was fair, and she began to take delight in

looking at it, and to desire it, and she plucked some of it and ate it, and gave it to her lord. Observe how Holy Writ speaks of this, telling how sin began in an inward manner; this inward sin went before and made way for evil desire, and the deed followed, the consequences of which are felt by all mankind. (S23)

He continues, identifying any anchoress who cannot yet see the connection between looking and leaping with Eve:

Hwa se hefde iseid to eue, þa ha weorp earst hire ehe þron: "A Eue, went te awei, þu warpest ehe o þi deað," hwet hefde ha iondsweret? "Me leoue sire, þu hauest woh. Hwerof chalengest tu me? þe eappel þet ich loki on is forbode me to eotene ant nawt to bihalden." þus walde Eue inohreaðe habben iondsweret. O mine leoue sustren, as eue haueð monie dehtren þe folhið hare moder, þe ondswerieð o þisse wise: "Me wenest to seið sum þet ich wulle leapen on him þah ich loki on him?" Godd wat, leoue suster, mare wunder ilomp. Eue, þi moder, leop efter hire ehnen, from þe ehe to þe eappel, from þe eappel iparais dun to þer eorðe, from þe eorðe to helle, þer ha lei i prisun fowr þusent ʒer ant mare, heo ant hire were ba, ant demde al hire ofsprung to leapen al efter hire to deað wiðuten ende. Biginnunge ant rote of al þis ilke reowðe wes aliht sihðe. þus ofte, as me seið, of lutel muchel waxeð. (T31–32)

If anyone had said to Eve, when she first cast her eyes upon [the apple]: "Ah Eve, turn away. You are casting your eyes upon your death," what would she have answered? "But dearest master, you are mistaken. Of what are you accusing me? I am forbidden to eat the apple at which I am looking; I am not forbidden to look at it." Thus Eve would have answered readily enough, my dear sisters, and she has many daughters who, following their mother, answer in the same way. "But do you think," someone will say, "that I shall leap upon him because I look at him?" God knows, my dear sister, more surprising things have happened. Your mother Eve leapt after her eyes had leapt; from the eye to the apple, from the apple in paradise down to earth, and from earth to hell where she remained, in prison, four thousand years and more, together with her husband, and she condemned all her children to leap after her, to endless death. The beginning and root of all this misery was a light glance. Thus, as they say, much often comes of little. (S23)

The underlying rationale of this radical transformation from a look to a leap is the author's simply stated moral of Eve's story: much can come from

little. It is a moral particularly suited to life in the tiny anchorhold. The
world that can enter the anchorhold might seem to the anchoress limited.
So also might the possibilities for evil seem few. Certainly the opportunities for physical activity are severely limited; the author does not presume,
as Aelred did, that his charges might actually escape through their windows for secret rendezvous.[48] But the author maintains that the smallest
uncalculated act, reinforced as it often is by human desire—any look, nod,
gesture, smile, or word—must affect the anchoress's inner life. Every act, in
short, is a *moral* act, on which hangs the tale of salvation. Because the anchoress's eyes and all her other senses are connected to her heart, no external act can remain unconnected to her inner life. Looking, though seemingly innocuous and certainly passive enough, can abruptly become leaping
in this tiny but concentrated spiritual landscape.

The anchoress, simply by virtue of being human, has already made the
most important leap from paradise to earth, from the desert to the world.
The interconnections among the windows of the anchorhold, the anchoress's eyes, and her leaping heart, are evidence enough that the anchoress's
spiritual life is far from stable and that she has left the desert ideal far behind her. If Anthony and Macarius, desert solitaries, are the anchoress's
models of holiness, she must also and primarily consider herself as the
daughter of Eve, Dinah, and Bathsheba, all sinners.[49] If her goal on the one
hand is to keep herself "unspotted from the world," it is on the other hand
a much humbler goal, which, as the author points out, is the goal of all
religions:

> Cleane ant shir inwit (consciencia), wiðuten weote of sunne þet ne
> beo þurh schrift ibet. Þis makeð þe leafdi riwle, þe riwleð ant rihteð
> ant smeðeð þe heorte ant te inwit of sunne for nawt ne makeð hire
> woh bute sunne ane. (T7)

> A clean, unblemished conscience, free from the awareness of sin that
> has not been forgiven through Confession. This is the work of the in-
> terior rule, the lady. It governs the heart and the conscience, ruling
> and guiding them and smoothing sin away from them, for it is only
> sin which makes the heart crooked. (S2)

If the anchoress should, like Judith, lead a hard life shut up in her chamber,
that life is defined by the most ordinary of Christian principles: faith, hope,
charity, humility, the keeping of the Ten Commandments, and frequent
confession (T8; S3). Thus the anchoress's position is presented as far more
paradoxical and complex than that of earlier desert solitaries. The windows of her anchorhold are a constant reminder that though she is a solitary, she does live in the world, and she is attracted to that world.

The anchorhold itself provides only the illusion of otherworldliness. The windows transform the anchorhold into a "unwalled city" (T40). Part II of the *Ancrene Wisse* is dense with references to the myriad of sense impressions that enter through the windows. Men and women continually call at the parlor window, and the anchoress's meals are delivered there. A cacophony is heard through the churchyard window: the cries of merchants, the laughter of dancers and children, the flattery of friends, the gossip of maidservants. All opportunities for touching are concentrated at the windows. It is as though the anchoress were in Christina's transparent cell, but now it is not Providence that protects her from the world, or conversely sends her out to fulfill its purpose. She, and not God, holds the key that controls her relationship with the world, because the attractiveness of the world, and therefore its danger, originates in her own heart. Thus, she must judge her heart's desire first, then open or close her windows accordingly. She must "find out from [her] maid" who her visitors are, then decide whether or not "it would be better to make ... excuses" and fasten her window (S28). She must learn to "easily recognize" (S37) flatterers and backbiters, so that she may "close [her] ears against [them], and if need be lock [her] windows" (S35). On the other hand, the anchoress is told that some visitors can do her no harm and might give her some pleasure. When good friends come for dinner, though the anchoress is not allowed to eat with them, she can wave to them through her window (T37; S30); she can also keep a cat for companionship (T213; S185) and chat with servants when she is ill or depressed (T217; S188). She is encouraged to keep friends in mind when she prays (T15; S9) and never to take the injunction that she live alone so seriously that she neglects to ask for outside help when she needs it (T116; S100). In short, the anchoress is constantly reminded that the life of a solitary has become a socialized and worldly life.

The *Ancrene Wisse* author is often cited for his use of homey detail. His injunction that the anchoress think about keeping a cat rather than a cow is probably the most frequently anthologized passage from the work.[50] R. M. Wilson, who notes that the author is "amusingly practical," remarks: "It is not surprising that such incidental illustration should prove more interesting to modern readers than the more serious religious instruction."[51] Another reader suggests that such "informal illumination" "obverts the monotony of a rigid didacticism."[52] But what these readers fail to notice is that such illustrations are essential to the author's view of life in the anchorhold. Such readers have also failed to learn the author's central lesson, that much can come from little. The fact is that the anchoress's battle is waged, not on the imaginary, larger-than-life field of the desert, but on the minute level of the everyday. Nothing—no action, no word, no thought, no desire—is incidental to the spiritual life of the anchoress. Her sensitivity to the moral consequences of her every act determines her spirituality. This is not Aelred's split psychological world where the inner life of holy meditations only begins after one has forced the world out of one's consciousness. The inner life here is largely defined by the anchoress's ability to recognize the continuity between inner and outer realities, and as a result to avoid sin by avoiding thoughtless contacts with the world.

But understanding that much comes from little, that worldly sights and sounds can disrupt her heart, has an added effect on the anchoress's spiritual life. For knowledge of the world cuts two ways in the author's view. On the one hand it is her acute perception of the world that helps her understand the necessity of "hald[unge] wiðinnen," insofar as she can, her human desires for sensual contact with the world. But on the other hand this same knowledge of the world—of both people and objects outside of her and the world of desires within her heart—can help her to understand and promote spiritual desires. The world is not only helpful to the anchoress's spiritual progress, it is essential.

The *Wisse* author, like the Victorine theologians before him and the Friars after him, thinks sacramentally. The world is not an incidental obstruction that men must bypass to arrive at spiritual knowledge. Rather, according to many twelfth-century theologians, the material world is the mirror of God's love. The same "sacramental sense" that Beryl Smalley cites as having given the Victorine exegetes "a new devotion to the letter of Scripture,"[53] gives the *Ancrene Wisse* author a new respect for, and confidence in, the minute details of creation to teach or mirror spiritual things. Thus no incident or desire is too worldly to illustrate God's love and the ways the anchoress can return that love. Barnyard animals, the habits of thieves, the calls of soap merchants, wrestlers' favorite holds, mothers' games with their children, and husbands' relations with their wives—all can be seen as illustrations of God's ways. In a negative sense, the anchoress *cannot* ignore these worldly activities because they exist not only outside her window, but within her memory. But in a positive sense she *should* not ignore them because they are her only mode of reference, the only objective correlative for her relationship with God.

Richard of St. Victor, in a work especially popular in England during the thirteenth century, makes use of the newly discovered spiritual value of the world in identifying Jacob's two wives, Rachel and Leah, with reason and affection:

> Accepit ... utraque illarum ancillam suam. Affectio, sensualitatem; ratio, imaginationem. Obsequitur sensualitas affectioni; imaginatio famulatur rationi. Intantum unaquaeque ancillarum dominae suae

necessaria esse cognoscitur, ut sine illis totus mundus nil eis posse conferre videretur. Nam sine imaginatione, ratio nihil sciret; sine sensualitate, affectio nil saperet. Utquid enim Lia circa labentium rerum amorem tam vehementer afficitur, nisi quia in eis, per ancillae suae (hoc est sensualitatis) obsequium, multiformiter delectatur. Item, cum scriptum sit: *Quia invisibilia Dei, a creatura mundi per ea, quae facta sunt, intellecta conspiciuntur* (Rom. 1), inde manifeste colligitur quia ad invisibilium cognitionem nunquam ratio assurgeret, nisi ei ancilla sua, imaginatio videlicet, rerum visibilium formam repraesentaret. Per rerum enim visibilium speciem surgit ad rerum invisibilium cognitionem, quoties ex his ad illam quamdam trahit similitudinem. Sed constat quia sine imaginatione corporalia nesciret, sine quorum cognitione ad coelestium contemplationem non ascenderet. Visibilia enim solus intuetur sensus carnis, invisibilia vero solus oculus videt cordis ... Discurrit ergo imaginatio (utpote ancilla) inter dominam et servum, inter rationem et sensum.[54]

Each of them ... receives her handmaid; the servant of the affections is sensation, that of reason is the imagination. But each of these handmaids is known to be necessary to her mistress, for without them the whole world would not be of use to them. For reason would know nothing without the imagination and the affections would feel nothing without the sensibility. For why is Leah so violently moved by the love of transitory things, if it be not that the services of her handmaid, the outer senses, give her a variety of delights? As it is written: "For the invisible things of Him from the creation of the world are clearly seen being understood by the things that are made" (Romans 1:20). From this we clearly see that the reason would never rise to the knowledge of invisible things unless her handmaid, the imagination, were to present to her the form of visible things. For by the image of visible things she rises to the knowledge of invisible things as often as she draws up a likeness between them in her mind. Clearly without the imagination she would have no knowledge of bodily things and without it she could not rise to the contemplation of heavenly things. For the outer sense alone perceives visible things and the eye of the heart alone, sees the invisible ... So the imagination like a handmaid runs between the lady and the servant, between the reason and the senses.[55]

As Richard points out, one cannot know or feel the presence of God without first knowing and feeling the things of the world. Leah's servant, sensation, might at times be too violently moved by things of the world, but if she were never moved at all, her mistress, affection, would never arrive at love of God.

The *Wisse* author uses the same image of the lady and the handmaiden to describe the relationship between the inner and outer rules. But whereas in his introduction the author makes the distinction between inner and outer seem clear-cut and unchanging—the outer rule exists only to support the inner—within the inner rule itself he comes much closer to Richard's complex understanding of the interdependence of inner life and external perceptions. Certainly the anchoress is to avoid careless "dallying" with the world by avoiding unnecessary looking, touching, talking, and hearing. But this denial of the senses—"damming up" her mouth, closing her ears, locking her windows—results not in the elimination of sense activity, or deadness, as Aelred might suppose, but rather in the concentration of it in her imagination (or her heart) for another purpose. The author repeatedly refers to the concentrated heart, and its opposite, the heart that has squandered or scattered its emotional energies:

Ant þet witeð to soðe þet eauer se þes wittes beoð mare isprengde utward, se ha lease wendeð inward. (T49)

Understand the truth of this, that the more these senses are scattered over external things, the less they can function inwardly. (S40)

As ȝe mahe seon weater, hwen me punt hit ant stoppeð hit biuore wel þet hit ne mahe duneward, þenne is hit inedd aȝein forte climben uppart, ant ȝe al þisses weis pundeð ower wordes, forstoppið ower þohtes, as ȝe wulleð þet ha climben ant hehin toward heouene ant nawt ne fallen duneward ant to fleoten ȝont te worlt, as deð muchel chaffle. (T39)

Just as you may see water, when it has been firmly stopped and dammed so that it cannot flow downwards, forced to go back and climb upwards, in just this way you should dam up your speech and your thoughts, if you want them to climb and rise up toward heaven instead of falling downwards and being scattered about the world as much idle talk is. (S32)

[Lengthy talk] of a drope waxeð into a muche flod þe adrencheð þe sawle, for wið þe fleotinde word tofleoteð þe heorte, swa þet longe þrefter ne mei ha beon riht igederet togederes. (T41)

[F]rom being a mere drop, [lengthy talk] grows into a vast flood which drowns the soul, for as the words flow the heart becomes dissi-

pated, so that for a long time afterwards it cannot be truly recol-
lected. (S33)

Thus the anchoress is not asked to forgo sense knowledge, as though she
were dead, but only to store it up in her heart for a purpose other than the
immediate gratification of her desires. As Richard of St. Victor points out,
all the sights and sounds and desires of the world, once transformed by the
imagination, contribute to spiritual knowing.

The knowledge that results is complex; it is not the world-denying "hidden" knowledge of the *Cloud of Unknowing,* which seeks to create a spiritual
state wherein the thought "of alle þe cretures at euer God maad . . . schal
be casten down and keuerid wið a cloud of forʒetying."[56] Nor, on the
other hand, is it the "frantic and misguided" allegorizing of the late Middle
Ages, typified by the fifteenth-century mystic, Henry of Suso, who

> eats three quarters of an apple in honor of the trinity and the remain-
> ing quarter in commemoration of "the love with which the heavenly
> Mother gave her tender child Jesus an apple to eat"; and in conse-
> quence Suso eats the last quarter with the paring, since little boys do
> not peel their apples; he does not eat it after Christmas, for then the
> baby Jesus was too young to eat apples.[57]

It is not this facile, almost mindless correspondence between the things of
the world (in this case eating an apple) and spiritual things (here the
Trinity and the childhood of Christ) that the *Ancrene Wisse* author is after.
The correspondences he encourages are much more plausible, and psychologically more helpful. How the anchoress must make use of worldly concerns even in advancing her spiritual growth can be seen in two sets of
passages in the *Ancrene Wisse.* The first concerns overcoming temptations,
the second concerns arriving at her goal of love for Christ.

In an extraordinary passage in part IV, "On Temptations," the author
asserts his faith in the imagination to use earthly knowledge and desires to
overcome earthly temptations. While such an idea might not seem out of
place in a work addressed to laymen, whose everyday cares and wishes form
an important part of the texture of their lives, its appearance is surprising
in a work directed toward solitaries, who are so often presumed to have cut
themselves off from such mundane concerns. After listing and explaining
the more traditional spiritual helps in warding off temptations, including
prayers and meditations, the author turns to a less usual method:

> Nawt ane hali meditatiuns, as of ure lauerd ant of alle his werkes ant
> of alle his wordes, of þe deore leafdi ant of alle hali halhen, ah oþres

þohtes sum chearre i meadlese fondunges habbeð iholpen, fowr cunne nomeliche to þeo þe beoð of flesches fondunges meadlese asailet: dredfule, wunderfule, gleadfule, ant sorhfule, *willes wiðute neod arearet iþe heorte;* as þenchen hwet tu waldest don ȝef . . . me ȝeide "Fur, fur!" þet te chirche bearnde, ȝef þu herdest burgurs breoke þine wahes—þeos ant oþre þulliche dredfule þohtes. Wunderfule ant gleadfule: as ȝef þu sehe Iesu Crist ant herdest him easki þe hwet te were leouest efter þi saluatiun ant þine leoueste freond of þing o þisse liue, ant beode þe cheosen, . . . ȝef me come ant talde þe þet mon þet te is leouest, þurh sum miracle as þurh steuene of heouene, weren icoren to pape, ant alle oþre swucche. Wunderfule ant sorhfule: as ȝef þu herdest seggen þet mon þet te is leouest were ferliche adrenct, islein oþer imurðret, þet tine sustren weren in hare hus forbearnde. Þulliche þohtes ofte i fleschliche sawlen wrencheð ut sonre fleschliche temptatiuns þen sum of þe oþre earre.   (T124-125; my emphasis)

Besides holy meditations on Our Lord, on all that He said and did, on our dear Lady and on all the holy saints, other thoughts too have sometimes been found helpful in the face of continual temptations, and for those who are much attacked by temptations of the flesh, thoughts of the following four kinds particularly: thoughts inspiring fear, thoughts inspiring wonder, thoughts inspiring joy, and thoughts inspiring sorrow, *feelings stirred up in the heart without any actual occasion.* For example, thinking what you would do if . . . people were shouting, "Fire, fire!" because the church was burning; or if you heard burglars breaking into your house—these and other such thoughts inspiring fear; then, thoughts inspiring wonder and joy, for example if you were to see Jesus Christ and hear Him asking you what you would like best, next to your own salvation and that of your dearest friends, of all things in this life, and offering you your choice . . . or if anyone were to come and tell you that a man most dear to you had by some miracle, say a voice from heaven, been elected pope, and other thoughts of the same kind; then, thoughts inspiring wonder and sorrow, for example if you heard that someone very dear to you have been suddenly drowned, or slain, or murdered, or that your sisters had been burned in their house. Such thoughts as these will often root out carnal temptations from carnal minds more quickly than those mentioned earlier.   (S107; my emphasis)

The passage is especially illuminating if we compare it with Aelred's more traditional remedies for fleshy temptations. For Aelred, we recall, temptations of the flesh are to be countered with severe asceticism; the more severe the temptation, the more complete the denial of the flesh that gave rise to it. But the *Ancrene Wisse* author refuses to advise the anchoress simply to deny her "carnal mind." On the contrary, he encourages her to recall and manipulate her common and irreducibly human desires and fears—her hopes for her friends' worldly advancement, her fear of bodily harm, her sadness at the death of one close to her. Such mundane concerns, which might at other times draw her into sin, here give her comfort when she feels most alone. In this instance, it is not so much that the author shows his sensitivity to the solitary's loneliness by, as one critic puts it, "imaginatively breaking down the walls of the cell" to people the anchoress's lonely world with desert heroes and saints;[58] rather, and more to the point, the author effectively reminds the anchoress that she has within her memory and imagination the resources to do the job herself, not by imagining heroic desert solitaries, but by consciously "stirring up in [her] heart" her worldly and human concern for very real friends. Here, paradoxically, the anchoress's attachment to the world—thoughts about family, friends, and security—is precisely what keeps her unstained by sin.

That the author recognizes the possibility of such worldly thoughts in the anchorhold as fantasizing that one's best friend has been elected pope is proof enough that he does not expect that an anchoress, merely by virtue of being locked in a cell, can detach herself from the world. That he encourages the anchoress to count on such thoughts, indeed purposely to call them to mind at times, is proof that this author, like Richard of St. Victor and unlike Aelred of Rievaulx, recognizes the anchoress's power to manipulate worldly fantasies to suit her psychological and spiritual needs.

In the passage we have just looked at the author encourages worldly thoughts to overcome worldly temptations. But in another set of passages the author goes further and asks the anchoress to use this same imaginative power, again based upon her worldly attachments, to make concentrate and to satisfy her love for Christ.

The quality of love that the *Ancrene Wisse* author promotes is very similar to that which is implicit in Aelred's meditations: a love of Christ that is sensual, human, and homey in its details. The difference is that while Aelred could depict no path or process by which a solitary, cut off from all worldly desires, could arrive at this love, the *Ancrene Wisse* author can treat the subject of love as the logical conclusion of his belief that a solitary cannot and should not escape the world altogether. The anchoress who attempts not to eradicate but only to contain and concentrate her human desires within her heart can use them in defining her love for Christ. The relationship the anchoress should seek with Christ is invariably described in the *Ancrene Wisse* in terms of the human relationships she has willingly forgone, though the desire for them remains and accumulates.

The most obvious relationship the anchoress cannot have on earth is a sexual relationship with an earthly husband. The author delivers some of his sternest warnings on the subject of chastity. but when he comes to describe the love between Christ and the anchoress, his language, largely borrowed from the Canticle of Canticles and from St. Bernard, is explicitly sexual. The kiss of peace that precedes communion at Mass is described in terms of an imagined, but nevertheless sexual embrace:

> Efter þe measse cos, hwen þe preost sacreð, þer forȝeoteð al þe world, þer beoð al ut of bodi, þer i sperclinde luue bicluppeð ower leofmon, þe in to ower breostes bur is iliht of heouene, ant haldeð him heteueste aþet he habbe iȝettet ow al þet ȝe eauer easkið. (T21)

> After the kiss of peace in the Mass, when the priest communicates, forget the world, be completely out of the body, and with burning love embrace your Beloved who has come down from heaven to your heart's bower, and hold Him fast until He has granted all that you ask. (S14)

Though the author asks the anchoress here to "forget the world," what he is actually suggesting is that the anchoress manipulate her human desires for sexual union. In part VII, the anchoress is directed not to *forget* her sexual yearnings for men, but to "stretch" those yearnings beyond this world toward Christ:

> Streche þi luue to Iesu Crist; þu hauest him iwunnen. Rin him wið ase muche luue as þu hauest sum mon sum chearre. He is þin to don wið al þet tu wilnest. (T208)

> Stretch out your love to Jesus Christ. You have won Him! Touch Him with as much love as you sometimes feel for a man. He is yours to do with all that you will. (S180)

In this love relationship, the anchoress feels the power of having so concentrated her energies. Her reward for having limited her contact with earthly men is that she has complete freedom in imagining an intense and sensual relationship with Christ.

It is not only the sexual relationship that Christ satisfies for the anchoress. He is presented also as the embodiment of the anchoress's desires for motherhood, courtship, and close friendship.[59] Christ is imagined as the teasing mother who plays hide and seek with her darling child (T119; S102), as the protective mother "full of pity, [who] puts herself between her child and the stern, angry father who is going to strike it" (T187; S162), as the young husband who tests his new wife's devotion (T112-13; S97), the confidant who encourages the anchoress to complain to Him of those who have done her harm (T53; S43). In part VII, "On Love," the love relationship between Christ and the anchoress is explicitly defined in terms of various human love relationships. The most famous, of course, is the extended image of Christ as the knightly wooer. But Christ is also described here as the most forgiving husband, the sacrificing mother, and generous friend.

Such worldly and human loves fall short of the otherworldly mysticism that critics have at times tried to find in the *Ancrene Wisse*.[60] As should be evident by now, mysticism would serve for the author no useful purpose in a work that establishes the anchorhold and the anchoress's heart as essentially worldly environments. The *Wisse* author has been defined as a mystical writer primarily because he borrows frequently from the mystical writings of St. Bernard. Certainly the work of recent critics in bringing to light the author's indebtedness to Bernardine sources is important,[61] but it must also be emphasized that the author borrows selectively, ignoring and sometimes suppressing Bernard's descriptions of mystical flight and concentrating instead upon what Bernard called the "contemplation of the heart," which is, by definition, a "carnal" experience:

> Et nota amorem cordis quodammodo esse carnalem, quod magis erga carnem Christi, et quae in carne Christus gessit vel iussit, cor humanum afficiat. Hoc repletus amore, facile ad omnem de huiusmodi sermonem compungitur. Nihil audit libentius, nihil legit studiosius, nihil frequentius recolit, nihil suavius meditatur ... Adstat oranti Hominis Dei sacra imago, aut nascentis, aut lactentis, aut docentis, aut morientis, aut resurgentis, aut ascendentis; et quidquid tale occurrerit, vel stringat necesse est animum in amore virtutum, vel carnis exturbet vitia, fuget illecebras, desideria sedet. Hanc ego abitror praecipuam invisibili Deo fuisse causam, quod voluit in carne videri et cum hominibus homo conversari, ut carnalium videlicet, qui nisi carnaliter amare non poterant, cunctas primo ad suae carnis salutarem amorem affectiones retraheret, atque ita gradatim ad amorem perduceret spiritualem.[62]

Notice that the love of the heart is, in a certain sense carnal, because our hearts are attracted most toward the humanity of Christ and the things he did or commanded while in the flesh. The heart that is filled with this love is quickly touched by every word on this subject. Nothing else is as pleasant to listen to, or is read with as much interest, nothing is as frequently in remembrance or as sweet in reflection ... The soul at prayer should have before it a sacred image of the God-man, in his birth or infancy or as He was teaching, or dying, or rising, or ascending. Whatever form it takes this image must bind the soul with the love of virtue and expel carnal vices, eliminate temptations and quiet desires. I think this is the principal reason why the invisible God willed to be seen in the flesh and to converse with man as a man. He wanted to recapture the affections of carnal men who were unable to love in any other way, by first drawing them to the salutary love of His own humanity, and then gradually to raise them to a spiritual love.[63]

For Bernard, this carnal and worldly attraction to Christ as a man is but the first stage of a love that gradually leaves the world behind, moving from "carnal" to "rational" to "spiritual" love.[64] For the *Ancrene Wisse* author, "carnal love" is what the anchoress most needs; if he has any further program in mind, it is nowhere evident in his book. Its absence is most noticeable in part VII, the culmination of his treatment of love and the chapter that most often insists that the anchoress cultivate a human and sensual, not a mystical, contact with Christ.

Having established from the opening paragraph of the inner rule onwards that the anchoress is a vulnerable human being with worldly desires that can be dangerous but are nevertheless inevitable, the author offers her the compensation of a creaturely and sensual love of Christ. He knows full well that the anchoress cannot forget or be dead to her human desires for friends, lovers, suitors, and children—in short, for the world. He also knows that constantly denying one's desires does not, as Aelred would suppose, eliminate them, but only makes them more powerful as they accumulate in the heart. But the author suggests that with that power, now transformed into an imaginative power, the anchoress can actually summon Christ's presence at will. He describes Mary, here envisioned as the ideal anchoress because she spoke so rarely, as able to command Christ's presence in her womb:

Ure deore wurðe leafdi seinte Marie, þe ah to alle wummen to beo forbisne, wes of se lutel speche þet nohwer in hali writ ne finde we þet ha spec bute fowr siðen. Ah for se selt speche hire wordes weren heuie ant hefden muche mihte ... Hire forme wordes þet we redeð of weren þa ha ondswerede Gabriel þen engel, ant teo weren se mihtie

þet wið þet ha seide, Ecce ancilla domini, fiat michi secundum uer-
bum tuum, ed tis word godes sune ant soð godd bicom mon, ant te
lauerd þet al þe world ne mahte nawte bifon bitunde him inwið hire
meidnes wombe.   (T41–42)

Our dear Lady St. Mary, who ought to be the model for all women,
spoke so little that we find her words recorded in Holy Scripture only
four times, but because she spoke so seldom her words had great
weight, and great power ... The first of her words that we read were
those with which she answered the angel Gabriel, and they were of
such power that as [soon as] she said *Behold the handmaid of the Lord.
Be it done unto me according to thy word,* the Son of God who was truly
God, became Man, and that Lord whom the whole world could not
contain enclosed Himself in her maiden womb.   (S33–34)

The paradox implied here is one I have been discussing throughout this
chapter. The anchoress who was traditionally asked to force the whole
world out of her tiny anchorhold and her heart, is here asked to receive
into her heart what the whole world was too small to contain: Christ. If
she can manage to retain all her human desires, while narrowly enclosed,
she can make of her heart an anchorhold for Christ, the most perfect recluse of all:

Ant nes he him seolf reclus i Maries wombe? þeos twa þing limpeð to
ancre: nearowðe ant bitterness, for wombe is nearow wununge, þer
ure lauerd wes reclus, ant tis word Marie ... spealeð bitternesse. ȝef
ȝe þenne i nearow stude þolieð bitterness, ȝe beoð his feolahes reclus,
as he wes i Marie wombe. Beo ȝe ibunden inwið fowr large wahes?
Ant he in a nearow cader, i neilet o rode, i stanene þruh bicluset hete
feste. Marie wombe ant þis þruh weren his ancre huses.   (T192–193)

And was not He Himself a recluse in Mary's womb? These two things
belong properly to an anchoress: narrowness of room, and bitterness;
for the womb, where Our Lord was a recluse, is a narrow dwelling,
and this word "Mary" ... means bitterness. If you then suffer bitter
things in a narrow place you are His fellow-recluses, since He was a
recluse in Mary's womb. Are you confined within four great walls?
He was confined in a narrow cradle, confined when He was nailed to
the cross, and fast enclosed in a sepulchre of stone. Mary's womb and
this sepulchre were His anchor-houses.   (S167)

But Christ confined himself in Mary's womb not to hide from the world
but to lead the most human, the most earthly life of any man. The result of

Christ's confinement, and the result of the anchoress's confinement as well,
is not that they feel *less* than others or that they are dead to the world, but
that they are more alive and feel more than others, because their energies
are so concentrated:

> Swuch grure hefde his monliche flesch aʒein þe derue pinen þet hit
> schulde drehen; þet nes na feorlich wunder, for eauer se flesch is
> cwickre, se þe reopunge þrof ant te hurt is sarre. Alutel hurt i þe ehe
> derueð mare þen deð a muchel i þe hele, for þe flesch is deaddre.
> Euch monnes flesch is dead aʒein þet wes godes flesch, as þet te wes
> inumen of þe tendre meiden. Ant naþing neauer nes þrin þet hit
> adeadede, ah eauer wes iliche cwic of þet cwike godd head þe wunede
> þrinne. (T60–61)

> His human flesh felt such apprehension at the cruel torments it was
> about to suffer; and that is not a strange or astonishing thing, for the
> more living the flesh, the sharper the sensation and the hurt. A slight
> wound in the eye hurts more than a great one in the heel, for there
> the flesh is more dead. The flesh of all human beings is dead, com-
> pared with the state of God's flesh, which had been taken from the
> tender maiden, and into which nothing ever entered that should kill
> it, but which was perpetually and constantly living, with the life of
> the living Godhead dwelling in it.   (S49–50)

To be "perpetually and constantly living" is the anchoress's difficult task.
In part VI, "On Penance," where the author describes the elect of God as
three different kinds of people, he identifies anchoresses not with those
who are dead to the world, but with those most alive. The three categories
include those living in the world, those dead to the world, and those alive
with suffering, having joined Christ on the cross:[65]

> Lokið, leoue sustren, hu þis steire is herre þen eani beo of þe oþre.
> Þe pilegrim i þe wordes wei, þah he ga forðward toward te ham of
> heouene, he sið ant hereð unnet ant spekeð umbe hwile, wreaðeð
> him for weohes, ant moni þing mei letten him of his Iurnee. Þe deade
> nis namare of scheome þen of menske, of heard þen of nesche, for he
> ne feldeð nowðer, ant forþi ne ofearneð he nowðer wa ne wunne. Ah
> þe þe is o rode ant haueð blisse þrof, he wendeð scheome to menske,
> ant wa in to wunne ant ofearneð forþi hure ouer hure . . . þus lo rihte
> ancres ne beoð nawt ane pilegrimes, ne ʒet nawt ane deade, ah beoð
> of þeos þridde, for al hare blisse is forte beon ahonget sariliche scheo-
> meliche wið Iesu on his rode. (T180)

See, dear sisters, how this degree is higher than any of the others. The pilgrim on the path of the world, although he is going forward towards the heavenly home, sees and hears things that are idle, and sometimes speaks such things, is angered by wrongs and can be hindered in his journey by many matters. The dead man cares no more for honour than for shame, for luxury than for austerity, for he feels neither, and therefore he earns neither sorrow nor joy; but the man who is on the cross, and takes joy in that, turns shame into honour and pain into joy and therefore deserves a passing reward . . . See then, true anchoresses are not only pilgrims, nor yet only dead people, but are of this third kind, for all their joy lies in being crucified in pain and dishonour with Jesus on His cross.   (S156)

The author in this passage takes his argument for the importance of the world one step further. It is not just that an anchoress cannot be dead to the world because she is a part of it. Here the author suggests that even if she could become indifferent to the world, she would be taking the easy way to salvation, the detached, desertlike way that substitutes apathy for love. To renounce the world altogether is also to renounce the only means human beings have for loving Christ, by turning to Him in His human guises, as lover, husband, father, mother, friend, and protector.

There can be no stronger evidence of the author's commitment to what Bernard would call "carnal love" than the famous Christ-knight story told at the end of the final chapter of the inner rule. Where we might most expect, if this were a mystical work, a description of mystical rapture as the ultimate reward of the solitary life, we find instead a romance, a delicate, courtly story about a hardhearted lady who disdainfully refuses to love. The lady lives much like an anchoress, "poure" and imprisoned alone within an "eorðene castel" (T198), surrounded by enemies. The author in earlier chapters frequently described the anchorhold as a castle under siege, usually for the purpose of stressing the need for spiritual self-protection. But in this story he points to a more serious danger. For the lady described here has become so intent upon protecting herself from her enemies in the world that she has become hardhearted and unable to recognize or respond to the one man who can help her. Having shut out the world, she has also shut out Christ, here presented as a courtly wooer, who offers aid to the lady in return for her love but is shunned. In the author's exegesis of the story he concentrates first upon the significance of the Christ-knight and his repeated attempt to win the proud lady's love. But he returns at the end to the lady herself to point to the dangers of hardheartedness: "Nis nan þet mahe edlutien, þet ha ne mot him luuien" (T204) ("There is no one who can hide herself away in order to escape loving Him" [S177]).

In the author's view, there can be no escapism in the anchorhold. To become "hidden" can no longer be considered the final goal of the solitary. She has entered the anchorhold not to escape the world, but to transform what could be her doom into her joy.

This is the final meaning of the author's seemingly simple moral tag, "of lutel, muchel waxeð." If a mere look at the world can result in the doom of all mankind, as it did in Eve's case, so too can the joys, pains, and sorrows of the insignificant world be transformed into an intensely human love of Christ.

But the author takes a great risk in presenting such a close relationship between the solitary and the world. Because there can be no escape in the anchorhold, there is inevitably a myriad of possibilities for sin; therefore, the *Ancrene Wisse* author must discuss with great care sin and its ultimate remedy, confession.

3

Self and the Sacrament of Confession

ERARD SITWELL, after summarizing the contents of the *Ancrene Wisse,* makes the following observation about its part divisions:

> Now if these divisions be considered it will be noticed that apart from one on public prayer and one on external rules there are two (II and III) which may be said to deal with the pursuit of virtue, how to guard against external and internal sins, and there is one (VII) on Love, which sets out ... general principles of the Christian life ... What is surprising is to find three sections [parts IV, V, and VI], equal to nearly half the whole work, devoted respectively to temptations, confession, and penance ... I think they legitimately raise the question whether they apply to the anchoresses at all, or whether the author happened to be interested in the subject matter of them and included them in his treatise for no other reason ... [T]he latter was more probably the case ... They are in no way necessary and it might be fairly argued that they are unsuitable.[1]

The translator of the *Ancrene Wisse,* M. B. Salu, drawing upon Sitwell's argument, goes even further in suggesting that "parts IV, V, and VI may themselves be an insertion by the author of his own previously written work," designed for a different audience.[2]

Given Sitwell's attempt to find mysticism as the key to spiritual life in the anchorhold, it is understandable that he would find the author's interest in sin and confession disconcerting. But his explanation of the discrepancy—that these sections were not written with the anchoresses in mind at all—seriously undermines the unity of the work, a subject on which the *Wisse* author is particularly insistent. He takes every opportunity to point out how carefully he has put his book together. Thus, he concludes his opening comments by almost proudly describing the unity of his work:

> Nu, mine leoue sustren, þis boc ich todeale on eahte destinctiuns, þet
> ȝe cleopieð dalen, ant euch wiðute monglunge spekeð al bi him seolf
> of sunderliche þinges, ant þah euchan riht falleð efter oðer, ant is þe
> leatere eauer iteiet to þe earre. (Ti1)

Now, my dear sisters, I am dividing this book into eight sections or parts. Each part has a different subject, and while there is no mingling of one subject with another, yet the parts are consecutive, each following naturally the one before.   (S6)

He even keeps count of every section, pointing out at the end of each section how many parts he has completed and what the next part will discuss, "as ich bihet þruppe," ("as I promised formerly" [T153; S132]). Just before part V ("Confession") in particular, the author takes time out to point directly to the unity of his book: "Neomeð ȝeme hu euch an dale falleð in to oþer as ich þear seide" ("Notice how each part leads to the next, as I said [earlier] that it would" [T153; S132]). Furthermore the author's remarks about confession are not, as Sitwell implies, confined to parts IV, V, and VI, but are liberally scattered throughout the work and turn up at conspicuously important points. Thus, the term "schrift" (confession) occurs no fewer than three times in the introduction alone, where the author outlines his purpose; part II, the opening of the inner rule, begins with at least an indirect allusion to the confession cycle in the story of David's heart, which leaps out in sin, laments, then returns; and part III opens with the pelican story, which the author overtly connects with the sin-sorrow-confession cycle. So whether or not the author's interest in confession is peculiar or misplaced in a work written for anchoresses, it is at least pervasive.

That the author was determined to include and dwell upon the subject of confession in this book for solitaries is certain.[3] *Why* he does so is a much more difficult question to answer. Certainly Sitwell is correct in calling the author a child of his time, and at least part of the answer does reside in widespread contemporary interest in the sacrament of penance. This chapter will, therefore, survey the well-documented history of the confession controversy, first in relation to the rise of individuality in the twelfth and early thirteenth centuries, and then as it influenced part V of the *Ancrene Wisse* in particular.

Sitwell, in his introduction to the *Ancrene Riwle,* isolates two "factors" that

conspired to make it likely that the author of the *Ancrene Riwle* should have had a particular interest in . . . moral or pastoral theology. The first was the appearance about this time of manuals for confessors [which were] primarily and evidently the outcome of the movement for the scientific treatment of theology which took place in the twelfth century.

The second factor, according to Sitwell, was Canon Twenty-One of the Fourth Lateran Council of 1215 "in which it was laid down that all the faithful must go to confession and Holy Communion at least once a year."[4] But both of these factors can be better understood as results, though not the final results, of a complicated debate with which the *Wisse* author was familiar than as factors conspiring in themselves to stimulate his interest in confession.

The confession controversy arose in the twelfth century simultaneously with the Church's increased commitment to life in the world. Underlying the concept of frequent confession is a belief that one can continually reassess and realign one's spiritual goals without withdrawing to a monastery. A controversy arose concerning how to turn this belief into a theologically valid practice. Several questions were debated: who should confess, how often, to whom, and for what purpose. But at the center of the debate stood only one issue: how could the acts of the penitent (his sorrow for and recounting of his sins), and the acts of the confessor (that representative of the Church who absolved and levied penances), be so balanced as to secure God's forgiveness of men's sins?

The question of individuality is crucial here, for central to the confession controversy was the relatively new belief that the internal and highly subjective acts of the penitent are at least as important to the process of forgiveness as any official and external act of the priest or the Church. That, in the words of one modern theologian, the question of "the relationship between exterior and interior penance still seems to be insufficiently expressed" to this day indicates the complexity of the problem.[5]

Before the twelfth century little attempt was made to relate the two. Interior penance was hardly a question, and the emphasis was heavily placed upon exterior penance of a grand and public sort.[6] The early Church Fathers, in fact, questioned whether the sins one committed after baptism could be remitted at all. Begrudgingly, Tertullian allows one extra penance (after baptism), per Christian, per lifetime:

> Haec ... venena ejus [the devil] providens Deus, clausa licet ignoscentiae janua, et intinctionis sera obstructa, aliquid adhuc permisit patere. Collocavit in vestibulo poenitentiam secundam, quae pulsantibus patefaciat: sed jam semel, quia jam secundo. Sed amplius nunquam, quia proxime frustra. Non enim et hoc semel satis est?

> God foresaw these poisons of his [the devil] and, even though the door of forgiveness was closed and made impassable by the bar of baptism, He yet allows it to stand open. In the vestibule He has established a second penance which may open to those who knock; but

only once, since it is already the second time; but never again, for the next time it will be of no profit ... After all, is not this once enough?[7]

There is good reason why nearly all of the Church Fathers refer to the practice as "penance" rather than "confession": very little importance is attached to the practice of telling one's sins, so little, in fact, that modern theologians continue to argue whether or not in the patristic age any private confession was practiced at all.[8] Penances were often indiscriminately imposed upon all Christians during fixed liturgical seasons, notably Lent. In the more particular cases, where the Christian took advantage of his option for one extra penance, the Church's great concern was not with the confession, but with the penance itself, which was generally public, involving a somewhat elaborate ceremony that proclaimed the sinner's admission into a special order of penitents. The "priest-penitentiary's" duty, as described by one historian, was "constant surveillance" to see that penitents performed their penances and did not approach the altar until they had been accepted back into the congregation by the bishop.[9] The bishop pronounced absolution only after the penance was completed, not, as today, after the confession of sins. Even after such elaborate penance absolution was not assured; until the twelfth century the evidence of forms of absolution shows that the bishop's words were really only a prayer *requesting* absolution.[10] As late as the sixth century, councils were still insisting on a single penance, though by this time much evidence indicates that the practice of allowing more than one penance was being observed, especially in the Celtic Church, which had the advantage of being far from the institutional center of the Catholic Church at Rome and was therefore free to establish the first system of private penance.[11]

Whether imposed publicly by the bishop in what was known as solemn or public penance, or privately by abbots or priests in the Celtic penitential "tariff" system, the penances were in any case exterior, that is involving some form of bodily chastisement, and severe. Penances lasting several years and sometimes for life were not unusual, even as late as the last decades of the eleventh century. Needless to say, with penances this severe, confession was not frequent and was often confined to the deathbed, which offered the advantage of the penitent's rarely surviving long enough to perform the required penance. Another solution to the problem of severe penances was to allow the penitent to "pay" for his sins monetarily by offering to the local monastery a sum of money, goods, or services to cover each year of penance.[12]

In this view of the economy of salvation the emphasis was on economy, and money payments are only one indication of the precision of the system. The earliest penitential manuals, written in Ireland and England, list quantitative or "tariff penances," which simply equate specific penances and particular sins. Little attention was paid to the interior state of the penitent, either to his motivation when he committed the sins or to his remorse or lack thereof when he made his confession.[13]

The neglect of such questions as the extent of the sinner's remorse and resolve to avoid the sin in the future is made clear in the following penance, imposed by a Norman priest upon his own soldiers following the battle of Hastings:

> Qui magno praelio scit se hominem occidisse, secundum numerum hominum pro unoquoque uno anno poeniteat. Pro unoquoque quem percussit, si nescit eum inde mortuum fuisse; si numerum retinet, pro unoquoque quadraginta diebus poeniteat, sive continue, sive per intervalla. Si autem percussorum vel occisorum numerum ignorat, ad arbitrium episcopi sui, quoad vivit, uno die in hebdomada poeniteat; aut si potest, vel ecclesiam faciendo, vel ecclesiam largiendo perpetua eleemosyna redimat.

> Anyone who knows that he killed a man in the great battle must do penance for one year for each man that he killed. Anyone who wounded a man, and does not know whether he killed him or not, must do penance for forty days for each man that he thus struck (if he can remember the number), either continuously or at intervals. Anyone who does not know the number of those he killed must, at the discretion of his bishop, do penance for one day in each week for the remainder of his life; or, if he can, let him redeem his sins by a perpetual alms, either by building or by endowing a church.[14]

We have here what is almost a Catch-22, because the soldiers were presumably sent out to kill the enemy, yet the more men they killed the more penance they were expected to perform. If they were expected to do penance, it is not likely that they were also expected to be repentant. Indeed, as Colin Morris, who cites this passage, points out, "since the supposed penitents were soldiers it was very probable that they would repeat the offenses."[15] While the passage implies that the soldiers were being asked to engage in a certain kind of self-examination—to determine how many of the enemy they left behind in what condition—this reflection on the past is curiously cut off from action and feeling in the present or future. That is, self-examination does not lead to any self-reflection, nor obviously can it lead to any change of heart. One's acts, both sinful and penitential, are somehow external to oneself, or, put more clearly, to one's feelings about those acts. Not only is it assumed that whether performed or paid for, by whomever in whatever state of mind, the penance suffices, but furthermore, the sinful act itself is in this case quite automatic, for soldiers in battle *will* kill.

Thus, if the early penitential system was harsh, there was also something very arbitrary, even hopeless, about the relationship between men's acts and God's forgiveness. The same qualities are reflected in, and partially explained by, the prevailing justification for the Incarnation—that sacrificial act that reestablished the bond between God and man that had been broken by Adam and Eve's sin. Christians today associate Christ's birth and death with all that is merciful, forgiving, and human in Church doctrine. But it was not always so, and in pre-twelfth-century theology, men, and even Christ, played only a minor and passive role in what was essentially a feudal battle of wits between clever potentates—God and the devil.

A. Hamilton Thompson summarizes what came to be known as the "devil's rights" theory of the Redemption:

> The theory, derived through Origen, gained ground that man, as a consequence of the Fall, had been subjected to the power of the devil, and that the sacrifice of Christ was demanded to free him from this thralldom to a personal master. It was an act of redemption, a payment made by God to the devil for the ransom of a slave. Such a payment could be made only in the person of one who was sinless and therefore free from the devil's power. On the other hand, it was inconceivable that the devil would accept a sinless ransom; that would be payment without an equivalent. It was necessary, therefore, that he should enter into the bargain without certainty of the true nature of the offering from which he expected to obtain compensation, and in the hope that Christ was a man liable to succumb to temptation to sin. The Incarnation was thus designed to deceive him and keep him in suspense, and of this successful deception the death of Christ was the climax. This once achieved, the work of redemption was completed: when once the devil witnessed the triumph of Christ over death, he knew himself defrauded where he had expected to get the full advantage of the transaction.

The trick turns on God's outwitting the archdeceiver Satan. Thus, as Thompson points out, Augustine's image for the Incarnation is a divine "mousetrap," in which God caught the devil. For St. Gregory, it was a hook, baited for the devil with the humanity of Christ, behind which hid the "sharp point of His divinity."[16]

Man has little to do with this story, except as slave or bait; at best he is a pawn fought over by two kings. It is no wonder that, in this game, men did not feel quite in control of their own sinfulness and repentance. As R. W. Southern points out:

> The warlike and resourceful God who had outwitted Satan was not easily to be bent to the milder ways of mercy. Although by his strategem God had wrenched Man from the hold of the Devil, it was not at all clear that he had given him any means of escaping the renewed assertion of the Devil's rights arising from actual sins: those could only be atoned for by immense penances and abundant alms.[17]

A man's change of heart or resolve to sin no more hardly counted for much in such a system. This God was more interested in strict payment.

Yet side by side with this system of severe and precise penances indiscriminately imposed existed another penitential system of sorts, which Jean Charles Payen describes as "une conversion dramatique et bouleversante."[18] The dramatic conversion is not often considered as part of the early penitential system, with good reason, because its assumptions seem far removed from the tariff system. This highly personal form of penance, which I will call the monastic penitential system, centers upon *metanoia,* or a change of heart, a profound realization of one's sins that forces a dramatic reversal of one's life. It need not always be as dramatic as St. Paul's falling off his horse, or Augustine's mad frenzy in his garden; it could instead take the form of entry into a monastery, and to some extent monasticism was the institutionalized form of this conversion to repentance.[19] Yet when the decision to enter the local monastery became more routine than dramatic, a more spectacular and sudden conversion came into vogue. Payen cites several examples from the period he calls "l'âge des prophetes (ixe — xie siècles)," and he notes that many of the spokesmen for the eremitic reform experienced profound and sudden conversions.[20] What is interesting about these dramatic conversions is that, although called "monastic" for the sake of convenience, they were not imposed from without, either by the Church or the monastic structure, though they often resulted ultimately in the penitent's joining or forming an order. They are, I think, the first indication we have of the belief that repentance could be extrasacramental and intensely personal.

Both to show this penitential sensibility at work in one who is not a monk and to show how the assumptions underlying this penitential "system" differ from those governing public penance, it will be useful to look at several passages from the memoirs of Guibert of Nogent (c. 1150), the author of what has been called the first "comprehensive autobiography in Medieval Latin."[21] Guibert mentions several of the "bouleversantes" conversions to which Payen alludes. But the most interesting, both to readers and to Guibert himself, because it seriously affected his life, is the conversion of his mother.[22]

The retirement of Guibert's mother to a hermitage near the monastery at Fly may not be the sudden conversion I have been speaking about (for the woman seems to have been very religious all her life), but it is dramatic and spectacular enough, at least in the eyes of her then very young son, because it leaves him in effect an orphan:

> Cum sciret me prorsus orphanum, et nullam omnino habere sub qua niterer opem, parentum siquidem et affinium multiplex erat copia; at vero nullus qui puerulo in omnibus tenerrimo, pro indigentiis aetatulae sollicite curam ferret; victualium enim ac indumentorum etsi esset nulla necessitas, earum tamen providentiarum, quae illius aevi impotentiae conveniunt, quae sine feminis administrari non possunt, me saepius vexabat inopia. Cum ergo me sciret his addictum incuriis, timore et amore tuo, Deus, sua obdurante praecordia.

> She knew that I should be utterly an orphan with no one at all on whom to depend, for great as was my wealth of kinsfolk and connections, yet there was no one to give me the loving care a little child needs at such an age; though I did not lack for the necessities of food and clothing, I often suffered from the loss of that careful provision for the helplessness of tender years that only a woman can provide. As I said, although she knew that I would be condemned to such neglect, yet Thy love and fear, O God, hardened her heart.[23]

This is one of the earliest passages in medieval literature where we see the heroic conversion, not on a distant spiritual plain of the ideal, but instead from the point of view of the abandoned world itelf, as it were, embodied in the saint's son. The passage betrays Guibert's own misgivings about his mother's "conversion by renouncing the world." He seems at the same time edified and disappointed that God has "marvelously hardened her heart" against her own son. And for the mother also, conversion is not so automatic and wholehearted that she does not suffer at the moment of separation:

> Dum ad praedictum monasterium demigraret, transitum habens, tantis cordis lacerabatur aestibus ut castellum ipsum vel respicero pro tormento intolerabili sibi esset, acerbissima enim moestitia, dum co-

gitat quid ibidem reliquerit, mordebatur. Nimirum plane si veluti ab ejus corpore membra propria viderentur abrumpi, cum impiissimam et crudelem se profecto cognosceret.

When on the way to that monastery she passed below the stronghold where I remained, the sight of the castle gave intolerable anguish to her lacerated heart, stung with the bitter remembrance of what she had left behind. No wonder indeed if her limbs seemed to be torn from her body, since she knew for certain that she was a cruel and unnatural mother.[24]

Her breaking away from her child and friends had much the same effect as the excommunication of solemn or public penance—removal of the sinner from the community of the faithful to the order of penitents—but here the "penance" is self-imposed and proceeds from an inner conviction of sin. Furthermore, the conviction (and the torment) does not cease upon conversion, confession, and penance, but, at least in the case of Guibert's mother, grows more severe, so that she thinks more and more about her sins:

Confessio igitur veterum peccatorum, quoniam ipsam didicerat initium bonorum, quotidie pene nova cum fieret, semper animus ejusdem exactione praeteritorum suorum actuum versabatur, quid virgo ineunte sub aevo, quid virita, quid vidua studio jam possibiliore peregerit, cogitaverit, dixerit, semper rationis examinare thronum, et ad sacerdotis, imo ad Dei per ipsum cognitionem examinata deducere. Inde cum tantis videres feminam orare stridoribus, tanta spiritus anxietate tabescere, ut inter operandum cum dirissimis vix ullo modo cessarent deprecatoria verba singultibus.

Since she had learned the beginning of good deeds from the confession of her old sins, she repeated her confessions almost daily. Consequently, her mind was forever occupied in searching out her past deeds, what she had thought or done or said as a maiden of tender years, or in her married life, or as a widow with a wider range of activities, continually examining the seat of reason and bringing what she found to the knowledge of a priest, or rather to God through him. Then you might have seen the woman praying with such sharp sighs, pining away with such anguish of spirit that as she worshiped, there was scarcely ever a pause in the heart-rending sobs that went with her entreaties.[25]

Thus, this penitential sensibility does not, as with the tariff system exemplified earlier by the penance imposed after the battle of Hastings, cut the sinner off from her past sins, but instead makes the memory of that past all the more real. And all her weeping is not only over past sins, for, as could be expected from the constant "searching" and "examining," she had developed a very tender conscience that never gave her peace:

> Si quando vero exterorum hominum conventiculi ejus solitudinis quam amplectebatur admodum turbarentur; cum ipsa enim omnes, qui ipsius notionem attigerant, viri praesertim ac feminae nobiles, quoniam mire erat faceta et temperans gratissime loquebantur, ipsis discedentibus, si quid minus verum, si quid futile, si quid otiosum se colloquiis immersisset, illud in illius animo dici non potest quas parturiebat angustias, donec solitas aut compunctionis seu confessionis attingeret undas.
>
> Sed quantumcunque studium, quantacunque solicitudo ejus haberetur in talibus, nil fiduciae, nil securitatis menti ejus afferre poterat, quin semper lugeret, quin semper, an reatuum suorum posset mereri veniam, flebilissime rogitaret.

> Whenever assemblies of people from outside disturbed her beloved solitude—for all who were acquainted with her, especially men and women of noble rank, took pleasure in conversing with her because of her wondrous wit and forbearance—on their departure, every untrue, idle, or thoughtless word she had uttered during their talk began in her soul indescribable anguish until she reached the familiar waters of penance or confession.
>
> Whatever the zeal and anxiety she showed in such matters, she could win for her soul no confidence, no composure to stay her unceasing lamentations, her earnest and tearful questionings whether she could ever earn pardon for her offenses.[26]

As with the penitential tariff system, so too here there is no assurance of absolution. Yet there is at least the sense that the sinner's salvation depends somehow upon her acts—sorrow, anguish, zeal, and anxiety—and not upon canonical penance externally imposed. Confession is important to Guilbert's mother, but not particularly as a sacrament of the Church that assures absolution. Instead the emphasis is upon her preparation for the confession, her continual searching and anguish.

In fact her state of mind has little to do with the Church at all. Such a highly emotive sensibility could hardly be encouraged or incorporated by any institution and was, of its nature, restricted to the very few, whether monks or extraordinary laymen, who could continually subject themselves to such rigorous self-examination.[27] On this point the old penitential system had its advantages, for if it tended to be quantitative and impersonal, it

was also democratic, at least up to a point. Many bishops scorned the penitential manuals as "unauthoritative" and dangerous because penances var-
ied from book to book.[28] Nevertheless, a parish priest, armed with whatever manual came his way, could offer penance to all who approached him.
Burchard of Worms, in a penitentiary incorporated into the *Decretum*, defines the value of his work as follows:

> [This book] docet unumquemque sacerdotem, etiam simplicem,
> quomodo unicuique succurrere valeat, ordinato vel sine ordine, pau-
> peri, diviti, puero, juveni, seni, decrepito, sano, infirmo, in omni ae-
> tate et in utroque sexu.[29]

> This book teaches every priest, even an uneducated one, how he can
> bring help to every person, whether ordained or unordained; whether
> rich or poor; boy, youth, mature man, or decrepit old man, healthy or
> inform, of all ages, and of both sexes.

Yet the more personal penitential sensibility did have its appeal, in popular as well as more refined spirituality, as witnessed by the number of con-
version-repentance stories that appear in the literature of the twelfth and
thirteenth centuries.[30] Its importance, it seems to me, is that it suggested
to the popular imagination that an individual's direct and immediate response to sin was at least as important as the Church's penitential apparatus
in the economy of salvation. Again I use the word "economy" literally, for
in both systems—the tariff system, in which specific penance was matched
against particular sin, and the more personalized monastic system, in which
a whole penitential life was offered as expiation—the penance was considered as payment of a debt to God incurred by sin.[31] There was no question
but that God was the final judge and bondsman who decided whether the
payment was sufficient.

But beginning in the twelfth century the question did arise whether the
individual could be his own mediator, or whether he must rely solely upon
the Church to mediate for him—that is, whether forgiveness of sin could
be secured by interior repentance alone, or only through the efficacy of the
priest. When in the twelfth century all the sacraments came under close
scrutiny so that they could be defined and fixed, these two penitential systems first collided and then collapsed into one another, resulting in the
Church's adoption of a sacrament and system of penance that recognized
the importance of the acts of the penitent as well as the acts of the confessor.

The twelfth century has been called "the golden age of repentance," an
age that sought what Payen calls the "gift of tears," what monastic writers

usually called the "grace of compunction."[32] Though tears are merely the
external sign of interior sorrow for sin, nevertheless, the burden of many
sermons was simply a request for tears. Within the monasteries, St. Bernard was urging:

> Prosternere et tu in terram, amplectere [Christ's] pedes, placa osculis,
> riga lacrimis, quibus tamen non illum laves, sed te.

> Prostrate yourself on the ground, take hold of [Christ's] feet, soothe
> them with kisses, sprinkle them with your tears and so wash not
> them but yourself.[33]

But compunction was now no longer restricted to the monasteries,
though it originated there. St. Anselm was composing for noblewomen
prayers designed specifically to arouse tears of compunction:

> Sint mihi, domine . . . lacrimae meae panes die ac nocte, donec dicatur
> mihi: "ecce deus tuus"; donec audiam: "anima, ecce sponsus tuus."
> Pasce me interim singultibus meis, pota me interim fletibus meis, re-
> focila me doloribus meis.

> Lord . . . let my tears be my meat day and night, until they say to me,
> "Behold your God," until I hear, "Soul, behold your bridegroom."
> Meanwhile, let me be fed with griefs, and let my tears be my drink;
> comfort me with sorrows.[34]

Not only does the content of these emotional prayers concern tears, but
their very form is shaped by compunction. In the preface to a collection of
prayers originally written for the Countess Matilda, Anselm notes that the
reader should not consider the prayers as separate entities to be read
through completely, but rather he should read only enough to "stir up" his
mind to compunction:

> *Orationes sive meditationes* quae subscriptae sunt, quoniam ad excitan-
> dam legentis mentem ad dei amorem vel timorem, seu ad suimet dis-
> cussionem editae sunt . . . Nec debet intendere lector ut quamlibet
> earum totam perlegat, sed quantum sentit sibi deo adiuvante valere ad
> accendendum affectum orandi, vel quantum illum delectat. Nec ne-
> cesse habet aliquam semper a principio incipere, sed ubi magis illi
> placuerit. Ad hoc enim ipsum paragraphis sunt distinctae per partes,
> ut ubi elegerit incipiat aut desinat.

> The purpose of the prayers and meditations that follow is to stir up
> the mind of the reader to the love or fear of God, or to self-examina-

tion ... The reader should not trouble about reading the whole of any of them, but only as much as, by God's help, he finds useful in stirring up his spirit to pray ... Nor is it necessary for him always to begin at the beginning, but wherever he pleases. With this in mind the sections are divided into paragraphs, so that the reader can begin and leave off wherever he chooses.[35]

The conscious attempt to stir up the spirit to tears ran the risk of sentimentality—a routine equation of tears with repentance and/or love. This is the concern of another monastic writer, Aelred of Rievaulx, who tells a story of a young novice who questions his vocation to be a monk, because he can no longer, as he could while living in the world, shed tears for his sins. Aelred chides him for considering those tears so "precious," pointing out that a good stage play, or a well-told tale of King Arthur, can provoke tears. Tears are helpful in the spiritual life, Aelred points out, only because they help people to know themselves, but tears should never be equated with love.[36] Still, the cult of tears, especially outside the monastery, did not always have the refining influence of an Aelred, and often enough, especially in the later Middle Ages, feeling and faith were confused. But the very fact that they *could* be confused marks an important advance of twelfth-century theology, most easily observed in the newly emerging image of God.

The early penitential system, with its insistence upon strict satisfaction, proceeded from and reinforced the image of a just God insistent upon his legal rights. But beginning with Anselm a new image of a merciful God emerges, which concentrates on the close relationship between Christ and men. In the story of the Redemption, man is no longer a pawn lost in a game of wits between God and the devil. Instead, the devil is eliminated from the scheme altogether so that the story can emphasize, as R. W. Southern puts it, "the direct confrontation between God and Man."[37]

In *Cur Deus homo?* Anselm sets out to prove the necessity of a God-Man to man's salvation and God's satisfaction.[38] His argument is both elegant and complex. The devil's rights theory of the Incarnation offended Anselm, not from, as Southern terms it, a humanistic point of view, nor even from a logical point of view (indeed, as Southern notes, Anselm only increased his logical difficulties by omitting the devil from the Incarnation scheme), but from a feudal or legal standpoint. If God is the highest feudal lord, and if the devil first rebelled against this lord, how can he be said to have any rights at all? Removing the devil's rights in effect, and almost in spite of Anselm, opened the way to a new theory of the Incarnation based solely on God's mercy toward men. Characteristically, Anselm summarizes his argument in a feudal image that Southern describes as follows:

He likened the work of the Redemption to the action of a king whose people had all, except one, been guilty of a crime worthy of death. But the one innocent man, besides his innocence, offered to perform a service greater than the offence of all his fellow subjects put together. The king accepted this service and agreed that it should effect the pardon of all who wished for it, on the condition that they presented themselves on the day the service was performed. Moreover, even if they could not come on this day, provided they came on another day, they would receive their pardon.

As Southern points out, such a view of the Incarnation "left the door to salvation very wide open," and thus helped to undermine the necessity of very harsh penances in atonement for sins.[39] It left in place of the devil's rights theory a very tender feeling, delicately conveyed in Anselm's story, for the human side of Christ, who had now become more man's representative in an appeal to God's mercy, rather than God's "trick" on the devil.

Abelard, writing a generation later, went much further than Anselm by eliminating altogether the notion of payment of debt from the economy of the Redemption. According to Abelard, Christ became Man primarily (and perhaps only) to teach other men how to love:

> Nobis . . . videtur quod in hoc justificati sumus in sanguine Christi, et Deo reconciliati, quod per hanc singularem gratiam nobis exhibitam, quod Filiius suus nostram susceperit naturam, et in ipsos nos tam verbo quam exemplo instituendo usque ad mortem perstitit, nos sibi amplius per amorem astrixit, . . . Redemptio itaque nostra est illa summa in nobis per passionem Christi dilectio, quae non solum a servitute peccati liberat, sed veram nobis filiorum Dei libertatem acquirit, ut amore ejus potius quam timore cuncta impleamus.

> It seems to us that *this* is the way in which we have been justified in the blood of Christ, and reconciled to God: that by this singular favor shown to us (that his Son took our nature, and persevered until death, providing us with both teaching and example) he bound us more fully to himself by love . . . And so our redemption is that great love awoken in us by the passion of Christ, which not only frees us from the slavery of sin, but acquires for us the true liberty of the sons of God, that we may fulfill all things more by love of him than by fear.[40]

Neither theory of the Incarnation—the Anselmian nor the more radical Abelardian—won easy acceptance in the schools, and writers as influential as Peter Lombard fluctuated between the old devil's rights theory and the new, more humanistic justification for Christ's presence on earth.[41] The Lateran Council of 1215, which settled or at least stabilized so many controversies, remained notably silent on this issue, probably because of the weight of authority supporting the old theory. But outside of the schools the notion of God's mercy and Christ's humanity firmly took hold, as evidenced by the cult of tears mentioned earlier, the new devotion to the Virgin Mary, and the appearance of crucifixes emphasizing Christ's human suffering rather than his triumph over the devil.[42] And in the schools themselves, if there was no agreement on the technicalities of the logical argument over the necessity of the Incarnation, the tendency to accept the corollaries—God's prevailing mercy and his love for men—is evident, especially in the controversy over penance, easier to debate because it required no denial of such traditional and prestigious theories as the devil's rights proposition.

The dynamics of confession are, of course, similar to those of man's first rebirth in the Incarnation: both involve the payment of a debt incurred by sin, in the former actual sin and in the latter original sin. As with Incarnation theory, so too penance theory involves a triangular scheme, with the Church instead of the devil as the central third party that prevents man's direct confrontation with God. But in the twelfth century, just as the devil was being eliminated from the one theory, so too the Church was, for a short time at least, all but eliminated from the other. The problem in both controversies is virtually the same: who plays the leading part in achieving salvation? Whose acts weigh more heavily with God: those of the priest, representative of the Church, or those of the penitent himself? Given the new feeling for God's mercy and Christ's humanity, it is not difficult to predict that in the first phase of the controversy at least, man's role would be emphasized. Payen summarizes man's new position in a scheme that

> gives the person an active role in the remission of sins, insisting on the moral aspects of individual conduct. Man is in fact at the center of a psychomachia in which he is torn between soul and body, angels and devils, vices and virtues, but he maintains his free will and is never the passive plaything of grace or the devil. Whence the importance of individual conversion, which is always an act of freedom, and also the corollary importance of confession and repentance.[43]

From a historical viewpoint it seems that the problem was somehow to combine the old penitential tariff system, which had the advantage of accessibility and equality, but which emphasized quantitative satisfaction externally imposed by the Church, with the monastic penitential system, which relied upon interior and individual sorrow for sin to win remission. Given the tendency of the laity during this period to appropriate monastic concepts, which I traced earlier regarding religious rules, it is not difficult to predict that the monastic system would prove very influential.

The most influential document in the confession controversy was a pseudo-Augustinian treatise, *De vera et falsa poenitentia*, written sometime in the second half of the eleventh century, and treating the subjects of sin, confession, and penance.[44] One of the most influential sections of the treatise, chapter ten, is a justification of the increasingly popular practice of confessing to laymen. The very fact that such a practice was popular in the eleventh and twelfth centuries is interesting enough, for, as Amédée Teetaert points out, it proves that in the popular mind at least confession itself was of value apart from the absolution granted by a priest.[45] But the Pseudo-Augustine's justification of the practice and his insistence on the obligation of confession to laymen in certain cases is even more interesting in its emphasis upon the emotional or interior life of the sinner. While the practice of confessing to laymen gradually died out in the course of the thirteenth century (as the sacramental aspects of confession gained prominence), nevertheless the theory of confession that justified such a practice helped to change radically the medieval concept of penance.[46]

The theory expressed in the *De vera et falsa poenitentia* and reiterated by many twelfth-century theologians is as follows: the efficacy of confessing our sins—whether to priest or to layman—lies in the shame (*erubescentia*) or confusion that telling one's sins aloud naturally produces. In the absence of a priest it is this shame and confusion that wins the remission of sins from a merciful God. Thus "qui erubescit pro Christo (confitendo peccata) fit dignus misericordia."[47] It follows then that confessing to a priest is not necessary for absolution. In fact no man can effect another's absolution, though the priest can, according to the Pseudo-Augustine, accelerate sins' remission by his prayers. The priest is dispensable not only for providing absolution, but also for levying penances, for the shame aroused in confessing is itself a large part of the satisfaction God requires for sins: "Et quoniam verecundia magna est poena."[48] So the sinner to a large extent imposes his own penance upon himself, and this is true of every sinner, not just of rarified souls like Guibert's mother. Because shame is aroused by confession and at the same time provides most of the required penance, it follows that the more frequently one confesses, the better, whether to priest or to layman.[49] The *De vera et falsa poenitentia* provides one of the earliest justifications and means of encouraging recurrent confession, and brings to laymen what had always been an essentially cloistered penitential sensibility.

Confession to laymen was not considered, either by the Pseudo-Augustine or by the early scholastics, as a sacrament, for nowhere does the Pseudo-Augustine attribute to laymen the power to forgive sins.[50] The justification he provides is extrasacramental, based upon the shame and confusion aroused in confessing. Yet this justification does enter and assume an important place in debates attempting to fix the sacramentality of confession. For what the *De vera* has done is to shift the focus of attention away from the priest's power to absolve and from the importance of external satisfaction for sin, and instead to focus attention squarely upon the confession itself, particularly upon the sorrow and shame of the penitent himself. The Pseudo-Augustine's influence is evident throughout the short-lived but intense debate over the sacrament of confession.

Abelard characteristically takes the conclusions of the Pseudo-Augustine to their logical extreme, yet his conclusions concerning the subjectivity of penance are not so extreme that they cannot be followed and supported by most later twelfth-century thinkers.[51] Abelard's teaching on confession occupies the last third of his *Scito te ipsum* and logically follows his treatment of sin, which is integrally related to his theory of confession. Just as in the newly emerging confession theory it is not so much the external acts of absolution and satisfaction that are considered but the internal contrition of the sinner, so too in Abelard's definition of sin it is not the act itself that constitutes the sin, but the individual's intention preceding the act. For Abelard actions are morally neutral in themselves. Sin is not an external act, nor is it a vice that only makes us prone to evil; nor is sin, as it is for Augustine, an evil will, for "will" is too ambiguous a term for Abelard's taste.[52] Specifically, sin is the consent (consensus) to evil and

> peccare est creatorem contempnere, hoc est, id nequaquam facere propter ipsum quod credimus propter ipsum a nobis esse faciendum, vel non dimittere propter ipsum quod credimus esse dimittendum.

> to sin is to hold the Creator in contempt, that is, to do by no means on his account what we believe we ought to do for him, or not to forsake on his account what we believe we ought to forsake.[53]

The doctrine is important in many respects, but Robert Blomme emphasizes two. First, Abelard's definition depends upon man's own responsibility and knowledge of sin: "For Abelard, there can be no sin where there is merely a mistake; the responsibility of the man must always be engaged." Second, Abelard's definition emphasizes the interiority of sin. Sin occurs at the moment of consent, not when one actually commits the deed:[54]

Tunc uero consentimus ei quod non licet, cum nos ab eius perpetra-
tione nequaquam retrahimus parati penitus, si daretur facultas, illud
perficere. In hoc itaque proposito quisquis reperitur reatus perfectionem incurrit nec operis effectus super additus ad peccati augmen-
tum quicquam addit.

The time when we consent to what is unlawful is in fact when we in
no way draw back from its accomplishment and are inwardly ready, if
given the chance, to do it. Anyone who is found in this disposition
incurs the fullness of guilt; the addition of the performance adds
nothing to increase the sin.[55]

It naturally follows that if sin is essentially interior, then so too must
penance be. Penance is that "dolor atque contritio animi" that proceeds
from love of a merciful God, "quem tam benignum adtendimus." Sins are
forgiven at the moment we feel the "sigh" of remorse:

Cum hoc . . . gemitu et contritione cordis, quam ueram penitentiam
dicimus, peccatum non permanet, hoc est, contemptus Dei siue consensus in malum, quia karitas Dei hunc gemitum inspirans non pati-
tur culpam. In hoc statim gemitu Deo reconciliamur et precedentis
peccati ueniam assequimur, iuxta illud Prophetae, "Quacumque hora
peccator ingemuerit, saluus erit," hoc est, salute animae suae dignus
efficietur. Non ait, quo anno, uel quo mense, siue qua ebdomada, uel
quo die, sed qua hora, ut sine dilatione uenia dignum ostendat nec ei
penam aeternam deberi, in qua consistit condempnatio peccati.

With this sigh and contrition of heart which we call true repentance
sin does not remain, that is, the contempt of God or consent to evil,
because the charity of God which inspires this sigh does not put up
with fault. In this sigh we are instantly reconciled to God and we
gain pardon for the preceding sin, according to the Prophet: "In what
hour soever the sinner shall sigh, he shall be saved," that is, he will be
made worthy of the salvation of his soul. He did not say: in what year
or in what month or in what week or on what day, but in what hour,
so as to show that he is worthy of pardon without delay, and that
eternal punishment, in which the condemnation of sin consists, is not
owing to him.[56]

Such a subjective view of penance may seem to preclude altogether the
necessity of confessing one's sins, but such is not quite the case. D. E. Luscombe, Abelard's recent and thorough editor, notes that in other works
Abelard insists on the traditional obligation to confess.[57] But in the *Scito te*

ipsum, where Abelard is more interested in morality than in strict theology, he avoids meeting the issue head on. "For many reasons the faithful confess their sins to one another," Abelard notes, without touching on the *obligation* to do so. Later he notes that often confession is a matter of prudence, not duty, for confession to the wrong man or at the wrong time can do more spiritual harm than good. Nevertheless, though it is not necessary for absolution, which comes at the moment of contrition, confession is, according to Abelard, very useful. Contrition or inner sorrow remits the eternal punishment due for sin, but some temporal punishment does remain. Abelard notes that if the confessor is careful in his duty to assign appropriate penances, the sinner will have the advantage of being able to suffer here on earth rather than in purgatory, where all suffering is greater. Furthermore, the priest's prayers may help to mitigate the punishment. More important, and here Abelard relies directly upon the Pseudo-Augustine,

> in humilitate confessionis magna pars agitur satisfactionis, et in relaxatione penitentiae maiorem assequimur indulgentiam.

> in the humility of confession a large part of satisfaction is performed and we obtain a greater indulgence in the relaxation of our penance.[58]

The shame of confessing to another man and of accepting the punishment imposed by another reestablishes and makes up for the shame that was lacking when one consented to evil. Thus, because oral confession induces shame, and because shame is essential to the remission of sins, confession is exceedingly useful, though not indispensable.[59]

Although most of Abelard's statements concerning confession were neither refuted nor pronounced anathema at the Council of Sens (1140) and were accepted by later theologians, the obligation to confess, which Abelard deemphasized, had to be reasserted and the argument rearranged to emphasize the importance of the priest's role in the sacrament. Otherwise the Church would have been left with a completely internal sacrament, a contradiction in terms. Abelard had gone about as far as it was possible to go in the direction of the subjectivity of both sin and repentance, and now the pendulum had to swing back at least somewhat in the direction of the old external penitential system.

The scholastics following Abelard who insisted on the obligation to confess agreed that internal sorrow effected the remission of sin, but emphasized that the confession itself was both the outward sign (essential to any sacrament) of the contrition and that which facilitated greater or more perfect contrition by exciting shame.[60] Thus, for Peter Lombard, Peter of Poitiers, Alanus de Insulis, and Gratian, contrition and confession are inextricably bound together. Yet, for all these thinkers, it is still the contrition itself, though manifested and increased in confession, that works the remission.[61]

It is not difficult to see that the twelfth-century "contritionist" theory of penance is highly subjective and internalized.[62] Whether one has sinned or repented depends upon the individual's frame of mind, and depends, as Payen points out, upon a very emotionally sensitive mind at that: a tender conscience is essential to the system. Furthermore, because the scheme is so internalized, the priest's function, and therefore the Church's function, is minimal: the priest merely "declares" aloud the remission of the external punishment already granted at the moment of the individual's contrition and by praying and levying a penance, remits some of the temporal punishment due for sin. Although such a subjectivist theory is quite understandable as a reaction against the old penitential tariff system,[63] still, a more refined scheme was needed that gave equal weight to all the parts of the sacrament—contrition, confession, absolution, and satisfaction.

Beginning with Hugh of St. Victor, who in spite of considerable opposition in his time insisted that only the priest's absolution could remit the eternal punishment due for sin, the importance of absolution to the sacrament of penance was on the rise once more.[64] Canon Twenty-One of the Fourth Lateran Council of 1215 reestablished once for all (or at least for three hundred years, until the problem arose again during the Reformation) the necessity of absolution to the remission of sins, without, however, denying the importance of contrition and confession. Christians were obligated to confess their sins at least once a year to their own parish priest, who was to question the sinner carefully to judge the gravity of his sins, the extent of his sorrow, and, balancing these two, declare a penance.[65] Finally confession or penance had become a fixed sacrament, with all its parts contributing to its efficacy, and more or less satisfactory from both an "ecclesiological and a psychological point of view."[66]

Canon Twenty-One certainly did not solve all the problems connected with the sacrament. Another generation had passed before this most complicated of sacraments was neatly defined and made to fit into the sacramental framework by St. Thomas. Furthermore, earlier councils had already begun urging more frequent confession to no avail, so it seems that something more than Church pronouncements was needed.[67] The twelfth-century theologians I have been discussing provided at least half of what was needed: a penitential theory that emphasized equally faith in an individual's ability to recognize his own sins and feel remorse and faith in the sacramental power of the Church, which made what had formerly been an essentially monastic privilege and sensibility accessible to all.

What was now needed was a vehicle to move the new theory out of the schools and into the world. Two vehicles were actually used. The Friars were encouraged by several popes to preach repentance and hear confessions in every town in England and Europe.[68] But there was another network of men who could help to spread the new theory: parish priests, who, if properly informed themselves, could teach the doctrine of contrition at the same time that they administered the sacrament of confession. To inform parish priests a new genre of literature was born, or rather resurrected; the new *summae confessorum* bore at least some resemblance to the old Celtic tariff penitentiaries. The new manuals range from very scholarly, technical treatises on the efficacy of confession, to straightforward, almost homely explanations and aids for parish confessors. They form a major genre of thirteenth-century literature, called by one reader among the most "popular best sellers" of the age.[69]

The spirit and tone of the new *summae*, and even their purpose, are radically different from the old tariff penitentiaries and indicate how much penitential theory has changed. They rarely, if ever, list specific penances. Thomas of Chobham, in one of the most influential confession manuals, does devote a short section following his discussion of some sins to "what penance ought to be enjoined."[70] However, even here he rarely lists a specific penance, but rather gives general principles, often to the effect that the punishment should fit the sin, and should be enjoined "secundum prudentiam discreti sacerdotis."[71] In fact in some cases Thomas goes out of his way to avoid giving a specific penance. Though two sources that Thomas follows closely elsewhere list three years as the appropriate penance for "simple" fornication, Thomas claims that authorities have not set a specific penance for that sin.[72]

Rather than emphasize various penances for sins, Thomas undertakes to instruct parish priests, and through them the faithful, on the sacrament of penance. The priest's task in the confessional had become quite complicated, now that intention largely determined sinfulness and inner sorrow determined penance. As F. Broomfield points out, the priest "could no longer be considered as the administrator of a hard and fast penal code. He had become a judge in the full sense with the obligation to base his decisions on the principles of a newborn moral theology."[73] For one thing, the sinner's confession had now become extremely important, at least as important as satisfaction or penance, and the primary determinant of absolution, which was now given immediately after the confession and before the penance had been accomplished. The new manuals describe at some length the various necessary attributes of a good confession: it must be humble, speedy, frank, bitter, complete, and so on.[74] Furthermore, a more refined notion of sin required the priest to question the penitent closely about the motivations and "circumstances" surrounding each sin. Thomas of Chobham carefully names and defines the important circumstances sine quibus non potest sciri quantitas peccati, et nisi sciatur quantitas peccati, non potest sciri quanta penitentia alicui peccato sit iniungenda.[75]

without which the gravity of sins cannot be known, and if the gravity of sins is not known, neither can the proper penance for each sin be enjoined.

The circumstances are summarized in a little verse, easy to memorize: "quis, quid, ubi, quibus auxiliis, cur, quomodo, quando" (who, what, where, with what help, why, how, when); and the significance of each is explained. Later on, Thomas gives circumstances that might affect each particular sin, as well as circumstances that apply to various occupations; players and prostitutes and clerics must all be addressed differently.[76] Thomas seems almost to relish the variety and individuality of sin.

While the largest single article of Thomas's *Summa* concerns the specifics of various sins, still it occupies only one-third of the treatise that numbers close to six hundred pages in Broomfield's edition. Much of the rest is devoted to teaching the parish priest himself the basic tenets of the faith. Thus Thomas includes a long article about "what a priest ought to know," in addition to a careful and complete explanation of what penance is, its parts and efficacy, and the power given to priests to forgive sins.[77] Armed with such knowledge, the priest could, in turn, teach his parishioners. The almost tutorial contact between priest and penitent in confession offered a unique opportunity to teach parishioners, if not the theological subtleties of their faith, at least the Credo, some helpful prayers, and, most important, a method for examining their consciences with some awareness of the complexity of sin. Thus the parish priest became a genuine director of souls, a counselor, even "something of an artist since the doctrine of the circumstances of sin developed in the Faculty of the Arts" at Paris.[78]

If this marks a great advance in moral or practical theology, a greater one was soon to come. While in the early thirteenth century confession manuals were written for and studied by parish priests alone, by the end of the same century the audience had expanded significantly, as evidenced by the number of manuals written in the vernacular for laymen as well as priests. Payen notes that it was this proliferation of confession manuals that "makes . . . repentance the greatest of the sacraments, one which is at the very center of the Christian life."[79] In England especially, with its penchant for the practical and the concrete, confession manuals, at first for priests and later for laymen, flourished. The earliest known manual of the new type was written by an Englishman, Robert of Flamborough, and the most famous and popular of the handbooks in the vernacular is *Handlying Synne*,

Robert Brunne's translation of William of Waddington's *Manuel des peches*.[80]

The arrival of carefully detailed confession manuals, written in the vernacular for laymen, points up the great changes that had taken place in the Church's understanding of sin, confession, and repentance. At the turn of the thirteenth century, largely as a result of the controversies I have been discussing, a new branch of theology is born—moral theology—which has as its center the notion of conscience, entailing the individual Christian's awareness of and responsibility for his own sins. It is surely no accident that the notion of conscience comes to be refined at precisely the same moment that the confession controversy is resolved.[81] For in the new confession scheme, one's own conscience, once wounded by sin, urges repentance and sorrow. Repentance no longer depends upon such external forces as liturgical season or one's ability to pay a monk to complete one's penance. It is now an internal voice, operating constantly, that urges repentance and simultaneously assures forgiveness through God's mercy. One can repent continually, not only because the machinery now exists to facilitate more frequent confession, but also because the new image of a merciful God—interested enough in man's heart to send His Son to teach men how to love Him—engenders a hope that shame for sin and a sorrowful recognition of sins can move this God to forgive over and over again. Recognition of one's sins has become both easier and harder than it had been earlier. Abelard helped to take some of the blindness or coincidence out of the notion of sin: because sin requires the consent of conscience, Abelard argued, one cannot sin without knowing it. But on the other hand, all men were now asked to understand and analyze, with the help of their confessors, the motivations, attributes, and stages of sin.

The result of this new branch of theology, as D. E. Luscombe notes, is a new moral language "with which [man can] study his own character and conduct."[82] This language, which had been developed in the cloisters by Bernard, Anselm, and Aelred, and in the schools by Abelard, Peter the Chanter, and others, soon entered the popular realm. Moral theological concepts, such as intention, contrition, consent, and temptation, entered the popular literature as discussions of the "heart," which could be torn by indecision, wounded by sin, broken by remorse, and smoothed and healed in confession. It could almost be said that with the arrival of moral theology the pain and individuality of temptation, sin, and remorse now became the layman's privilege, and not just the saint's.

It is precisely this juxtaposition of the ordinary Christian and the saint that I suspect Gerard Sitwell finds so disconcerting in the passage quoted at the opening of this chapter, in which he questions whether sin and con-

fession are suitable subjects for anchoresses. But at the center of the confession controversy was a desire to bring the experiences of cloistered saints
and worldly sinners closer together by bringing the monastic penitential
sensibility and the sacrament of confession within reach of all Christians.
Admittedly the most obvious results of the controversy—Canon Twenty-
One of the Fourth Lateran Council and the proliferation of confession
manuals—had a more immediate impact upon the layman than upon those
very advanced in the spiritual life, who, like Guibert's mother, might have
been already accustomed to self-searching, sorrow for sin, and penance. But
the *Ancrene Wisse* author does not take for granted that his charges are far
advanced in the spiritual life. Nor, in fact, does he give any hint of a spiritual state so advanced that sin, and therefore confession, would no longer
be considerations. On the contrary, the possibility of frequent confession
informs the *Wisse* author's vision of the spiritual life of solitaries throughout the work, but most obviously in the section on the sacrament itself,
where the author develops his own theory of confession, carefully balancing inner experience and outward forms.

The *Ancrene Wisse* author, like many English writers of his time, is not
primarily interested in theological theory, except as it affects practical concerns. But his interest in the practical consequences of the confession controversy leads him to write, as part V of the *Ancrene Wisse*, a "schriftes boc,"
or confessional manual, for his charges. In that it is directed not toward
priests but toward penitents, and in that it is written, therefore, not in
Latin but in English, this confession manual is unique in early thirteenth-
century literature. Not until late in the century do vernacular manuals for
penitents reappear.[83]

Because this manual is not directed toward those who might be called
professionals, the author does not feel compelled to include any theoretical
or technical discussion of the sacramentality of confession. Yet it is possible to extraxt from his manual some idea of his position regarding the confession controversy.

The author divides his discussion of confession into two parts, the first
of which is much shorter than the second:

> Twa þinges neomed ȝeme of schrift i þe biginnunge: þe earre, of
> hwuch mihte hit beo, þe oþer, hwuch hit schule beon. Þis beoð nu as
> twa limen ant eiðer is todealet, þe earre o sixe, þe oþer o sixtene
> stucchen. (T153–154)

> Take note, now at the beginning, of two points about Confession,
> first, what power it has, and second, how it ought to be practiced.

These are like two branches, each with its divisions, the first having six, the second sixteen parts. (S133)

In the first part he sets out to "demonstrate" ("pruuie") the powers ("mihtes") of confession, which he later calls by their more technical name, the "efficaces" of the sacrament (T156). Most of what could be called the author's theory of confession can be extracted from this first "limen" or branch of the confession section, and it can be summarized as follows: contrition, or internal sorrow for sin, is intimately connected with confession, so connected that the author is unwilling to assign to either one alone the power to effect the remission of sins. Internal sorrow, while necessary, cannot alone bring the forgiveness of sins. Of the three traditional parts of the sacrament—contrition, confession, and satisfaction—the last is given the least attention. Canonical or set penance is waived in favor of the whole penitential life the anchoress leads.

The author's explanation of the efficacy of confession, though not technical, is complex and merits close analysis:

Schrift haueð monie mihtes, ah nulle ich of alle seggen bute sixe, þreo aȝein þe deouel, ant þreo on us seoluen. Schrift schent þen deouel, hackeð of his heaued, ant todreaueð his ferd. Schrift wescheð us of alle ure fulðen, ȝelt us alle ure luren, makeð us godes children. Eider haueð hise þreo. Pruuie we nu alle. (T154)

Confession has many powers, and I shall not speak of all of these, but only of six, three which operate against the devil, and three in ourselves. Confession confounds the devil, cuts off his head, and puts his army to rout. Confession washes us of all our impurities, gives back to us all that we had lost, and makes us children of God. Each of these has its three divisions. Let us now demonstrate all of them. (S133)

Having noted that his explanation makes no claim to being complete, he continues with his "proof," which takes the form of a moralization of the Biblical story of Judith and Holofernes:

Þe earste þreo beoð alle ischawde i Iudithe deden. Iudith, þet is schrift, as wes ȝare iseid, sloh Oloferne, þet is þe feond of helle. Turn þruppe þer we speken of fuhelene cunde þe beoð ieuenet to ancre. (T154)

The first three are all shown in the deeds of Judith. Judith, that is, Confession, as was said before, slew Holofernes, that is, the devil of hell. Turn up the place where we spoke of the nature of birds which are compared to anchoresses. (S133)

The author here takes pains to remind his readers that they have read of Judith before, in another context that might be relevant here. If we take the author's advice and turn back to part III, we will recall that both birds and Judith have contradictory characteristics in common with anchoresses: they live in the world and apart from it simultaneously. Judith represents the anchoress both because she lives a hard, lonely, sinless life, and because her name means confession. While in part III the author concentrated on the solitariness of the life, here he explores Judith's other relationship to anchoresses. He has not yet told us what power confession has for anchoresses, but he insists from the start that it will be particularly "suitable" (to use Gerard Sitwell's phrase) to anchoresses, because Judith represents both confession and the anchoritic life.

The author continues, telling the story of how Judith slew Holofernes, and explicating it:

Ha hackede of his heaued ant seoððen com ant schawde hit to þe burh preostes. Þenne is þe feond ischend, hwen me schaweð alle hise cweadschipes. His heaued is ihacket of ant he islein i þe mon sone se he eauer is riht sari for his sunnen ant haueð schrift on heorte. Ah he nis nawt þe ȝet ischend hwil his heaued is ihulet, as dude on earst Iudith, ear hit beo ischawet, þet is ear þe muð i schrift do ut þe heaued sunne, nawt te sunne ane, ah al þe biginnunge þrof ant te foreridles þe brohten in þe sunne, þet is þe deofles heaued þet me schal totreoden anan, as ich ear seide. Þenne flih his ferd anan as dude Olofernes, his wiheles ant his wrenches þet he us wið asaileð, doð ham alle o fluhte, ant te burh is arud þet ha hefden biset, þet is to seggen, þe sunfule is delifret. (T154)

She cut off his head and then went and showed it to the priests of the city. It is then that the devil is confounded, when we show up all his evil ways. His head is cut off and he is slain in a man as soon as he is truly sorry for his sins and has the intention of confessing in his heart. But the devil is not yet confounded while his head is hidden, as it was by Judith, and before it is shown forth, that is, before the mouth puts out the mortal sin in Confession, and not only the sin itself, but its whole beginning and the occasions which brought it about, that is, the head of the devil which must be trampled on at once, as I said before. Then his army, the tricks and strategems by which he attacks us, flees away immediately, as did that of Holofernes; they all take to flight, and the city which they were besieging is liberated, that is to say, the sinful man is set free.   (S133)

A comparison of this moralization with one given by Peter Lombard in the *Sentences* is instructive. Peter, along with many of his contemporaries, used the story of the ten lepers (Luke 17:12) to support the contritionist theory of confession. Peter Lombard tells the story briefly in the *Sentences*, emphasizing that the lepers were first cured by Christ, then sent to the priests to have themselves "declared" clean. The story illustrates, according to Lombard and other contritionists, that the priest's power is only a declarative power that comes *after* the fact of remission of sins by God, as a result of the sinner's contrition. Peter Lombard's conclusion is typical of the contritionist point of view:

> [God] [i]pse enim per se tantum dimittit peccatum, qui et animam mundat ab interiori macula, et a debito aeternae mortis solvit.
>
> Non autem hoc sacerdotibus concessit, quibus tamen tribuit potestatem solvendi et ligandi, id est, *ostendendi homines* ligatos vel solutos. Unde Dominus leprosum sanitati prius per se restituit, deinde ad sacerdotes misit, quorum judicio ostenderetur mundatus.   (my emphasis)

> [God] alone himself remits sin, who both cleanses the soul from interior stain and looses from the debt of eternal death.
>
> But he did not concede this to priests, and yet to them he gave the power of loosing and binding, that is of *showing men* to be bound or loosed. Hence the Lord by himself first restored the leper to health and then sent him to the priests that by their judgment he might be shown to be clean.   (my emphasis)[84]

By comparison with Peter Lombard's story, simply told and simply moralized, the *Wisse* author's exegesis is unusually dense, even by his own standards. The passages have their similarities: both authors are concerned with explicating the *order* of events in confession. But where Peter's point seems clear and unmistakable, the *Wisse* author's does not.

The most obvious reason is that the *Wisse* author makes the story central; he uses it to establish his point, not to support it. Where Peter Lombard uses technical, abstract notions of binding and loosing, internal stain and eternal debt, and remission of sin, the *Ancrene Wisse* author remains far more concrete and far less technical. But the reasons for the density of the author's story go beyond stylistic considerations. Quite simply, he does not want to draw Peter Lombard's conclusion, that sin is remitted before confession to the priest. So, instead of concentrating upon the obvious se-

quence of events in the Judith-Holofernes story—that Judith cut off Holofernes's head *before* she showed it to the priests—the author rearranges the
sequence of events with almost every sentence. At first it seems that the
order of events in confession should be to (1) confound the devil, (2) then
cut off his head, and (3) thus put his army to rout. But a few lines later it
seems that the anchoress can "cut off the devil's head" *first*, as soon as she is
"truly sorry" for her sins and has "the intention of confessing in [her]
heart" ("schrift in heorte"). *Then* she should "confound the devil" or put
him to shame by showing the already severed head of the devil to the priest
in confession. Later still, it seems that the devil's head is only cut off and
"trampled on" *after* or *as* it is shown forth to the priest in confession.

Not only is the sequence of events muddled, but also the parallels between the events of the story and the acts of confession are unclear. Is the
cutting off of the devil's head to be equated with the "true sorrow" that
precedes confession, or with the confession itself, where "the head of the
devil must be trampled on at once?" Are "confounding the devil" and
"cutting off his head" the same action?

Why all this confusion? Has the author become so caught up with rhetoric that he has lost his way? I think not. Surely the man who could so
carefully separate the subtle stages of Eve's sin in part II has a powerful
hold on his language and thought and could tell the story sequentially if he
wanted to. But if he had told the story only once, and moralized the events
in their "proper" order—Judith first cut off Holofernes's head, then
brought it to the priests of the city—he would have had to accept the theological conclusion that sins (the devil's or Holofernes's work) are forgiven
(or killed) *before* they are revealed to the priest in confession. The author
uses no theoretical terminology in this passage—there is not a trace of
Latin scholastic language—and yet it seems to me that he is exploring one
of the great theoretical issues of his time, involving the relationship between the acts of the penitent and the acts of the priest. The question is
clearly posed by Peter Lombard:

> Hic quaeri solet si peccatum omnino dimissum est a Deo per cordis
> contritionem, ex quo poenitens votum habuit confitendi, quid postea
> dimittatur ei a sacerdote.

> It is customary to ask here: if sin is wholly remitted by God through
> contrition of heart, from which the penitent has the intention of con-
> fessing, what is remitted to him later by the priest?[85]

The contritionists had gone too far: by so emphasizing the contrition of
the penitent, they had lost sight of the external aspects necessary to a sacrament. The *Ancrene Wisse* author, in his own way, tries to right the bal-

ance. He purposely *blurs* the distinction, so carefully set out by contritionists, between contrition and confession. By continually rearranging the events of his story the author suggests that the drama of confession is not a linear story but a circular one. Each "event" includes all the others. Confession is not several acts, but only one. Contrition and confession—cutting off the devil's head and confounding him—are inextricably bound together as two concurrent parts, one outer and one inner, of the same act, which results in the remission of sins. The age of extreme contritionism has passed, though it has certainly left its mark: internal sorrow for sin is necessary for forgiveness, but it can no longer be considered apart from oral confession to a priest. "Riht sarwe" (true sorrow) *means* "schrift in heorte" (the intention to confess in one's heart), which can only be realized in "schrift" of mouth.

Further on the author restates the point more succinctly, though again not in a technical manner. He restates the close bond between sorrow and confession, using the etymology of Judith's name again, but this time he allegorizes not a story but a relationship:

> Iudith, þe spealeð schrift, as ich ofte habbe iseid, wes Merarihtes dohter. Ant Iudas, þet is ec schrift, wiuede o Thamar. Merariht ant Thamar ba ha spealieð an on ebreische ledene. Neomeð nu ʒeorne ʒeme of þe bitacnunge. Ich hit segge scheortliche. Bitter sar ant schrift—þet an mot cumen of þe oþer, as Iudith dude of Merariht, ant ba beon somet ifeiet, as Iudas ant Thamar, for nowðer wiðuten oðer nis noht wurð oðer luter.   (T159)

> Judith (whose name means Confession, as I have reiterated), was the daughter of Merari, and Juda (whose name also means Confession) married Thamar. "Merari" and "Thamar" both have the same meaning in Hebrew. Now observe this meaning well. I give it briefly. Bitter sorrow and Confession—the one may come of the other as Judith did of Merari, and both may be joined together, as were Juda and Thamar, for neither is worth much, or worth anything, without the other.   (S137)

The author is unwilling to use just the Judith-Merari relationship as the exemplar of the relationship between sorrow and confession, for then it might be presumed that sorrow precedes in importance because it gives birth to confession. The Juda-Thamar marriage tie makes clear that neither sorrow nor confession is meaningful without the other.

Finally, in his discussion of how confession ought to be practiced, the author yet again reiterates his position vis à vis the contritionists, this time using at least some theoretical language. The eighth attribute of a good confession, he says, is shame. Shame had become a central technical term of contritionist theory: for many twelfth-century theologians, the sinner's shame alone effected the remission of sins. Though he makes use of the ideas of several contritionists in the passage that follows, the *Ancrene Wisse* author nevertheless comes to the conclusion that while shame is an essential part of the sacrament, it is only when that shame is externalized in confession that the sacrament exists:

> God riht is, wat crist, þet us scheomie biuore mon, þe forȝeten scheome þa we duden þe sunne biuore godes sihðe. Nam omnia nuda sunt et aperta oculis eius ad quem nobis sermo. "For al þet is al is naket," seið seinte Pawel, "ant open to his ehnen, wið hwam we schulen rikenin alle ure deden." Scheome is þe measte deal, as seint Austin seið, of ure penitence. Verecundia pars est magna penetentie. Ant sein Bernard seið þet na deorwurðe ȝimstan ne deliteð swa muchel mon to bihalden as deð godes ehe þe rude of monnes neb þe riht seið hise sunnen. Understond wel þis word. Schrift is a sacrement, ant euch sacrament haueð an ilicnesse utewið of þet hit wurcheð inwið, as hit is i fulluht, þe wesschunge wiðuten bitacneð þe wesschunge of sawle wiðinnen. Alswa i schrift, þe cwike rude of þe neb deð to understonden þet te sawle, þe wes bla ant nefde bute dead heow, haueð icaht cwic heow ant is irudet feire. Interior tamen penitentia non dicitur sacramentum, set exterior uel puplica uel solempnis.   (T169)

It is very right, Christ knows, that we, who forgot shame before God's eyes when we committed the sin, should bring shame upon ourselves in the eyes of man. *For all things are naked and open to his eyes to whom our speech is.* "All that there is is naked and open to his eyes," says St. Paul, "to whom we must render an account of our deeds." Shame, as St. Augustine says, is the greatest part of our penance. *Shame is the greatest part of penance*; and St. Bernard says that no precious jewel pleases the eye of man so much as God's eye is pleased by the redness of a man's face when he is confessing his sins rightly. See that you understand this thoroughly. Confession is a sacrament, and every sacrament has an outward sign of that which it performs inwardly, as for example in Baptism the outward washing signifies the interior washing of the soul. And so in Confession, the lively red of the face gives us to understand that the soul, which was pale, and had no more color than that of death, has taken on the hue of life and is made beautifully red. *But interior penance is not called a sacrament, only exterior, or public, or solemn penance is so called.*   (S146–147)

At first glance, the passage seems to follow the contritionist position. Echoing Abelard, the author first notes that the shame in confessing one's sins compensates for the lack of shame that allowed the sinner to consent to sin in the first place. Following Abelard again, he notes that shame is encouraged by our having to confess our sins aloud before another man. But the author does not then conclude with Abelard that, though confession is useful, the shame itself works the remission of sin. Instead, he avoids the theoretical issue and goes on to the value of shame in the third part of the sacrament, satisfaction. Again he relies upon contritionist theory, here directly quoting the Pseudo-Augustine's *De vera et falsa poenitentia*, in attributing to shame the greater part of satisfaction. Since Abelard also used this section of the *De vera*, it still seems possible that the *Wisse* author might finally draw the contritionist conclusion: that the sacrament of confession consists primarily of shame or inner contrition, which both assures eternal forgiveness for sin and provides most of the satisfaction due for sin.

But at this point the author abruptly changes course again and dwells through the rest of the passage on the definition of a sacrament and its application to confession. Every sacrament has an outward sign, he notes, and in confession the red blush of the shameful sinner is that sign. So shame is essential to the sacrament, as an outward sign is essential to every sacrament; but, while shame is a *sign* of forgiveness, it does not itself effect the forgiveness. Only the whole sacrament, including all its parts, can do that. The author stresses that only contrition and confession *combined* form the sacrament. While he has concentrated in this section on the value of shame as an attribute of a good confession, he ends the passage warning his readers not to misunderstand the relative value of interior and exterior penance: interior penance, or shame, while extremely important, does not constitute a sacrament; only what he calls "exterior penance" can be sacramental.

Had his charges been better versed in prescholastic terminology, the author's use of the phrase "exterior penance" in this context might have confused them.[86] In most theological writings, the term refers to the third part of the sacrament, namely satisfaction, or the canonical penance assigned by the priest. By the early thirteenth century, when the *Wisse* author was writing, satisfaction for sin was once again assuming some importance in confession theology. Most theologians called exterior penance, or satisfaction, the outward "sign" of the sacrament.[87] But the *Ancrene Wisse* author does not follow this trend; he assigns the shameful blush as the "sign" of the sacrament; and he is unwilling to assign any *sacramental* importance to satisfaction for sins. So, by "exterior penance" the author does not mean canonical penance.

What then does he mean when he speaks of "exterior or solemn or public penance" as the only proper forms of the sacrament? The clue is provided by the context. Toward the end of the twelfth century, the terms "public" and "solemn" penance reentered confession theory, having been temporarily ignored while theologians concentrated upon defining private confession. The practice of more formal penances, before the bishop or in public, was by now comparatively rare and strictly reserved for extreme cases when the sins in question had been themselves so publicly known as to scandalize the Church. But the theologians of the period, in an effort to be thorough, usually listed three kinds of sacramental penance—private, public, and solemn. This list occurs without variation in numerous confessional works.[88] The *Ancrene Wisse* author's source for his Latin quotation is, at present, unknown, and it is impossible to tell whether he himself changes "privata" to "exterior" or not. In any case, the author could only be referring to private penance as the first of three sacramental forms confession could take.

It is interesting to conjecture why the author might choose to emend his source's "privata" to "exterior," for the two words seem contradictory. In the context of the three forms of sacramental confession, private confession is actually the *least* externalized form, because it entails no public spectacle or humiliation. But the author has been concerned throughout the *Ancrene Wisse* with the paradox of private versus public, and outer versus inner, reality in the anchorhold. To become "hidden," the anchoress must paradoxically think of herself as exceedingly exposed and vulnerable to the world. Christ, born a recluse in Mary's womb, lived the most public life of any man. If the author had been drawn to confession theory for no other reason, the simple fact that the controversy centered upon the relationship of outer forms to inner acts would have fascinated him. The contritionists' solution of so concentrating on the inner experience of contrition as to eliminate the necessity of outward forms was unsatisfactory to the *Wisse* author because it eliminated the careful balance between inner and outer reality that distinguishes a sacrament and that also distinguishes the author's own mode of thought throughout the *Ancrene Wisse*. Though obviously interested in the private experience of confession, the author wants to emphasize that internal sorrow and shame depend upon the exterior act of confessing one's sins. Here, then, is a theological reason for calling private confession "exterior penance."

But there are also, I think, psychological reasons why the author might want to emphasize to the anchoress that internal sorrow must be externalized in confession. In the intensely private spiritual world of the anchoress private confession is the most externalizing act she can profitably perform.

After being taught previously in the *Wisse* to turn all her outward-bound energies inward, here she is being asked, in a sense, to turn herself inside out. She must no longer cover or protect her heart, but instead must uncover and expose it to the priest in confession. The reversal of energies might be quite a violent experience for the anchoress, and the author applies to the activity the equally violent images of spewing out and stripping naked:

> Culle al þe pot ut, þer speowe ut al þet wunder, þer wið fule wordes
> þet fulðe efter þet hit is tuki al towundre, swa þet ha drede þet ha
> hurte his earen þet hercneð hire sunnen. (T176)

> Let her pour out all that is in the pot, let her vomit out then all that
> monstrosity; and let her attack that uncleanness mercilessly for what
> it is, with foul words, so that she is afraid of hurting the ears of him
> who is hearing her sins. (S153)

"[D]espoile þe sunne ant make hit naket," ("Strip your sin . . . and let it become naked" [T164; S142]), the author advises, so that the anchoress can avoid imitating Adam and Eve, who,

> þa ha hefden i þe frumðe isuneget, gedereden leaues ant makeden
> wriheles of ham to hare schentfule limen. (T165)

> when they had sinned in the beginning, gathered leaves and made
> coverings of them for their shameful members. (S143)

The anchoress's sinful heart is here a "shameful member" that must be exposed. Given the otherwise "hidden" life of an anchoress, such exposure, even in private confession, must have seemed a most "exterior penance."

But, though the externalizing act of oral confession is the culmination of the sacrament for the *Wisse* author, he is equally interested in another intermediary level of activity, somewhere between private experience and exterior confession: the level of careful self-reflection that prepares the anchoress to confess aloud. Confession for the anchoress is not a spontaneous pouring forth, as the image of vomiting might suggest, but rather it is an act carefully arranged and organized in advance by the anchoress. Preparation for confession is an elaborate psychomachia in which the anchoress accuses herself, judges herself, and levies her own penance:

> Sein Austin leofliche us leareð: Ascendat homo tribunal mentis sue, si
> illud cogitat quod oportet eum exiberi ante tribunal Christi. Assit ac-
> cusatrix cogitatio, testis Consciencia, Carnifex timor, þet is, þenche
> mon o domes dei ant deme her him seoluen þus o þisse wise. Skile

sitte as domes mon up o þe dom seotel. Cume þrefter forð his þohtes
munegunge, wreie him ant bicleopie him of misliche sunnen: "Beal
ami, þis þu dudest þear, ant tis þear, ant tis þear, ant o þisse wise."
His inwit beo icnawes þrof ant beore witnesse: "Soð hit is, soð hit is.
þis ant muchele mare." Cume forð þrefter fearlac þurh þe deme
heast, þe heterliche hate: "Tac bind him heteueste, for he is deaðes
wurðe. Bind him swa euch lim þet he haueð wið isuneget, þet he ne
mahe wið ham sunegi namare." Fearlac haueð ibunden him hwen he
ne dear for fearlac sturie toward sunne. ȝet nis nawt þe deme þet is
skile ipaiet, þah he beo ibunden ant halde him wið sunnen, but ȝef
he abugge þe sunne þet he wrahte, ant cleopeð forð pine ant sorhe,
ant hat þet sorhe þersche inwið þe heorte wið sar bireowsunge, swa
þet hire suhie, ant pini þe flesch utewið mid feasten ant wið oþre
fleschliche sares. Hwa se o þisse wise biuoren þe muchele dom demeð
her him seoluen, eadi he is ant seli.   (T158)

St. Augustine . . . teaches us lovingly: *Reflecting that he must appear be-*
fore the tribunal of Christ, let man mount the tribunal of his own mind. Let
reflection be present as accuser, conscience as witness, and fear as executioner.
Let man think upon the Day of judgement and judge himself here in
this manner. Let Reason sit upon the judgement-seat, as judge. Then
let his Memory come forth and accuse him, and charge him with various sins. "Good friend, you have done this at one time, this at another, and this at another, and in this way." Let his conscience admit
it and bear witness to it: "It is true. It is true. This, and much more."
Then let Fear come forth at the command of the judge, who sternly
gives this order: "Take him and bind him fast, for he has deserved
death. Bind every limb with which he has sinned, in such a way that
he may never sin with them again." And when he dare not, for fear,
make any movement towards sin, then Fear has bound him. But the
judge, that is, Reason, is not yet satisfied, even though he is bound
and refrains from sin, unless he pays for the sin which he has committed; and he calls forth Pain and Sorrow and orders Sorrow to
scourge his heart inwardly with sore repentance until it gasps for
breath, and to torment the flesh outwardly with fasts and other bodily
hurts. Whoever judges himself here, in this way, before the great
Judgement, is blessed and happy.   (S136–137)

So before the anchoress ever enters the confessional she must "mount the
tribunal of [her] own mind." Given the author's elaborate instructions, it
is no wonder that he counsels that "confession ought to be considered for a
long time beforehand":

Of fif þinges wið þi wit gedere þine sunnen of alle þine ealdes: of childhad, of ȝuheðehad, gedere al togederes; þrefter gedere þe studen þet tu in wunedest ant þench ȝeorne hwet tu dudest in euch stude sunderliche ant in euch ealde; þrefter sech al ut ant trude þine sunnen bi þine fif wittes, þrefter bi alle þine limen i hwuch þu hauest isuneget meast oðer oftest; aleast sunderliche bi dahes ant bi tiden. (T174)

Recall your sins with these five points in mind: all your different ages, recalling all the sins of your childhood and youth; then recall the places in which you have lived and try hard to remember what you did in each place in turn and at every age; then search out all your sins and track them down according as they were committed with your five senses, and then according to all the parts of your body, and find out in which you have sinned most and most often; lastly, the days and times of each. (S151)

Such preparation must have been intensely personal as well as painful and is a far cry from that "confession," described earlier, of the Norman soldiers after the battle of Hastings, in which there was such a curious dissociation of the penitent from his past. In the *Ancrene Wisse*, preparation for confession entails exactly the opposite—a conscious reintegration of the anchoress's past, including her life before she entered the anchorhold, with her present. Each time memory confronts reason, the anchoress will be painfully aware that she is *not* dead after all, that her entrance to the anchorhold has not ended her life but merely changed its external aspects. Each time the anchoress prepares to confess she prepares an autobiography of sorts, consciously creating a continuity in her whole life. It is, of course, a painful continuity, for the thread that runs throughout is sin.

The author recognizes that this painful realization will naturally engender sorrow for sin: after memory has confronted reason, pain and sorrow are called forth, he notes. If the anchoress accuses herself properly, with sufficient self-reflection (the first attribute of a good confession [T156; S135]), then the second attribute, "bitterness," should naturally follow. But if sorrow is the result of self-reflection, that sorrow is also the subject for further reflection. The *Wisse* author, unlike many of his predecessors, is unwilling to assume that the sorrow that naturally results from recalling one's sins is "perfect contrition," sorrow arising solely from the awareness that one has offended God. Instead, in a method he has used before, the author asks the anchoress to try to rise to a more perfect and selfless contrition by first reflecting upon exclusively worldly sorrows.

Thus, the first situation that the author asks the anchoress to imagine is the sorrow attendant upon separation from one's family:

ʒef a mon hefde ilosed in a time of þe dei his feader ant his moder, his
sustren ant his breðren, ant al his cun ant alle his freond þet he eauer
hefde weren asteoruen ferliche, nalde he ouer alle men sorhful beon
ant sari as he eaðe mahte?   (T159)

If a man lost his father and his mother, his sisters and his brothers,
and all his relatives and all the friends he ever had suddenly died, all
this within one hour, would he not be the most sorrowing, the most
grieving of men, and might he not well be so?   (S137)

The author goes on to point out that while such sorrow would be great,
the sorrow of a man who has slain his heavenly family, specifically his
"gentle Heavenly Father and his dear Mother St. Mary," and all his children, "that is, his good works," should feel even more sorrow.

That the author asks the anchoress to rise to a religious sorrow by meditating on an exclusively worldly sorrow is typical and interesting, and that
it should be this particular sorrow is even more interesting. It seems to me,
and of course I can only speculate here, that the first "sorrow" an anchoress
might feel upon recalling her "childhood and youth" would be not the
saintly, spiritualized sorrow of having offended God, but instead the exclusively worldly sorrow of loss—loss of family and friends experienced by the
anchoress when she renounced them to enter her "grave." I suspect that
the *Ancrene Wisse* author wants to legitimize this feeling, or at least acknowledge it, even as he asks the anchoress to redirect the feeling of loss
toward her heavenly family.

The question might arise here that if the anchoress can do all that the
author has so far required—that is, prepare her confession by organized
self-reflection and in a sense prepare her sorrow by redirecting a worldly
sorrow toward God—if she is able to so combine contrition and confession
before she ever sees the priest, why must she repeat the process formally in
oral confession? The confession itself seems almost an anticlimax after such
great preparation. But the *Ancrene Wisse* author seems fully aware of the
psychological value of what he calls "pouring out" sins verbally in oral confession (T164). The image of vomiting suggests the purging effect of confessing aloud. Furthermore, the author speaks of the satisfaction of striking
hateful sins violently by speaking bluntly in confession (T162). When a
woman cleans her house, the author notes, she has only half-completed her
job when she has gathered all her dirt "on an heap" (T161); she must finally be rid of it, and "schuueð hit ut," or shove it out (T161).

Beyond the psychological satisfaction of pouring out one's sins is the
theological fact that the author takes for granted: sin is only forgiven when
it is confessed orally. He does not share the interest of some of his predecessors in pinpointing the exact moment of forgiveness, nor is he interested in

the theoretical question of by whose agency (priest's or penitent's) sins are remitted. Instead, he dwells only on the practical results of oral confession, which as a sacrament has the following "effects in us":

> Schrift wescheð us of alle ure fulðen, ȝelt us alle ure luren, makeð us godes children. (T154)

> Confession washes us of all our impurities, gives back to us all that we had lost, and makes us children of God. (S133)

By emphasizing both the self-reflection and oral confession, the *Wisse* author combines the most psychologically useful aspects of both contritionist and postcontritionist thought. Because he shares the postcontritionist's assurance that the sacrament of confession does result in the forgiveness of sins, he can afford to encourage the deep and constant self-reflection in which Guibert's mother engaged without condoning or encouraging the unceasing insecurity that so tormented Guibert's mother. Unlike that woman, whose every moment was tormented by the fear that nothing she could do would earn God's pardon for her sins, the anchoress is assured that *her* confessions, though preceded by painful self-reflection and shame, will earn pardon and will restabilize her life, restoring to her all that she feared she had lost.

Thus far this discussion has been confined to the interdependence the author sets up between contrition and confession. The other two subjects of confession theory, absolution and satisfaction, are of little importance to the *Wisse* author. Absolution is referred to only once, at the very end of part V, and then only in a subordinate clause.[89] Whether the author believes that the priest's absolution has only a declaratory value (the contritionist point of view), or whether he believes that the absolution is the agent of remission, is impossible to say. What is important to note, however, is that he chooses not to dwell on the subject of absolution at all, for his choice points out how very minor the author considers the role of the priest in the drama of confession to be. A priest is certainly necessary for confession, preferably, the author points out, a good priest (T176; S152). The anchoress is not advised that she may confess to a layman. But the priest is present almost as an observer rather than as a guide or even a participant. In fact, the by now traditional roles of priest and penitent are curiously reversed in the *Ancrene Wisse*. Most confession manuals of the early thirteenth century emphasize the priest's role as counselor and physician or leech, one who carefully and subtly draws out from the sinner a detailed confession of his sins. But in the *Ancrene Wisse* the anchoress is expected to prepare fully her own confession. The *ideal* confession, according to the author, is one in which the priest says nothing at all until the moment of absolution:

Me ne schal easki nan bute for neode ane, for of þe easkunge mei uuel fallen bute hit beo þe wisre.   (T173)

There ought to be no questioning except only in the case of necessity, for evil may come of questioning if it is not done with enough discretion.   (S150)

Like Abelard before him, this author has his doubts about the priest's power of discretion, though he avoids Abelard's conclusion, later condemned, that priests without discretion do not have the power to forgive sins. He knows that the anchoress is, in a sense, an amateur who needs to have the sixteen parts of confession

alle . . . tobroken . . . ow, mine leoue sustren, as me deð to children, þe mahten wið unbroke bread deien on hunger.   (T175)

broken . . . all up for you, my dear sisters, as people do for children, who, if their bread were not broken up for them, might die of hunger.   (S151)

But it is nevertheless with the anchoress, not the professional confessor, that the responsibility for a good confession lies. To this end the author even teaches the anchoress the theory of circumstances, translating for her all technical terms:

Abute sunne liggeð six þing þet hit hulieð, o Latin "circumstances," on Englisch "totagges" mahe beon icleopede: persone, stude, time, manere, tale, cause.   (T163)

There are six things connected with sin which conceal it, and which in Latin are called "circumstances." In English they may be called "totagges." They are: person, place, time, manner, number of times, and cause.   (S141)

He gives elaborate examples of each circumstance; his discussion of "cause" is typical:

Cause is hwi þu hit dudest, oðer hulpe oþre þerto, oðer þurh hwet hit bigon. "Sire, ich hit dude for delit," "for uuel luue," "for biȝete," "for fearlac," "for flatrunge." "Sire, ich hit dude for uuel, þah þer ne come nan of." "Sire, mi lihte ondswere oðer mine lihte lates tulden

him earst up o me." "Sire, of þis word com oðer, of þis dede wreaððe
ant vuele wordes." "Sire, þe acheisun is þis hwi þet uuel leasteð ȝet;
þus wac wes min heorte."   (T164)

The cause is why you did it, or helped others to do it, or how it
began. "Sir, I did it for pleasure," "out of evil love," "for the sake of
gain," "out of fear," "in order to flatter." "Sir, I did it with an evil
intention, even though no evil came of it." "Sir, a frivolous answer of
mine or my frivolous glances first attracted him to me." "Sir, this
conversation gave rise to another, this action gave rise to anger and
evil words." "Sir, the reason why the wrong is still continuing is this.
My heart was weak in this way."   (S142)

If the anchoress learns her lessons well, and examines her own conscience
properly, the priest's role as careful examiner will be minimal.

The *Ancrene Wisse* author further minimizes the priest's duties regarding
the assignment of a specific penance. He grants to the priest the power to
judge the gravity of sins according to the circumstances ("efter þe totagges
. . . he schal þe sunne demen mare oðer leasse" [T177]), and this power is
usually associated with assigning a penance. But this power seems irrelevant, because the author all but dismisses canonical penance, noting that,
under normal circumstances, the priest should refrain from assigning any
specific penance at all:

Þe preost ne þearf for na gult bute hit beo þe greattre leggen oþer
schrift on ow þen þet lif þet ȝe leadeð efter þeos riwle.   (T176)

The priest need not give you any penance outside the life which you
lead according to this rule, for any guilt, unless it is exceptional.   (S153)

The penance formula the author provides for confessors assigns as "penance" the very life the anchoress already leads:

Efter þe absolutiun, he schal þus seggen: "Al þet god þet tu eauer
dest, ant al þet vuel þet tu eauer þolest for þe luue of Iesu Crist
inwið þine ancre wahes, al ich engoini þe, al ich legge up o þe i re-
missiun of þeose ant i forȝeuenesse of alle þine sunnen."
(T176-177)

After the absolution he should say, "I enjoin and impose upon you,
for the remission of these sins and for the forgiveness of all your sins,
all the good that you ever perform and all the harm that you ever en-

dure for love of Jesus Christ within your anchoress's dwelling." (S153)

Here, it seems to me, the author has departed seriously from the spirit if
not the letter of postcontritionist theology. Technically speaking, the third
essential part of the sacrament is present—a penance of sorts *is* assigned.
And given the hard life led by a solitary, for her life to be assigned as her
penance makes a certain amount of sense and cannot be called a light penance. Indeed, it is a particularly hard penance, as the author later points
out, even a "martyrdom," because it does not end until death. But for that
very reason it is not a *sacramental* penance, because it is neither specific nor
variable, nor does the priest or the Church have any control over its assignment or its completion. Furthermore, when the author speaks in part VI of
penance (as opposed to confession, the subject of part V), he all but ignores sacramental penance, that penance assigned as payment for specific
sins. Though he ends part V by saying that it is only "natural" to follow
the subject of confession with a treatment of penance, his change in tone
and point of view at the opening of part VI is sudden, almost startling, to
anyone familiar with confession literature. We are told that the discussion
to follow concerns "deadbote," which, literally translated, means payment
for a deed. So we expect a discussion of penance as reparation for sin. Instead, we find a sympathetic exploration of the sufferings of the penitential
life and the rewards of that life, the joys of heaven.

The opening lines of part VI clearly indicate the change in tone. While
the author repeats almost exactly the words of the "penance" imposed at
the end of part V, the context is quite different:[90]

> Al is penitence, ant strong penitence, þet ȝe eauer dreheð, mine leoue
> sustren. Al þet ȝe eauer doð of god, al þet ȝe þolieð is ow martirdom
> i se derf ordre, for ȝe beoð niht ant dei up o godes rode. (T177)

> All that you suffer, my dear sisters, all is penance, and hard penance.
> All the good you ever do and everything that you suffer in such a
> hard "Order" is martyrdom for you, for you are night and day upon
> God's cross. (S154)

Suddenly the anchoress is no longer, as she was in part V, the accused sinner, assigned to do penance for her sinful life, but is now a saint, a martyr,
doing penance in imitation of Christ. Penance is not viewed as a penalty
for past sins but rather as a form of "glory" chosen by the elect few. The
orientation of time has been reversed: penance no longer looks backward
on the sinful past but instead looks forward to its reward in heaven and in

the love of Christ on earth. In part VI we leave behind the sacrament and theology of sinners and take up the theology of saints.

To summarize the author's complicated attitude toward the sacrament of confession: of the four aspects of the sacrament usually discussed—contrition, confession, absolution, and satisfaction—the author is almost exclusively interested in the first two. More specifically, he concentrates upon the interdependence of contrition and confession as the internal and external aspects of the sacrament. Throughout the *Ancrene Wisse* the author has stressed the dependence of internal or spiritual well-being upon careful attention to exterior things. Twelfth-century theories concerning the efficacy of confession aid the author in emphasizing the same dependence regarding confession. Internal sorrow for sin—including shame, bitterness, and humility—are essential to the sacrament, but can only be fully realized by being arranged and ordered and made concrete in oral confession, the external side of the sacrament. Absolution and satisfaction, though mentioned by the author, are glossed over, perhaps because, like prescriptive religious rules, they are so external to the penitent that they run the risk of encouraging a mechanical performance of the sacrament.

The author's argument is practical or psychological rather than theoretical: he wishes to place the responsibility for a good confession with the individual anchoress herself rather than with the priest or the Church. In this respect he does not follow the postcontritionist trend toward reasserting the Church's power in the sacrament of confession. Such an assertion would not have served the author's purpose. He uses only those theological aspects of the confession controversy that reinforce his notion of the ideal spiritual state: a heart that is calm because it is "wiðuten weote of sunne þet ne beo þurh schrift ibet" ("free from the awareness of sin that has not been forgiven through confession" [T7; S2]) but is at the same time alive with the awareness of its own responsibility in the sin-repentance cycle. Thus he emphasizes only those aspects of the sacrament—contrition and confession—that encourage an awareness of sin but at the same time ensure forgiveness.

4

Self-Awareness and Sin

A MARKED change in the *Ancrene Wisse* author's attitude toward the anchoress occurs at the opening of part VI: while in part V he views her as a sinner who must confess, in part VI he views her as a saint whose life of penance imitates Christ's suffering. Such an abrupt reversal has led at least one reader, J. H. Gray, to conclude that the link between these parts is both artificial and "misleading." Even more "contrived," he maintains, is the link between parts IV ("Temptations") and V.[1] There, after discussing primarily the traditional remedies for temptation—prayers, meditations, and the like—the author says that his next chapter will consider confession, the most efficacious remedy of all for temptations:

> Moni cunnes fondunge is i þis feorðe dale, misliche frouren ant monifalde saluen. Ure lauerd ʒeoue ow grace þet ha ow moten helpen. Of alle þe oðre þenne is schrift þe biheueste. Of hit schal beon þe fifte dale. (T153)

> In this fourth part there is temptation of many kinds, various comforts and many different remedies. May our Lord grant grace that these may help you. Confession is the most efficacious of them all, and the fifth part will be about this. (S132)

But, as Gray points out, confession is not a remedy for temptation, but for sin, the result of *giving in* to temptations. Beginning with what Gray calls these "clumsy" linkings, he builds a case to support the contention of M. B. Salu and Gerard Sitwell, that parts IV and V do not belong to the *Ancrene Wisse* but rather "once formed a separate treatise on penance and were later adopted and incorporated into the *Ancrene Riwle*."[2] Not only are the links between the parts dubious, but so also is the subject matter. Gray notes that "Parts Four and Five are moral theology in a treatise which is otherwise almost entirely a conventional work of monastic asceticism." Finally, Gray echoes Sitwell in insisting that parts IV and V "are eminently unsuitable to serve as reading matter for female recluses."[3]

Understanding the place of sin and confession in the *Wisse* author's thought is crucial. While Gray, Sitwell, and Salu are the only critics to question overtly the unity of the *Ancrene Wisse,* most other critics simply ignore the author's extensive discussion of sin and confession, which, as Sitwell points out, accounts for nearly one-third of his book. This chapter will therefore examine in detail a point I have touched upon several times before: the *Wisse* author's encouragement throughout his work of an awareness of sin in the anchorhold, which confession both facilitates and soothes.

Starting from the premise that the *Ancrene Wisse* is a "conventional work of monastic asceticism," one would indeed have difficulty explaining the author's abrupt reversal at the opening of part IV. As the branch of theology that helps the ordinary Christian distinguish right from wrong, moral theology could be called the theology of sinners and as such would seem to have no place in a work devoted to the theology of saints, or monastic asceticism. Yet the juxtaposition of saints and sinners is not peculiar to the transition between parts V and VI; it pervades the *Wisse* from beginning to end. I have been contending in this book that the *Ancrene Wisse* is not an essentially monastic work, but that the author continually reinterprets monastic asceticism in terms of the new moral theology. In earlier chapters I examined briefly some intellectual controversies and solutions that support and lend credence to the author's reinterpretation of the formerly monastic concept of a religious rule and the solitary life. A review of the results of the author's interest in moral theology will prove useful.

The earliest passage wherein the author translates the theology of saints into a theology for sinners occurs in his introduction, where he defines his religious rule. The goal of the inner rule, he states, is "the one rule regarding cleanness of heart." In explicating the Latin phrase "puritatem cordis" the author for the first time juxtaposes moral theology and monastic asceticism. "Puritas cordis" is usually considered a strictly monastic concept, derived ultimately from Cassian, the early monastic writer upon whom St. Benedict so often relies in his *Rule.* For Cassian the phrase refers to the highest goal of the monk; after moving through the stages of fear, compunction, humility, mortification, and the driving out of all faults, he finally arrives at "puritatem cordis," or perfect love.[4] But the *Ancrene Wisse* author no sooner quotes the monastic phrase than he "declassifies" it, in a sense. Purity of heart is not, for him, the elite rule of a few, a specialized monastic goal, but instead is that basic concept "circa quam uersatur tota religio."

The author's own translation of the complete Latin phrase makes clear his preference for the universally applicable terms of moral theology:

Nu þenne is hit swa þet alle ancren mahen wel halden an riwle? Quantum ad puritatem cordis, circa quam uersatur tota religio, þet is alle

mahen ant ahen halden a riwle ononte purte of heorte, þet is cleane
ant schir inwit (consciencia), wiðuten weote of sunne þet ne beo
þurh schrift ibet ... Þeos riwle is imaket nawt o monnes fundles, ah
is of godes heaste; forþi ha is eauer an wiðute changunge, ant alle
ahen hire in an eauer to halden.   (T7)

Now then, is it possible for all anchoresses to follow one rule? All
may and ought to keep one rule *regarding cleanness of heart* (*the concern
of all religion*), that is, a clean, unblemished conscience, free from the
awareness of sin that has not been forgiven through Confession. . . .
This rule is not an invention of man, but is part of what God commands; therefore it remains always the same, without changing, and
all are bound to follow it always and unchangingly.   (S2)

Purity of heart, the monastic term, is here translated "a clean conscience," a
concept that was developed and explored by moral theologians of the late
twelfth century. The goal of the anchoress is not peculiar to the solitary
life, nor even to the monastic orders, but is, in fact, the goal of all men:
salvation. Any other rules, specifically, *monastic* rules of fasting, prayers, and
vigils, are men's inventions, mere tools or mechanical aids.

Thus, from the very start the *Wisse* author announces his interest in
moral theology, the theology of right and wrong, that centers around

luue ant eadmodnesse ant þolemodnesse, threoweschipe ant haldunge
of þe alde ten heastes, Schrift ant penitence.   (T8)

love, humility and patience, fidelity and the keeping of the ten ancient Commandments, Confession and penance.   (S3)

Monastic asceticism certainly enters into the work, but even as the author
outlines the monastic virtues in parts II and III, he is drawn toward a theology of the world, and with good reason. His charges are not monks or
hermits, alone in private deserts. Living as they do in the middle of town,
their separation from the world is but an illusion. The ideal and the real,
the saint and the sinner—the anchoress partakes of both worlds. The author recognizes that he must teach her to deal with both.

Parts II and III are companion pieces, purporting to teach the anchoress
to guard her outward senses and her inner feelings. Both impulses are essentially monastic ideals, based on the premise that one can be dead to the
world. But although each part opens with a portrayal of the ideal anchoress, alive within because she is dead without, each quickly reverts to a
story seriously at odds with the stated ideal.

The argument of part II is that the anchoress, to be holy, should protect her heart by guarding her five senses. She should, then, be the *antithesis* of sinners like Lucifer, Eve, Dinah, and Bathsheba, who let their eyes wander. But what about David, whose story precedes all the others and serves as a prelude to part II? Though he was "God's darling," he nevertheless let his heart leap out into sin through the window of his eyes. He "lamented" its loss, however, and his heart "returned." What is his relationship to the anchoress? Is he, and by extension, is she, a saint or a sinner? Does David's story fall into the category of monastic asceticism or moral theology?

Clearly the story of David cuts two ways. Regarding the stated subject of part II—custody of the senses—even the holiest of men is a negative model. Like Eve, David allowed his heart to stray, and as a result he sinned. The anchoress is counseled to be holier than David and more saintly, by guarding her senses well. But David's story, though it is a story of sin, nevertheless has a happy ending. His heart leapt out, but it returned as a result of his sorrow. In terms of moral theology, which, as the author notes in his introduction, guides the conscience to an awareness of sin and on to repentance, David is a positive model for the anchoress. In other words, as a saint the anchoress must avoid sin by depriving her senses. But if she should fail from time to time in this monastic pursuit, she can and ought to turn to the theology of sinners, by learning to recognize her sin, repent of it, and win back her heart. Thus the model of David as the sinner who recognizes his sins looks forward to part V ("Confession").

So too does the model presented at the opening of part III. As with the story of David, the pelican image has contrary implications. The pelican who lives alone in the wilderness might represent the saintly anchoress, secluded in her anchorhold, but he might also, at times, represent the anchoress frustrated and angry in her seclusion. Of course, in the context of part III—regulating inward feelings—the angry pelican, murderer of his own children, is a negative model. The anchoress, should, like the pelican of the Psalms, live alone and untouched by worldly emotions. But the angry pelican, viewed as a moral theological model can also be saved. The angry pelican, like the angry anchoress, can "right" himself, by drawing forth from his heart the "blood of sin," becoming repentant, and exposing his sin "to the priest in confession."

It seems to me that parts II and III, though ostensibly addressing monastic goals, provide ample preparation for the author's concern with sin and confession—the touchstones of moral theology—in parts IV and V. In part IV ("Temptations"), the tension the author has created between saint and sinner reaches its peak. For all the comforts and remedies offered to the tempted *saint* in part IV, it is the reality, the subtlety, the inescapability of *sin* that carries the emotional force of the section. In part V, for the first and only time in the *Ancrene Wisse,* all tension is released. No longer able to think of herself as a saint, the anchoress can uncover her sinfulness in a purging, thorough, thoughtful confession. But in admitting her sinfulness, she is paradoxically transformed once again into a saint, with an "unspotted heart" and a "clean conscience," and, therefore, can once again be addressed in part VI as the saintly martyr suffering for the love of Christ, rather than in repayment for past sins.

Before the anchoress can appreciate confession's power to transform her from sinner into saint, however, she must learn how light a leap connects saint with sinner. The image of sin as a "liht lupe," first presented at the very beginning of the inner rule in the stories of David's, Lucifer's, and Eve's leaps into sin, is finally fully developed in part IV ("Temptations").

Part IV opens in much the same way as the two preceding parts, with a story. But whereas the author earlier chose to leave unexplored the ambiguity of the stories of David and the pelican, in part IV he tells his story twice, giving two possible endings:

Sec mon haueð estaz swiðe dredfule. Þet an is hwen he ne feleð nawt his ahne secnesse, ant forþi ne secheð nawt leche ne lechecreft, ne easkeð namon read ant asteorueð ferliche ear me least wene. Þis is þe ancre þe nat nawt hwet is fondunge; to þeos spekeð þe engel i þe apocalipse: . . . "Þu seist þe nis neod na medecine, ah þu art blind iheortet ne ne sist nawt hu þu art poure ant naket of halinesse ant gasteliche wrecche." Þet oþer dredfule estat þet te seke haueð is al frommard þis, þet is hwen he feleð se muchel angoise þet he ne mei þolien þet me hondli his sar ne þet me him heale. Þis is sum ancre þe feleð se swiðe hire fondunges ant is se sare ofdred þet na gastelich cunfort ne mei hire gleadien, ne makien to understonden þet ha mahen ant schulen þurh ham þe betere beon iborhen. (T92-93)

When a man is ill there are two conditions to be feared. One is that he should not be aware of his own disease, and therefore seek neither leech nor leechcraft, ask advice from nobody, and suddenly die when it is least expected. This is the case of the anchoress who does not know what temptation is, and to her the angel in the Apocalypse speaks . . . "You say you do not need medicine, but you are blind of heart; you do not see that you are poor and naked of any holiness, and spiritually destitute." The other condition to be feared in a sick man is altogether different from this, and that is that he should feel so much pain that he cannot bear anyone to touch his sore, or to cure him. This is the case of the anchoress who is so very much aware of her temptations and so sorely afraid, that no spiritual comfort can cheer her or make her understand that through them she can and should achieve salvation the more worthily. (S78)

To help the anchoress avoid the first possibility, the author will, in this part, teach her "what temptation is," how various it is, how subtle, how frequent, how crafty. But the author is also perfectly aware that in teaching the anchoress to avoid sudden death by becoming alert to the symptoms, he might instead condemn her to a slow, more painful death resulting from obsession with symptoms and neglect of the cure. To avoid this second possibility the author will offer the anchoress "comforts," which take the form of justifications for temptations, and "remedies" or method of overcoming temptations before they lead to sin.

The author knows well that he (and the anchoress too if she learns her lessons well) walks a tightrope in this venture of dealing with temptations. The author must teach the anchoress enough so that she avoids the pitfall of presumption, the result of too little knowledge of self. But he must not present the possibility of temptations so strongly that the anchoress falls into despair, the result of what could be called too much self-knowledge. The relationship between presumption and despair has been a favorite theme of the author's throughout the work.

In his introduction he advised against solemn vows to keep the outer rule for fear that breaking them "would cause too much pain," resulting in despair, "a state without hope or faith in your salvation" (S4). At the end of part III the opposite possibility arises: the anchoress "whose life is holy and exalted," who can momentarily "fly in contemplation," must be grounded by earthly temptations, "the falling sickness" of sparrows, and "fall to the earth lest she fall into pride" or presumption (S77). In part V the anchoress, in her confession, must balance hope of God's mercy with fear of his justice:

Hope ant dred schulen aa beon imengt togederes. Þis forte bitacnin, wes i þe alde lahe ihaten þet te twa grindelstanes ne schulde namon twinnin. Þe neoðere, þe lið stille ant bereð heui charge, bitacneð fearlac, þe teieð mon from sunne ant is iheueget her wið heard forte beo quite of heardre. Þe vuerne stan bitacneð hope, þe eorneð ant stureð hire igode werkes eauer, wið trust of muche mede. Þeos twa namon ne parti from, for as sein Gregoire seið: Spes sine timore luxuriat in presumptionem. Timor sine spe degenerat in desperationem. Dred wiðuten hope makeð mon untrusten, ant hope wiðute dred makeð ouertrusten. (T170)

Hope and fear must always be mingled. It was to signify this that it was decreed in the Old Law that two millstones should not be separated. The lower one, which lies still and bears a heavy load, signifies the fear which holds man back from sin, and is here made heavy with hard things, so as to be free of harder hereafter. The upper stone signifies hope, which runs and busies itself with good works always trusting to be greatly rewarded. Let no man separate these two, one from the other, for as St. Gregory says: *Hope without fear grows rankly into presumption. Fear without hope degenerates into despair.*   (S147)

As the image of the two grindstones suggests, the anchoress's life is a carefully balanced tension between hope and fear. The tension is the *ideal,* because the two grindstones *should* work against each other, grinding away at the anchoress's heart. Though such pressure might be painful, its absence leads the anchoress toward presumption or despair, "of all sins those nearest to the gates of hell" (S148).

The author's interest in hope and fear, and their extremes, presumption and despair, is but another manifestation of the saints-and-sinners theme. Presumption, or spiritual pride, is the worst enemy of the saint, the man who so consistently avoids sin that he comes to believe himself beyond sinning. Despair, on the other hand, is the pitfall of the sinner, who recognizes too well that he has sinned again and again. That the author continually returns to these possibilities is further evidence that he views the anchoress as both saint and sinner. The spiritual life of an anchoress is never static; it rises and falls like the movement of the sparrow at the end of part III. Given that she can never expect to stand still, the anchoress must be prepared to deal with both the dangers that beset saints and those that prevent sinners from returning to sanctity.

Part IV opens with an address to the "holy" and "good" saint:

Ne wene nan of heh lif þet ha ne beo itemptet. Mare beoð þe gode þe beoð iclumben hehe, itemptet þen þe wake.   (T92)

Let no one of holy life think that she will not be tempted. The good, who have climbed high, are more greatly tempted than the weak.   (S78)

The author first proves his point imagistically by quickly transforming the holy anchoress, who, as a bird in part III had "climbed high," into the "mate" of various crawling and earthbound beasts.[5] These beasts, representatives of the seven deadly sins, together with the anchoress, produce a variety of sinful offspring. The seven deadly sins were, of course, a well-known classification of sin. Equally conventional was the practice of associating sins with animals, though there was no fixed system of associating particular sins with particular beasts.

Morton Bloomfield, in *The Seven Deadly Sins*, credits the *Wisse* author as the first English writer to attempt a sustained systematic personification of the sins as animals. The result, he notes, "is fresh and vivid, and one of the best pieces of description in our early literature."[6] But the *Ancrene Wisse* author's interest in the subject goes far beyond a simple concretization of sins as various animals. After describing the animals he notes that each of them has numerous offspring, and each of the offspring has even more numerous guises. At this point the author makes an almost frightening transition from allegory to life: the guises are devastatingly specific. Pride might be imagined as a devouring lion, but its eleventh cub looks more like an anchoress who reads *Cosmopolitan:*

> þe ealleofte hwelp is efted wið supersticiuns, wið semblanz ant wið sines, as beoren on heh þe heaued, crenge wið swire, lokin o siden, bihalden on hokere, winche mid ehe, binde seode mid te muð, wið hond oðer wið heaued makie scuter signe, warpe schonke ouer schench, sitten oðer gan stif as ha istaket were, luue lokin o mon, speoken as an innocent ant wlispin for þen anes. Her to falleð of ueil, of heaued clað, of euche oðer clað, to ouegart acemunge, oðer in hweowunge oðer ipinchunge, gurdles ant gurdunge o dameiseles wise, scleaterunge mid smirles fule fluðrunges, heowin her, litien leor, pinchin bruhen oðer bencin ham uppart wið wete fingres. (T102–103)

The eleventh cub is fed with superstitions, with postures and gestures, such as carrying the head high, curving the neck haughtily, giving sidelong or scornful looks, blinking the eyes, pursing up the mouth, making signs of derision with the hands or with the head, throwing one leg over the other, sitting or walking stiffly like one tied to a stake, giving affectionate looks to men, speaking like an innocent and affecting a lisp. Here belongs one's attention to the veil covering the head, and to all the other clothes; excessive care about adornment, as to coloring or pleating; girdles and girdling the waist like a girl living in the world; daubing unguents on pimples, coloring the hair or the cheeks, plucking the eyebrows or pushing them up with moistened fingers. (S88)

At times the examples are even further concretized with highly realistic internal monologues. The eighth offspring of the Serpent of Envy is Suspicion:

> Þet is misortrowunge bi mon oðer bi wummon wiðuten witer tacne, þenchen: "Þis semblant ha makeð. Þis ha seið oðer deð me

forte gremien, hokerin, oðer hearmin," ant þet hwen þe oþer neauer
þideward ne þencheð. Herto falleð fals dom þet godd forbeot swiðe,
as þenchen oðer seggen: "ȝe ne luueð ha me nawt. Hereof ha wreide
me. Lo nu ha speokeð of me, þe twa, þe þreo, oðer þe ma, þe sitteð
togederes. Swuch ha is, ant swuch, ant for uuel ha hit dude." (T104)

That is, distrusting a man or a woman without sure proof, thinking:
"This is a pretence she is making. She is saying or doing this in order
to make me angry, to deride me, or to do me some harm," and this
when no such thing has occurred to the other person. Here belongs
false judgment, which God sternly condemns, as when someone
thinks or says: "Yes, she doesn't like me. She has accused me of such
and such. Look now how they are talking about me, the two of them"
(or three, or more), "sitting there together. She is this, and that, and
she did it with evil intent." (S89)

We can see in this method a precursor to the exempla used by vernacular
sermon writers who tried to keep their lay audiences' attention by illustrat-
ing the various sins with moralized tales that were usually amusing, and
sometimes bawdy. Yet there is nothing rollicking or even diverting about
the *Wisse* author's stories. They are told not about fabliau characters who
lived once upon a time but about human anchoresses in plausible situa-
tions, and their responses are at least understandable, if not admirable.

As the specific examples pile up the author becomes almost frustrated by
the variety, declaring it an impossible task to set down all the possible
manifestations of sin. The anchoress must finish the job herself:

Monie ma hwelpes þen ich habbe inempnet haueð þe liun of prude,
ah abute þeose studieð wel swiðe, for ich ga lihtliche ouer, ne do
bute nempni ham; ah ȝe eauer ihwer se ich ga swiðere uorð, leaueð
þer lengest, for þer ich feðeri on a word tene oðer tweolue. (T103)

The Lion of pride has many more cubs than these I have named, but
give these diligent attention, for I have merely touched upon them
and named them; but concentrate most wherever I have passed more
rapidly, for there I have loaded one word with ten or twelve possibilities. (S88)

The more possibilities he names, then, the more apparent it should become
to the anchoress that the possibilities for sin are endless. At one point, the
author becomes almost indignant, cutting short his description of the Fox
of Covetousness to order the anchoress to complete the section on tempta-

tions herself. His phrases, he notes again, are "weighted with sense"
("ifeðeret"):

> ȝe mote makien, þet wite ȝe, i moni word muche strengðe, þenchen
> longe þerabuten, ant bi þet ilke an word understonden monie þe
> limpeð þer to, for ȝef ich schulde writen al, hwenne come ich to
> ende? (T106)

> You can, as you know, amplify some phrases, to draw out their
> meaning, and here, by this phrase, understand what it implies, for if I
> should write out the whole myself, when should I come to an
> end? (S91)

Finally, he gives the anchoress a lesson in classifying all manner of sins
for herself:

> Ne nat ich na sunne þet ne mei beon ilead oðer to an of ham seouene
> oðer to hare streones. Unsteaðeluest bileaue aȝein gode lare—nis hit
> te spece of prude, inobedience? . . . Neomunge of husel in eani heaued
> sunne, oðer ei oþer sacrement—nis hit te spece of prude þet ich cleo-
> pede presumptio? ȝef me wat hwuch sunne hit is; ȝef me hit nat
> nawt, þenne is hit ȝemeeles under accidie, þet ich slawðe cleopede.
> Þe ne warneð oðer of his uuel oðer of his biȝete. Nis hit slaw
> ȝemeles oðer attri onde? (T108)

> I do not know of any sin which cannot be connected either with one
> of these seven or with their offspring. Inconstant faith in God's
> teaching—is not that disobedience, and a species of pride? . . . Com-
> municating, or receiving any other sacrament while in a state of mor-
> tal sin—is not that the species of pride which I called *Presumption?*
> This, if one is conscious of it as such. If not, then it is negligence and
> comes under *accidie,* which I have called Sloth. If one person does not
> let another know of some impending advantage or disadvantage, is
> that not slothful negligence or venomous envy? (S92–93)

And on the author goes, through a multitude of sins, ranging from treach-
ery to abortion. The catalog is so long, and so specific, that one suspects
that this author, like Thomas of Chobham, takes a certain delight in the
variety of sin. But his delight again turns to frustration at the end of the
passage, where he reiterates that

> alle sunnen sunderliche bi hare nomeliche nomen ne mahte namon
> rikenin. Ah i þeo þe ich habbe iseid, alle oþre beoð bilokene. Ant nis,

ich wene, namon þe ne mei understonden him of his sunne nomeliche under sum of þe ilke imeane þe beoð her iwritene. (T109)

no one can enumerate all the sins there are, one after another, giving
each its special name, but in those that I have mentioned, all the rest
are included, and I do not think there is any man who cannot recognize a particular sin of his own under one of the groups here recorded. (S93)

In these passages, the author indicates one purpose for the long section
of the deadly sins: to teach the anchoress how to classify her own sins. This
purpose looks forward to part V ("Confession"), where the sinful anchoress is instructed to examine her conscience according to the seven deadly
sins:

Bigin earst ed prude, ant sech alle þe bohes þrof, as ha beoð þruppe
iwritene hwuch fulle to þe. Þrefter alswa of onde, ant ga we swa duneward rawe bi rawe, aþet to þe leaste, ant drah togedere al þe team
under þe moder. (T172)

Begin first with pride, and examine all its ramifications, as they are
recorded above, to see which of them applies to you. Then do the
same with envy, and let us work downwards taking one sin after another, to the last, and put together all the offspring under the mother
sin. (S149)

In this respect, part IV shares the same purpose and method with the confession manuals, which classified a wide variety of sins for the confessor.
But such classification is only useful to the anchoress *after* she has sinned.
The categorizing process does not prevent sin, nor does it even isolate sin,
except after the fact. So throughout this long section the author seems to
address the anchoress as a sinner who can only name her sins and classify
them after she has committed them and analyzed them.

But the section on the seven deadly sins has a contrary purpose, more in
keeping with the stated object of part IV: to teach the anchoress to avoid
sin by recognizing the hatefulness of its concrete forms. At the end of the
enumeration of the sins the author abruptly returns to the rhetoric of
saints, who should always "shun" sin:

Nu ʒe habbeð ane dale iherd, mine leoue sustren, of þeo þe me
cleopeð þe seoue modersunnen, ant of hare teames, . . . ant hwi ha
beoð swiðe to heatien ant to schunien. (T12)

Now you have heard one part of this treatment, my dear sisters, of those things which are called the seven mother sins, and about their offspring ... and why they are greatly to be hated and to be shunned. (S96–97)

The author could have stopped here, leaving the anchoress with two rather simple precepts: to hate and shun sin if she wants to remain holy; and, if she sometimes fails in this endeavor, at least to learn to recognize sins committed and learn to classify and examine them in confession. She is, in other words, advised to follow David's example and be a saint if she can, and if she cannot, she can at least recognize when she has become a sinner. But there is a gray area between these two rather static possibilities—the area of temptation—that has been thus far unexplored. To avoid sin the anchoress must learn to recognize its beginnings in temptation. And temptation, unlike sin, involves not a simple "leap," but a long, subtle process that fascinates the author.

The process, the author notes, is "often concealed and hidden" ("ihud ofte ant dearne" [T114; S99]), by the devil, and crafty "deceiver of hell" ("þe sweoke of helle" [T115; S99]). The devil, in the *Ancrene Wisse* as in most other medieval writings, is a being with a real existence, who tempts the anchoress, though the *Wisse* author is careful to point out repeatedly that he has no power over her except by her own consent.[7] If the anchoress can only recognize the devil in all his disguises she can defeat him. But therein lies the difficulty. The devil, as the author presents him, is so crafty that he is at times all but impossible to recognize. If the author does not eliminate the notion of devils, he does create a devil who is almost the anchoress's double. To tempt an anchoress, the devil becomes an expert in the anchoritic life, making himself the "trusty counsellor" of the anchoress:

ʒet is meast dred of hwen þe sweoke of helle eggeð to a þing þet þuncheð swiðe god mid alle, ant is þah sawle bone ant wei to deadlich sunne. Swa he deð as ofte as he ne mei wið open uuel cuðen his strengðe. "Na," he seið, "ne mei ich nawt makien þeos to sungin þurh ʒiuernesse, ant ich chulle, as þe wreastleare, wrenchen hire þiderward as ha meast dreaieð,ant warpen hire o þet half ant breiden ferliche adun ear ha least wene," ant eggeð hire toward se muchel abstinence þet ha is þe unstrengre i godes seruise, ant to leaden se heard lif ant pinin swa þet te licome þet te sawle asteorue. He bihalt an oþer þet he ne mei nanesweis makien luðere iþoncket, se luueful ant se reowðful is hire heorte; "Ich chulle makien hire," he seið, "to

reowðful mid alle. Ich schal don hire se muchel þet ha schal luuien
ahte, þenchen leasse of godd ant leosen hire fame"; ant put þenne a
þulli þonc in hire softe heorte: "Seinte Marie, naueð þe mon oðer þe
wummon meoseise, ant namon nule don ham nawt. Me walde me ʒef
ich bede, ant swa ich mahte helpen ham ant don on ham ealmesse."
Bringeð hire on to gederin ant ʒeouen al earst to poure, forðre to oðer
freond, aleast makien feaste ant wurðen al worldlich, forschuppet of
ancre to huswif of halle. Godd wat swuch feaste makeð sum hore.
Weneð þet ha wel do, as dusie ant adotede doð hire to understonden;
flatrið hire of freolac, herieð ant heoueð up þe ealmese þet ha deð.
Hu wide ha is icnawen, ant heo let wel of ant leapeð in orhel. Sum
seið inohreaðe þet ha gedereð hord, swa þet hire hus mei ant heo ba
beon irobbet. Reowðe ouer reowðe. Þus þe traitre of helle makeð
him treowe readesmon.   (T115)

There is most need to fear when the deceiver of hell incites one to
something which seems very good but which is destruction to the
soul leading to mortal sin. He does this whenever he cannot show his
strength by means that are clearly evil. "No," he says, "I cannot make
this one sin through gluttony, but I will push her further to the side
towards which she is already leaning, and throw her on that side, and
suddenly fall upon her when she least expects it." He urges her on to
such great abstinence that she becomes the less strong in God's service, and to lead so hard a life and to make her body suffer so much
that her soul itself dies. He considers someone else, and seeing that he
is unable to induce evil thoughts in her, so loving is her heart, and so
full of compassion, "I shall make her," he says, "too compassionate. I
shall work upon her so much that she will come to love worldly pos-
sessions, and think less of God, and lose her good name." Then he
puts into her tender heart some such thought as this: "St. Mary!
What distress this man" (or this woman) "is in, and no one will do
anything for them. People would do something for my sake if I asked
them, and in that way I might help the suffering and give them
alms." He draws her on to start collecting, to give it all, at first, to the
poor, then later to her friends, and lastly to hold a feast and to become thoroughly worldly, transformed from an anchoress into the
lady of a great house. Such a feast, God knows, can make a woman
into a whore. She thinks herself to be doing good, and so foolish,
stupid people give her to understand. They flatter her for her liber-
ality, they praise and make much of the alms which she gives. How
widely-known she is! And she is pleased by this, and leaps into pride.

Soon people are saying that she is making a store of precious things, so that she and her house are liable to be robbed. Misery on misery! Thus the deceiver of hell makes himself into a trusty counsellor! (S99-100)

Here the devil is a parody of the conscientious anchoress, who also understands what any anchoress who reads the *Ancrene Wisse* should by now know: much can come from little. He knows the anchoress's habit of mind so thoroughly that he can use her own spiritual impulses—whether toward asceticism or toward compassion—against her. The choice presented to the anchoress in this passage is not holiness *versus* sin; in this world of subtle process, holiness can *become* sin.

Besides playing the role of anchoress, the devil also parodies the healing power of confession. As one seeks in confession a wise physician who will discover and soothe the particular wounds of each individual penitent, so too the devil as the evil physician mixes each of his "medicines" to the taste of the individual. Though the devil maintains an existence and a self outside the individual imagination, he can, if only by trial and error, come to know the anchoress better than she knows herself and can present her with temptations tailor-made for her particular susceptibilities:

Lut beoð i þis world, oðer nan mid alle, þet ne beo wið hare sum oðerhwile itemptet. He haueð se monie buistes ful of his letuaires, þe luðere leche of helle, þe forsakeð an, he beot an oðer forð anan riht, þe þridde, þe feorðe ant swa eauer forð aþet he cume o swuch þet me on ende underuo, ant he þenne wið þet birleð him ilome. Þencheð her of þe tale of his ampoiles. (T116-117)

There are few or none in this world who are not tempted by one or other [temptation] at some time. He has so many cases full of his medicines, the evil physician of hell, that if anyone refuses one, he at once offers them another, a third, a fourth, and so on until at last he comes to one which is accepted, and this he pours out for him over and over again. Think now of the number of his phials! (S100-101)[8]

The thought could be quite frightening. The conception of the devil is not so "modern" as to suggest that he is only a faculty of the human mind; nevertheless, he *is* a mind reader, so skillful, and so persistent, that he can find a way into any anchoress's heart.

While the anchoress is thinking of the endless variety of the devil's ways, and probably of her own vulnerability to temptation, the author wisely makes a transition to the "comforts" and "remedies" against temptation. The comforts are, in fact, various justifications for temptation. The one most often remarked upon is the sixth comfort:

> Þe seste confort is þet ure lauerd, hwen he þoleð þet we beon itemp-
> tet, he pleieð wið us as þe moder wið hire ȝunge deorling. Flið from
> him ant hut hire, ant let him sitten ane ant lokin ȝeorne abuten cleo-
> pien "Dame, Dame," ant wepen ane hwile, ant þenne, wið spredde
> earmes, leapeð lahhinde forð, cluppeð ant cusseð ant wipeð his
> ehnen. Swa ure lauerd let us ane iwurðen oðer hwile, ant wiðdraheð
> his grace, his cunfort ant his elne, þet we ne findeð swetnesse i na
> þing þet we wel doð, ne sauur of heorte, ant þah i þet ilke point ne
> luueð us ure lauerd neauer þe leasse, ah deð hit for muche
> luue.   (T118-119)

The sixth comfort is that Our Lord, when he allows us to be tempted, is playing with us as a mother with her darling child. She runs away from him and hides, and leaves him on his own, and he looks around for her, calling "Mama! Mama!" and crying a little, and then she runs out to him quickly, her arms outspread, and she puts them round him, and kisses him, and wipes his eyes. In the same way, Our Lord sometimes leaves us alone for a while and withdraws His grace, His comfort and consolation, so that we find no pleasure in doing things well, and our heart's savour is gone. And yet, at that very moment Our Lord is not loving us any the less, but is doing this out of His great love for us.   (S102)

The vivid image was often used in later religious works, most notably in *The Chastising of God's Children,* whose title and subject matter are largely drawn from this passage of the *Ancrene Wisse.*[9] What is remarkable about the passage is not only its "homeyness," but also the portrait of God as loving game player. In the early Middle Ages God was seen as a deceiver who, in the Incarnation "trick," matched wits with the deceiver of hell. Here, of course, the image has been considerably softened and humanized, in keeping with the newer view of God as loving and merciful parent. But nevertheless, the image does have its darker, or at least more unpleasant implications. This mother, and thus this God, are deceiving the anchoress. The story is paralleled by one told earlier in part IV, of God as the "wise" husband, who at first pretends not to notice his new wife's faults, but later

> makeð him swiðe sturne, ant went te grimme toð to forte fondin
> ȝetten ȝef he mahte hire luue toward him unfestnin. Alest, hwen he

understont þet ha is al wel ituht, ne for þing þet ne deð hire ne luueð
him þe leasse, . . . þenne schaweð he hire þet he hire luueð swete-
liche. (T113)

pretends to be very stern, and puts on a fierce expression in order to
try whether he might still remove her love from him. Finally, when
he sees that she has been well disciplined and that she loves him no
less for anything that he does to her . . . then he shows her that he
loves her dearly. (S97)

Both stories are variations on the patient Griselda tale, which Chaucer
and his contemporaries found so edifying, but which many modern readers
find distasteful, even cruel. But, in the context of part IV of the *Ancrene
Wisse,* the stories do have their usefulness as "comforts" for the tempted anchoress. The image of God as playful deceiver balances the image of the
devil as wily and malicious deceiver. If the devil has one quality upon
which the author insistently dwells, it is his craftiness. Just imagining the
variety of his schemes, let alone experiencing them, could drive an anchoress to distraction. But if, at times, the anchoress can think of temptation
as a game, not the cruel, unpredictable game of the devil, but the loving
game between mother and child, or husband and wife, then perhaps, at
those times, she can see the devil's game for the parody that it is. To recognize the devil's ways as a perverse imitation of God's loving game (loving,
because God stacks the deck in the anchoress's favor, while the devil does
not), might, at times, give the anchoress enough confidence to "laugh the
old *ape* loudly to scorn" (lahheð þe alde *eape* lude to bismere" [T126;
S109]).

The comfort only works, of course, when the anchoress does recognize
the devil's game. Thus devil and anchoress partake in a game of wits. To
show how much cunning is required to beat the devil at his own game, the
author makes ingenious use of the old devil's rights theory, this time making the Christ-Man (and not His Father) the cunning trickster:

Þurh þe strengðe of eadmodnesse he weorp þe þurs of helle. Þe ʒape
wreastlere nimeð ʒeme hwet turn his fere ne kunne nawt þet he wið
wreastleð, for wið þet turn he mei him unmundlunge warpen. Alswa
dude ure lauerd, ant seh hu feole þe grimme wreastlere of helle breid
up on his hupe ant weorp wið þe hanche turn in to galnesse, þe
rixleð i þe lenden, hef on heh monie ant wende abuten wið ham ant
swong ham, þurh prude, dun in to helle grunde. Þohte ure lauerd, þe
biheold al þis: "Ich schal do þe a turn þet tu ne cuðest neauer, ne ne
maht neauer cunnen, þe turn of eadmodnesse, þet is þe fallinde

turn," ant feol from heouene to eorðe, ant strahte him swa be þe
eorðe þet te feond wende þet he were al eorðlich, ant wes bilurd wið
þet turn.   (T144-145)

Through the strength of humility He threw down the devil of hell. A
cunning wrestler observes which stratagem is unknown to the man
with whom he is to wrestle, for by it he can throw him unawares.
This is what Our Lord did. He saw how many the grim wrestler of
hell caught upon his hip and threw, with a twist of his haunch, into
lechery, which rules the loins, how he lifted up many and walked
about with them and then swung them, through pride, down into
the pit of hell. Our Lord, seeing all this, thought: "I shall play you a
trick which you have never known and which you could never know,
the trick of humility, that is, the falling stratagem"; and He fell,
down from heaven to earth, and lay stretched out upon the earth in
such a way that the devil thought that He was completely of the
earth, and he was deceived by this stratagem.   (S124-125)

The anchoress, like Christ, and like the devil (and, for that matter, like the
author too), must be cunning. "A wise subtlety," the author points out,
echoing a proverb that the clever nightingale in *The Owl and the Nightingale* used to bolster her rather untenable position, "is better than a crude
strength" ("Betere is wis liste þen luðer strengðe" [T138; S119]).[10] Physical strength and endurance are useful tricks for obvious and exterior
temptations, but for "interior" and "hidden" temptations, "wisdom ant
gasteliche strengðe" ("wisdom and spiritual strength" [T94; S79]) are required.
    While the comfort of seeing temptation as a child's game can allay the
anchoress's fears and release the tension of temptation momentarily, the
more deadly game goes on. The author, even while he explains the comforts and remedies against temptations, introduces more evidence of the
devil's cunning. The most forceful reminder comes in the form of a long
and powerful digression. Toward the end of part IV the author takes up
the subject of the sacraments as trustworthy remedies against temptations:

ʒe schulen bileaue habben þet al hali chirche deð, red, oþer singeð,
ant alle hire sacremenz strengeð ow gasteliche, ah nan ase forð ase
þis, for hit bringeð to noht al þes deofles wiheles.   (T138)

You must trust in the fact that all that Holy Church does, all that she
reads or sings, and all her sacraments strengthen you spiritually; trust
in nothing so much as this, for it brings to naught all the wiles of the
devil.   (S119)

The very mention of the devil's wiles seems to remind the author of the subject that most interests him, for at this point he returns to several new variations of the devil's stratagems against anchoresses, variations that, I think, would shake anyone's trust:

[Trust] nan ase forð ase þis, for hit bringeð to noht al þes deofles wiheles, awt ane his strengðes ant his stronge turnes, ah deð his wiltfule crokes, his wrenchfule wicchecreftes, ant alle his ʒulunges, ase lease swefnes, false schawunges, dredfule offearunges, fikele ant sweokele reades, ah þah hit were o godes half ant god forte donne. For þet is his unwrench, as ich ear seide, þet hali men meast dredeð, þet he haueð moni hali mon grimliche biʒulet. Hwen he ne mei mawt bringen to nan open vuel, he sput to a þing þet þuncheð god. "Þu schuldest," he seið," beo mildre, ant leoten iwurðe þi chast. Nawt trubli þin heorte ant sturien in to wreaððe." Þis he seið forþi þet tu ne schuldest nawt chastien for hire gult ne tuhte wel þi meiden, ant bringe þe in to ʒemeles i stude of eadmodnesse. Eft riht þer toʒeines: "Ne let tu hire na gult toʒeues," he seið. "ʒef þu wult þet ha drede þe, hald hire nearowe. Rihtwisnesse," he seið, "mot beo nede sturne." Ant þus he liteð cruelte wið heow of rihtwisnesse . . . Betere is wis liste þen luðer strengðe. Hwen þu hauest longe iwaket ant schuldest gan to slepen, "Nu is uertu," he seið, "wakien hwen hit greueð þe. Sei ʒet a Nocturne." For hwi deð he swa? For þet tu schuldest slepen eft hwen time were to wakien. Eft riht þer toʒeines. (T138–139)

Trust in nothing so much as this, for it brings to naught all the wiles of the devil, not only his feats of strength, but also his cunning stratagems, his wily witchcraft, and all his deceptions such as misleading dreams, false visions, shocks which fill you with fear, flattering but deceitful advice even about things done for God's glory, actions good in themselves. For this is his evil cunning, as I said before, of which holy people are most afraid, and by which he has deceived many a holy man. When he cannot bring someone to that which is manifestly evil, he urges them toward something which has the appearance of good. "Thou shouldst," he says, "be more indulgent and not insist on meting out punishment; thou shouldst not let thy heart be troubled and roused to anger." He says this to prevent you from punishing your maidservant for her faults, and training her properly, thus making you negligent instead of forebearing. And then in direct contradiction of this: "Do not let any of her faults go unnoticed," he says. "If you want her to be in awe of you, keep her strictly. Justice," he says, "must of necessity be stern." And in this way, he gives to cru-

elty the colour of justice . . . A wise subtlety is better than a crude
strength. When you have been keeping vigil for a long time, and
ought to go to sleep, he will say, "It would be virtuous to keep awake
now that it is difficult. Say another nocturn." Why does he do this?
So that you will fall asleep later, when it is time to get up. And again
the contrary of this.   (S119-120)

And so on. The wiliness of the devil, and how he craftily plays upon each
of the anchoress's moods, clearly fascinates the author. He does, eventually,
return to the efficacy of the sacraments (particularly the Eucharist) in
combating temptations:

> I þulliche temptatiuns nis nan se wis ne se war, bute godd him warni,
> þet nis bigilet ofte. Ah þis hehe sacrement [Holy Eucharist], in hardi
> bileaue, *ouer alle oðre þing* unwrið hise wrenches ant brekeð hise
> strengðes.   (T139; my emphasis)

> In temptations such as these there is no one so prudent or cautious
> that he is not often deceived, unless God himself instructs him. But
> his holy sacrament [Holy Eucharist], taken in firm faith, lays bare his
> trickeries and breaks his strength *better than anything else.* (S120; my
> emphasis)

Though the Eucharist might work "better than anything else," still,
what would really be necessary to avoid being deceived by all temptations
is instruction from "God Himself." But the anchoress has only her rule
master. And in just now playing the devil's advocate the author has shown
the anchoress how even his own book, the *Ancrene Wisse,* could be used
against her. That the outer rule, concerning training of servants, keeping
vigils, and the like, can become an occasion for sin is a familiar theme; the
author has already taken great pains to bring this lesson home to the anchoress. But here he shows how even his most basic and unerring inner
rule—to keep her heart untroubled, "even," and "smooth" by practicing,
among other virtues, patience and humility—can also be incorporated into
the devil's act, and used as an excuse for negligence. Here it is the devil (or
the author in devil's disguise) who counsels the anchoress to ignore her
duty to reprimand her servant because she should not "trouble" and "stir
up" ("trubli" and "sturien") her heart.
     In this long digression the author brings to light the final implications
of his opening remarks about the nature of religious rules. Any written or
fixed external rule, even the one written by as ingenious and flexible a man
as this author, is finally only "monnes fundles," man's invention, and can

therefore be perverted for evil use. What is finally required of the anchoress, and of all Christians, is not strict or literal adherence to a written set
of laws, but instead, choices determined by internalized ethical judgments.
Perhaps that is why the author cuts off the digression here, not to return to
his subject (remedies against temptations to lechery), but rather to disgress
again on the importance of the "ʒeteward," or gatekeeper to the anchoress's heart, her "heorte ehnen," or heart's eye, which must constantly engage in "busi warschipe sundri god from uuel" ("unceasing discrimination
between good and evil" [T139-141; S120-121]).

What has interested the author most in part IV is that the distinction
between good and evil is rarely simple. The more rules one has, that is, the
more distinctions one can make, the more material with which the devil
can work. He can make virtually any evil seem like a good, and vice versa.
This is not to say, of course, that the devil is all-powerful. With "God
himself" instructing her, the anchoress could perceive all the devil's deceptions. But with only her rule master to teach her to be "wis" and "war"
(prudent and cautious) she cannot hope to win every time. At this point
even the author, who has created a whole world for the anchoress, is power-
less to sustain her in it. The anchoress cannot forever avoid sin.

In a sense, the point of part IV, or at least the point of the selections I
have been discussing, is to convince the anchoress that she probably has
sinned in the past, and probably will sin again. Indeed, the devil who
tempts the anchoress, and the author who teaches her the devil's ways, are
closely related in this section. In incorporating his own admonition—
"nawt trubli þin heorte"—into the devil's monologue, the author reminds
us that part of his purpose in part IV has been *to trouble* the anchoress's
heart by making her aware of the multitude of subtle temptations that will
beset her. His obvious purpose, of course, is to teach her about temptations
so that she can avoid giving in to them. But in specifying the process of
temptation so convincingly, in playing the devil's part so well, the author
has taken the risk of producing the opposite effect: that is, he may be
tempting the anchoress himself. The devil's methods and those of the author are alarmingly similar. The devil, says the author, can, when all else
fails, "bifulen hire wið þoht of alde sunnen, hwen he ne mei wið neowe"
("taint [the anchoress] with the thought of past sins when he cannot with
new") and bring back the sin so vividly that she begins to "savour" it all
over again (T140-141; S121). But so too the author himself can, by paint-
ing temptation so vividly, suggest *future* sins that the anchoress never
dreamed of, but now might.

Aware of the problem, the author breaks off his discussion of lechery, for
example, shying away from the specifics for once and reverting to the

vague (but provocative) "I ȝuheðe me deð wundres" ("In youth strange
things are done" [T106; S92]). Of the offspring of lechery, the author declares:

> [Those] ich mei speoken of for scheome, ne ne dear for drede, leste
> sum leorni mare uuel þen ha con ant beo þrof itemptet. (T107)

> [Of those] I may not speak, out of shame, and dare not, for fear any-
> one should learn more of evil than she already knows, and should be
> thereby tempted. (S91)

Yet as he pointed out earlier, even "to name" ("nempnin") a sin—and the
author has certainly done much more than that—can serve to "soil hearts
that are already clean" ("sulen cleane heorten" [T106; S91]).

This comparison between the ways of the devil and the ways of the author is not meant to prove that the *Ancrene Wisse* author actually sets out
to tempt the anchoress. But I think it can be said that the author seems
aware of the paradoxical effects of knowledge: the knowledge that leads to
sin and the knowledge that helps one to avoid sin are identical—knowledge of the devil, the flesh, and the world. Because the author has provided
the anchoress with this knowledge—throughout the work, but especially
in part IV—it seems highly "suitable" indeed that he provide her with the
ultimate remedy, confession, by which she can regain her lost innocence
and become "unwemmet," unspotted, once more.

In a way J. H. Gray is correct in saying that the author confuses sin and
temptation in the link joining parts IV and V, for it is true that confession
is the remedy for sin, not for temptation. But the author has not simply
clumsily linked the two parts, making a misleading theological error for
the sake of rhetorical continuity. He certainly knows the difference between temptation and sin, for on numerous occasions in part IV he refers
to the "voluntary" nature of sin, to the "consent of the reason" necessary
before temptation becomes sin.[11] But while he seems sure of the theological difference between temptation and sin, he is not so sure of the *psychological* difference. For the devil's temptations, as the author presents them,
seem, at times, like strikingly good appeals to the anchoress's reason. Furthermore, the devil proceeds, as in his attack upon the compassionate anchoress, so slowly, in such minute steps, that it might be exceedingly difficult to decide where the temptation ends and the sin begins.

It is finally psychology, or internalized ethics, and not theology, that is
the touchstone of the author's treatment of sin and confession. Given his
subtle, psychological treatment of sin, it makes perfect sense that he should
include a discursive treatment of the most psychological of sacraments in

part V. It is also reasonable that, in his treatment of confession, the author should deemphasize the external (though theologically necessary) aspects of confession—absolution and satisfaction—to concentrate upon the internal and psychologically essential elements of the sacrament—inner contrition and a purging, thorough confession that seeks to uncover not only sins, but also their beginnings and motivations in temptations. Finally, it is also understandable that the author should blur the theological distinctions among the various parts of confession, because he sees both sin and repentance as processes whose psychological parts cannot easily be distinguished.

Inner awareness is the author's goal for his charges. Though he sometimes calls it "spotlessness" or "purity of heart," his definition of those terms, presented first in his introduction, then reiterated throughout the work, makes clear that this goal is not a state but a process. The inner rule, which is also as the author notes the goal of all religions, is a "cleane ant schir inwit, consciencia, wiðuten weote of sunne þet ne beo þurh schrift ibet" ("clean, unblemished conscience, free from the awareness of sin that has not been forgiven through confession"). "Weote" and "inwit" result not in any systematized, fixed theological rule, but rather in an inner life that is an endlessly repeated process: moving from innocence through contact with the world, temptation, sin, suffering, repentance, and back to love and innocence once more.

The subtlety and specificity with which the *Wisse* author examines the inner life is ample evidence of his central interest in promoting individuality in the solitary life rather than the more traditional otherworldly goals usually set for solitaries. In this interest the author reflects the complex world of late twelfth-century and early thirteenth-century thought, a world in which various systems of thought first collided, then fused to produce a rather new set of values centering upon the individual rather than the community. In particular, the author writes at a time when the traditional distinction between an elite theology for monks and a theology for laymen collapses, resulting in a new moral theology, equally applicable to all Christians because its field of study is the variety and individuality of human conduct. Once the world is viewed as inescapable, because it signifies not simply an outer reality, but a psychological reality that we all carry within us, then the whole notion of monasticism as withdrawal from the world is open to question, and the new religious ideal is dominated by the notion of conscience, the moral reflection of the outer world that exists in all men at all times. The movement is away from a cloistered, static view of the world, away from any view that considers the world as separable from the self. It is a movement toward a view of human experience that emphasizes the continuity of internal and external experience. This view is nowhere better described in the Middle Ages than in the *Ancrene Wisse*. Its author constructs a concentrated but complete world for his audience in which the once comforting but finally misleading distinctions between inner and outer experience, the cloister and the world, saint and sinner, and even good and evil, are systematically blurred so as to encourage a spiritual life of continual process, and of continual tension, relieved only in confession. If the anchoress seems to have withdrawn from the world, she has done so to confront more directly the ever-changing world of herself.

Notes
Index

Notes

Introduction

1. Augustine, *Confessions*, trans. R. S. Pine-Coffin (Middlesex: Penguin, 1961), p. 223.

2. Charles Homer Haskins, *The Renaissance of the Twelfth Century* (Cambridge, Mass.: Harvard University Press, 1927). Haskins, as well as more recent scholars, defines the Twelfth-Century Renaissance loosely, so that it encompasses not only the twelfth century but also the several decades preceding and following it; see pp. 6–10.

3. R. W. Southern, *The Making of the Middle Ages* (New Haven: Yale University Press, 1953), p. 221.

4. Ibid., p. 222.

5. See Colin Morris's brief but illuminating discussion in *The Discovery of the Individual, 1050–1200* (New York: Harper and Row, 1972), particularly pp. 64–79.

6. See, for example, R. W. Chambers, *On the Continuity of English Prose* (1932; rpt. London: Oxford University Press, 1950), p. xcvi; R. M. Wilson, *Early Middle English Literature* (London: Methuen, 1939), p. 129; Geoffrey Shepherd, ed., *Ancrene Wisse: Parts Six and Seven* (1959; rpt. New York: Barnes and Noble Imports, 1972), p. ix.

7. Though there is a sizable body of literature devoted to the *Ancrene Wisse,* almost all of it relates to historical questions. See, however, Geoffrey Shepherd's important introduction to *Ancrene Wisse: Parts Six and Seven* and the recent imagery study by Janet Grayson, *Structure and Imagery in "Ancrene Wisse"* (Hanover, N.H.: University Press of New England, 1974).

8. See *Oxford English Dictionary,* "inwit" (1), and *Middle English Dictionary,* "inwit" (4). *An Anglo-Saxon Dictionary's* entries under "inwid, inwit" indicate that in Anglo-Saxon the word has only derogatory meanings: guile, deceit, fraud, evil. Only during the Twelfth-Century Renaissance and, presumably first in the *Ancrene Wisse,* does the term come to refer to conscience.

9. Beatrice White, "The Date of the *Ancrene Riwle,*" *Modern Language Review,* 40 (1945), 206–207, and Shepherd, *Ancrene Wisse: Parts Six and Seven,* p. 57.

10. E. J. Dobson reviews and adds to the body of evidence supporting all these facts in *The Origins of "Ancrene Wisse"* (Oxford: Clarendon Press, 1976). He ends his highly technical and closely argued study by tentatively naming the *Ancrene Wisse* author as Brian of Lingen, about whom we know very little but who at least could have written the work if Dobson's detective work is correct. On the dating

of the *Ancrene Wisse* see Dobson's earlier study, "The Date and Composition of the *Ancrene Wisse*," *Proceedings of the British Academy*, 52 (1967), 181-208, as well as C. H. Talbot's ground-breaking essay, "Some Notes on the Dating of the *Ancrene Riwle*," *Neophilologus*, 40 (1956), 38-50. That the *Ancrene Wisse* was originally composed in English was first argued persuasively by D. M. E. Dymes, "The Original Language of the *Ancrene Riwle*," *Essays and Studies*, 9 (1924), 31-49; see also R. W. Chambers, "Recent Research upon the *Ancren Riwle*," *Review of English Studies*, 1 (1925), 5-13. Chambers in the same essay carefully summarizes the argument of those who favor a Latin or French original and of those who argue for an early twelfth-century date of composition. On the dialect of the work see J. R. R. Tolkien's classic study, "*Ancrene Wisse* and *Hali Meiðhad*," *Essays and Studies*, 14 (1929), 104-126. For a more complete bibliography of studies devoted to the *Ancrene Wisse* see *The Manual of the Writings in Middle English*, 1050-1500, gen. ed. J. Burke Severs (Hamden, Conn.: Archon, 1970), II, 650-654.

11. A most useful discussion of the term "medieval humanism" appears in R. W. Southern's *Medieval Humanism and Other Studies* (New York: Harper and Row, 1970), pp. 29-60.

12. The first step toward an annotated edition of the *Ancrene Wisse* was taken by Geoffrey Shepherd in his very useful edition of two parts of the work, *Ancrene Wisse: Parts Six and Seven*, with the most extensive annotation available for any portion of the *Ancrene Wisse*. Shepherd's notes give some indication of the *Wisse* author's wide reading and eclecticism. E. J. Dobson, *Moralities on the Gospels* (Oxford: Oxford University Press, 1975), recently discovered an important new source of the *Ancrene Wisse*, the *Moralia super Evangelia* (c. 1200-1215?). The work of Dobson and particularly of Shepherd represents the most substantial research to date on the sources of the *Ancrene Wisse*.

1. Self and Religious Rules

1. The title *Regula monasteriorum* is preferred, although *Regula monachorum* often appears; see E. Cuthbert Butler's scholarly edition, *S. Benedicti regula monasteriorum*, 3rd ed. (Freiberg: Herder, 1935), and Leonard Doyle, trans., *St. Benedict's Rule for Monasteries* (Collegeville, Minn.: St. John's Abbey Press, 1948), pp. iii-iv. All references and translations are to the edition and translation of Justin McCann, *The Rule of St. Benedict in Latin and English* (Westminster, Md.: The Newman Press, 1952). Citations appear in the text and refer to chapter only.

2. The following religious rules composed for solitaries and secular canons all depend heavily upon the Rule of St. Benedict. Grimlaic's *Regulae solitariorum (c.* 900), *Patrologia Latina* (hereafter *PL*), 103, cols. 575-664; allusions to St. Benedict's Rule appear throughout the work but are especially frequent in the opening chapters; see, for example, cols. 577D, 578C and D, and 579B, as well as the remarks of L. Gougaud, *Ermites et reclus* (Vienne, France: Ligugé, 1928), p. 63. Peter the Venerable's letter to the hermit Gilbert (c. 1133-1138), often referred to as his rule, closely follows the Rule of St. Benedict; see *The Letters of Peter the Venerable*, ed. Giles Constable, 2 vols. (Cambridge, Mass.: Harvard University Press, 1967), I,

27–41, and II, 70. Peter the Venerable's reliance upon Benedict's Rule is discussed by Jean Leclercq in "Pierre le Vénérable et l'érémitisme clunisien," *Studia Anselmiana: Petrus Venerabilis, 1156-1956*, ed. Giles Constable and James Kritzeck (Rome: Herder, 1956), pp. 99–120. Aelred of Rievaulx's *De vita eremitica* (c. 1160), to which the *Ancrene Wisse* is frequently compared, also relies heavily upon St. Benedict's Rule. The Latin text of Aelred's Rule has been edited by Charles Dumont, *La Vie de recluse et la prière pastorale de Aelred de Rievaulx*, Sources Chrétiennes, 76 (Paris: Editions du Cerf, 1961). Dumont describes the work as "une adaptation de la règle de saint Benoit, dont on reconnaîtra facilement l'ordonnance générale, et à de nombreux détails, l'interprétation cistercienne telle qu'elle devait être donnée au noviciat de Rievaulx," p. 13. Mary Paul Macpherson, in her translation of the work, *Rule of Life for a Recluse*, in *Works of Aelred of Rievaulx*, vol. I, *Treatises and the Pastoral Prayer* (Spencer, Mass.: Cistercian Publications, 1971), notes the continual allusions to St. Benedict's Rule. Early rules for secular canons, most notably Chrodegang's *Regula canonicorum* (c. 753), *PL*, 89, cols. 1097-1120, are also essentially Benedictine. See J. C. Dickinson, *The Origins of the Austin Canons and Their Introduction into England* (London: Society for Promoting Christian Knowledge, 1950), pp. 16–20. The only influential religious rule that does not depend upon the Benedictine model is the so-called Rule of St. Augustine, developed as a religious rule sometime before the mid-twelfth century.

3. See, for example, Shepherd, *Ancrene Wisse: Parts Six and Seven*, p. xxix.

4. Ibid., p. xxxvii: "We have in the *Rule* a rule which is more than the usual rule." For the alternate title see James Morton, *The Ancren Riwle: A Treatise on the Rules and Duties of Monastic Life* (London: Camden Society, 1853), p. v, who emphatically pronounces *Ancren Riwle* to be "the original and proper title." Though later scholars recognized that Morton's title was merely a translation of the Latin "Regulae inclusarum" added in a seventeenth-century hand to only one manuscript of the work, and that Morton's Middle English translation was grammatically incorrect, most have been satisfied with correcting the grammar to *Ancrene Riwle* (adding the genitive case ending) and otherwise letting Morton's title stand. Only one critic, Francis Magoun, has chosen to argue vigorously against what he repeatedly refers to as Morton's "invented" title, "urg[ing] that the designation *Ancrene Riwle* be altogether dropped and that *Ancrene Wisse* be used in its place." As Magoun points out, only the latter title has any manuscript authority at all: "The text in Ms. *Corpus Christi College Cambridge*, No. 402 is the only English text of this work to have a title of any sort and . . . there it is *Ancrene Wisse*, 'the way or mode of the life of recluses.' All positive evidence favors this title not merely because it is the only contemporary title, but because the manuscript in which it occurs is among the oldest and, more important, offers the most correct text." See Magoun, "*Ancrene Wisse* vs. *Ancren Riwle*," *ELH*, 4 (1937), 112-113. Magoun's argument, though it seems quite persuasive to me, has been ignored by many critics, who use the title *Ancrene Wisse* only when referring to the Corpus manuscript in particular. E. J. Dobson, in his recent studies of the origins of the work, is a notable exception, although he accepts the title *Ancrene Wisse* somewhat reluctantly. See Dobson, *The Origins of "Ancrene Wisse,"* pp. 51–53. Critical reluctance to use the work's

contemporary and therefore most authoritative title may arise from the difficulty in
determining the exact meaning of the otherwise unrecorded noun "wisse." For the
range of possible meanings, see *An Anglo-Saxon Dictionary:* "wis," "wise," and
"wisian"; *Oxford English Dictionary:* "wis," "wise"; Dobson, *The Origins of "Ancrene
Wisse,"* p. 52; and Winifred Felperin, "The Art of Perfection: Art and Instruction
in the *Ancrene Riwle,"* (Ph.D. diss. Harvard University, 1966), p. 176. Felperin
suggests that the term "may well be a translation of the Latin 'scientia,' the technical term in Cassian's *Collations* for structured, comprehensive inquiry"; she refers
the reader to *Collatio* XIV, "De spiritali scientia," *PL,* 49, col. 953.

    5. Gerard Sitwell, "Introduction," *The Ancrene Riwle,* trans. M. B. Salu, p. xi;
J. A. W. Bennett and G. V. Smithers, eds., *Early Middle English Verse and Prose,*
2nd ed. (Oxford: Clarendon Press, 1968), p. 223.

    6. See, for example, Hope Emily Allen, "The Origin of the *Ancren Riwle,"*
PMLA, 33 (1918), 448-492, and Vincent McNabb, "The Authorship of the *Ancren Riwle,"* *Modern Language Review,* 11 (1916), 1-5.

    7. See Derek Brewer, "Two Notes on the Augustinian . . . Origin of the *Ancrene
Riwle,"* *Notes and Queries,* n.s. 3 (1956), 232-235, McNabb, "The Authorship of the
Ancren Riwle," pp. 1-8, and Allen, "The Origin of the *Ancren Riwle,"* pp. 474-546.
Most scholars now accept 1215-1222 as the period during which the *Ancrene Wisse*
was written; see Chambers, "Recent Research upon the *Ancren Riwle,"* pp. 1-20;
Talbot, "Some Notes on the Dating of the *Ancrene Riwle,"* pp. 38-50; and Dobson,
"The Date and Composition of the *Ancrene Wisse,"* pp. 181-208.

    8. Dobson, *The Origins of "Ancrene Wisse,"* p. 17.

    9. Ibid., p. 21. Vincent McNabb, "The Authorship of the *Ancren Riwle,"* p. 1,
was the first scholar to note this quotation from the Augustinian Rule in the *Ancrene Wisse.* Dobson creates an inaccurate impression of the length of the passage
the *Ancrene Wisse* author quotes by printing a lengthy section of the Augustinian
Rule that he says is "directly quoted in Part II of *Ancrene Wisse."* In fact, as Dobson's italics silently suggest, only fourteen words of the passage are directly quoted.
They are: "Inpudicus oculus inpudici cordis est nuncius: Augustinus . . . non
solum appetere, sed appeti uelle criminosum." This passage is missing from the
Corpus manuscript, but see *The English Text of the Ancrene Riwle (Edited from Cotton MS. Nero A. XIV),* ed. Mabel Day, Early English Text Society, 225 (London:
Oxford University Press, 1952), p. 26. For further discussion of Dobson's sometimes confusing sense of literary dependency, see Siegfried Wenzel's review in *Spe-
culum,* 53 (1978), 355.

    10. Dobson, *The Origins of "Ancrene Wisse,"* p. 17.

    11. Ibid., pp. 18-19. Janet Grayson, *Structure and Imagery in "Ancrene Wisse,"* pp.
8-15, first brought this piece of formal symbolism to light.

    12. It has often been noted that the *Ancrene Wisse* author's division of his book
into outer and inner rules is borrowed from Aelred of Rievaulx. See, for example,
Grayson, *Structure and Imagery in "Ancrene Wisse,"* p. 4, and Shepherd, *Ancrene
Wisse: Parts Six and Seven,* pp. xxxvi–xxxvii. Although it is probably true that the
author borrows the terms from Aelred, the distinctions in the *Ancrene Wisse* between the two rules are much sharper than for Aelred, whose classification seems

an arbitrary division of otherwise indistinguishable material. In fact, Aelred's Rule is heavily dependent upon St. Benedict's largely external rule, and he has some difficulty fitting the inner rule into his scheme at all.

13. For the early history of the term *regula,* see Adalbert de Vogüé, "Sub regula vel abbate," in *Rule and Life: An Interdisciplinary Symposium,* ed. Basil Pennington (Spencer, Mass.: Cistercian Publications, 1971), pp. 23–25.

14. "Nobis autem desidiosis et male viventibus atque negligentibus, rubor confusionis est. Quisquis ergo ad patriam caelestem festinas, hanc minimam inchoationis regulam descriptam adjuvante Christo perfice; et tunc demum ad majora, quae supra commemoravimus, doctrinae virtutumque culmina Deo protegente pervenies" (chapter 73). Benedict here leaves ambiguous the question of whether the future referred to as coming "at length under God's protection" will occur during this life or the next. But he ends his prologue with the conviction that monks will live in the monastery and in accordance with the Rule until death: "Ab ipsius numquam magisterio discedentes, in ejus doctrina usque *ad mortem in monasterio perseverantes,* passionibus Christi per patientiam participemur, ut et regni ejus mereamur esse consortes" (my emphasis).

15. E. Cuthbert Butler, *Benedictine Monachism: Studies in Benedictine Life and Rule* (1924; rpt. New York: Barnes and Noble, 1962), p. 45; see also especially pp. 58, 300–301. For further discussion of the importance of obedience in St. Benedict's Rule, see Vogüé, "Sub regula vel abbate," pp. 23–24, and the brief but illuminating discussions by R. W. Southern in *The Making of the Middle Ages,* pp. 223–225, and *Western Society and the Church in the Middle Ages* (Middlesex: Penguin, 1970), p. 220.

16. See Jean Leclercq, "Profession according to the Rule of St. Benedict," in *Rule and Life: An Interdisciplinary Symposium,* pp. 117–149. While I draw frequently upon Leclercq's thorough research and have found it invaluable, all conclusions concerning St. Benedict's Rule and the Cistercians are my own and are often at variance with those of Leclercq, who finds far more flexibility in St. Benedict's Rule than I have been able to discover. For further discussion of the early history of Benedictine monasticism see David Knowles, *From Pachomius to Ignatius: A Study in the Constitutional History of the Religious Orders* (Oxford: Clarendon Press, 1966), and *The Monastic Order in England: A History of Its Development from the Times of St. Dunstan to the Fourth Lateran Council,* 2nd ed. (Cambridge: Cambridge University Press, 1963); Butler, *Benedictine Monachism;* Herbert Workman, *The Evolution of the Monastic Ideal: From the Earliest Times Down to the Coming of the Friars* (1913; rpt. Boston: Beacon Press, 1962); and Norman Cantor, "The Crisis of Western Monasticism, 1050–1130," *American Historical Review,* 66 (October 1960), 47–67.

17. Southern, *Western Society,* p. 257.

18. Knowles, *From Pachomius to Ignatius,* p. 22. On the Cistercian impulse to regulate every detail of daily life see Southern, *Western Society,* pp. 251–259. For an opposing view see Leclercq, "Profession according to the Rule of St. Benedict," pp. 138–139.

19. Dickinson, *The Origins of the Austin Canons,* pp. 26–58.

20. The complicated history of the term and its meanings is discussed by Dickinson, *The Origins of the Austin Canons*, pp. 37, 51–53, and 60–62.

21. Ibid., pp. 54–58, and 62–72. See also Southern, *Western Society*, pp. 241–242. The document known as the *Regula Augustini* is printed as an appendix in Dickinson, pp. 273–279. The letter that forms the core of the Rule is translated in *St. Augustine: Letters*, trans. Wilfred Parsons (New York: Cima, 1956), V, no. 211, 38–51.

22. Dickinson, *The Origins of the Austin Canons*, pp. 269–270.

23. Ibid., Appendix II, p. 275; *St. Augustine: Letters*, pp. 43–44.

24. Dickinson, *The Origins of the Austin Canons*, pp. 275, 279; *St. Augustine: Letters*, p. 51.

25. Southern, *Western Society*, p. 242.

26. Peter de Honestis writes his *Regula clericorum* (c. 1119) because he can find no evidence of the Fathers having written a "sure, fixed and adequate rule" for clerks: "Utrum quis sanctorum Patrum propheticae et apostolicae doctrinae servans exempla, et scrutans interna, clericis in unum commorantibus, certam fixamque et sufficientem regulam et ordinis canonici singularum varietatum, quaeque negotia continentem dictaverit" (*PL*, 163, col. 703). see Dickinson, *The Origins of the Austin Canons*, p. 62, n. 2.

27. For a discussion of the wide variety of religious groups who adopted the Augustinian Rule see Southern, *Western Society*, pp. 242–250, and Dickinson, *The Origins of the Austin Canons*, pp. 83–90.

28. Such arguments were made by both Peter the Venerable of Cluny and Bernard of Clairvaux. Yet, even as these two influential representatives of the black and white monks argued on behalf of moderation, they continued to attack the customs of each other's order as betrayals of the letter or the spirit of St. Benedict's Rule. See especially Peter the Venerable's famous letter to St. Bernard, which the *Ancrene Wisse* author may have known, in *The Letters of Peter the Venerable*, I, 52–101. Hope Emily Allen, in "The Origin of the *Ancren Riwle*," pp. 517 ff., suggests that the *Ancrene Wisse* author borrows from this letter in his introduction.

29. M. D. Chenu, *Nature, Man, and Society in the Twelfth Century: Essays on New Theological Perspectives in the Latin West*, ed. and trans. Jerome Taylor and Lester K. Little (Chicago: University of Chicago Press, 1968), p. 259. The discussion that follows draws frequently from two of Chenu's extraordinary essays: "Monks, Canons, and Laymen in Search of the Apostolic Life," pp. 202–238, and "The Evangelical Awakening," pp. 239–269.

30. See Shepherd, *Ancrene Wisse: Parts Six and Seven*, p. xxix, who notes that "apart from the Bible, no writing affords more points of contact with the *Rule* in themes, development of themes, and in common quotations than does the *Verbum abbreviatum* of Peter the Chanter." These contacts deserve much closer examination, especially because Shepherd himself refers relatively infrequently to the *Verbum abbreviatum* in his notes to Parts Six and Seven of the *Ancrene Wisse*.

31. *PL*, 205, cols. 233–239. Quoted and translated in Chenu, *Nature, Man, and Society in the Twelfth Century*, pp. 256–257. See also John Baldwin, *Masters, Princes, and Merchants: The Social Views of Peter the Chanter and His Circle* (Princeton: Princeton University Press, 1970), I, 315–316, and II, 212.

32. For a brief biography of Jacques de Vitry see Baldwin, *Masters, Princes, and Merchants,* pp. 38–39.

33. Jacques de Vitry, *Libri duo quorum prior orientalis . . . alter occidentalis historiae* (Douai, 1597), p. 357. Quoted and translated in Chenu, *Nature, Man, and Society in the Twelfth Century,* pp. 221–222. For additional evidence of the popularity of this extended meaning of *regulares* see François Vandenbrouke et al., *The Spirituality of the Middle Ages,* trans. Benedictines of Holmes-Edon Abbey, *History of Christian Spirituality* (London: Burns and Oates, 1968), II 257–258. Of particular interest are the remarks of Gerhoh of Reichersberg in *De aedificio Dei, PL,* 194, col. 1302. Vandenbrouke translates: "Every class, every profession without exception, possesses in the Catholic faith and the teaching of the apostles a rule suited to his own circumstances, and, by fighting as it behoves it under this rule, will obtain the crown." See also Chenu, *Nature, Man, and Society in the Twelfth Century,* p. 222.

34. Quoted in translation in Chenu, *Nature, Man, and Society in the Twelfth Century,* p. 239. Francis is said to have presented the briefest of rules, now lost, to Pope Innocent. But his remark indicates that, in Francis's view, the rule of the gospel should precede his or any other formal rule. See Vandenbrouke et al., *The Spirituality of the Middle Ages,* p. 290, and John R. H. Moorman, *The History of the Franciscan order from Its Origins to the Year 1517* (Oxford: Clarendon Press, 1968), p. 11.

35. Chenu, *Nature, Man, and Society in the Twelfth Century,* p. 247.

36. Thomas of Celano, *Vita prima S. Francisci, Analecta Franciscana* (Florence, 1926–1941), X, 26. Quoted and translated in Chenu, *Nature, Man, and Society in the Twelfth Century,* p. 257, n. 28.

37. Chenu, "The Evangelical Awakening," in *Nature, Man, and Society in the Twelfth Century,* pp. 239–269.

38. See Moorman, *The History of the Franciscan Order,* pp. 46–52. Even the *Ancrene Wisse* author, in later versions of his work addressed to a larger group of anchoresses, suggests the need for a more formally organized religious life. See, for example, T130–131.

39. See Allen, "The Origin of the *Ancren Riwle,*" p. 487, and Dobson, *The Origins of "Ancrene Wisse,"* pp. 48–50. Both scholars suggest that the *Wisse* author himself is the anchoresses' current chaplain. Dobson also assumes that the anchoresses already professed the Rule of St. Augustine. He identifies the anchoresses with the nuns of Limebrook Priory, located several miles from Wigmore Abbey, a Victorine house, and suggests on the basis of very slender evidence that the anchoresses were Augustinian canonesses at the time the *Ancrene Wisse* was written. In fact, the earliest reference to an Augustinian connection at Limebrook occurs in 1279, at least fifty years after the *Ancrene Wisse* was written. It is quite possible that Limebrook Priory was not organized as an Augustinian house until some time after the *Ancrene Wisse* was written and much of Dobson's evidence suggests as much (see pp. 180–181). Indeed, if the anchoresses already professed the Rule of St. Augustine, it would be all the more remarkable that the *Ancrene Wisse* author never refers directly to this rule.

40. See T8–9, and 211.

41. The anchoresses are advised, for example, not to fast on bread and water without permission, to dress comfortably and warmly, and not to wear penitential

hair garments or discipline themselves with scourges and the like, see T211–214. Derek Brewer ("Two Notes on the Augustinian . . . Origin of the *Ancrene Riwle*," pp. 232–235) and E. J. Dobson (*The Origins of "Ancrene Wisse,"* p. 27–54) have traced a number of these rules to the moderate Augustinian tradition.

42. See Allen, "The Origin of the *Ancren Riwle*," p. 516. Allen notes the anchoresses' "eagerness for a rule" that would give them a "settled connection" with some established order. Her discussion is perceptive, although it is part of her argument for an impossibly early date for the *Ancrene Wisse*. The *Wisse* author belongs not, as Allen believed, to a small "liberal minority" of early twelfth-century writers "who took a very spiritualized view of orders," but to a more substantial and more radical group of nonmonastic writers of the early thirteenth century who opposed the formalism of all established rules.

43. Because the *Wisse* author borrows frequently from Peter the Chanter's *Verbum abbreviatum*, it is quite likely that Peter's chapter on religious rules was known to him, and it is a probable source for his remarks on religious rules. On the other hand, St. Francis's remarks on religious rules, while they indicate a skepticism about rules analogous to that of the *Ancrene Wisse* author, are not a likely source. Though the author, in later versions of his book, shows great admiration for the new orders of friars, his original version, preserved in Cotton MS. Nero A. XIV, shows no knowledge of the new mendicant orders. A number of scholars have noted the absence of any mention of the friars in the earliest version of the *Ancrene Wisse*, because that important omission helps to establish the work's latest possible date of composition; see, for example, Chambers, "Recent Research upon the *Ancren Riwle*," p. 16.

44. Dobson, *The Origins of "Ancrene Wisse,"* p. 26, suggests a possible echo of the author's etymological discussion in the opening of a commentary on the Rule of St. Augustine attributed to Hugh of St. Victor.

45. Here I have supplied my own translation, because Salu's strays unusually far from the author's words. All bracketed translations are my own and will not be noted hereafter.

46. Contemporary evidence suggests that the author might have had good reason to urge his charges to be particularly suspicious of visiting bishops. *The Life of Christina of Markyate: A Twelfth Century Recluse,* ed. and trans. C. H. Talbot (Oxford: Clarendon Press, 1959), provides numerous examples of the repeated attempts of corrupt bishops and other high Church officials to seduce Christina or otherwise thwart her desire to become a nun. I am thinking especially of Christina's encounter with Ralph Flambard, the bishop of Durham, which Christina's biographer notes as "the beginning of all the frightful troubles that followed" in her life.

47. The author reiterates the point at the opening of his final chapter, "External Rules": "Biuoren on earst ich seide þet ȝe ne schulden nawiht, as i vu, bihaten forte halden nan of þe uttre riwlen. Þet ilke ich segge ȝetten . . . ȝe ȝet moten changin, hwen se ȝe eauer wulleð, þeose for betere"(T210). ("I said earlier, at the beginning, that you should certainly not promise to keep anything of the exterior rules as if under a vow, and I say so again . . . [Y]ou yourselves must change these for better ones whenever you will" [S182]). The chapters of the *Ancrene Wisse,*

which the author calls "destinctiuns" or "dalen," have been given appropriate and convenient titles by Salu in her translation.

48. Walter Ullmann, *The Individual and Society in the Middle Ages* (Baltimore: Johns Hopkins University Press, 1966), p. x. The context of Ullmann's remark is a discussion of the interrelationship among feudalism, law, obedience, and individualism. He does not mention the religious vow of obedience, but the point nevertheless applies.

49. *Liber de praecepto et dispensatione, PL,* 182, col. 874.

50. Hope Emily Allen, "The Origin of the *Ancren Riwle*," p. 531, cites both John of Salisbury (*Polycraticus,* c. 1150-1161) and Peter of Blois (d. 1212) as writers who used St. James's definition of religion to combat more formal and legalistic definitions of religious rules. John Dickinson, *The Origins of the Austin Canons,* p. 176, cites Arno of Reichersberg (d. 1175), who also used the same passage from St. James's Epistle to defend the legitimacy of the order of canons against frequent Cistercian attacks. Peter of Blois is the most likely source for this passage in the *Ancrene Wisse,* because the author elsewhere borrows frequently from Peter's works; see Shepherd, *Ancrene Wisse: Parts Six and Seven,* pp. 41, 48, 51, 53, 58, 61, 64. Allen, though she is the only scholar to mention Peter of Blois in connection with this passage, could not recognize Peter as a source so long as she insisted that the *Ancrene Wisse* was written in the first half of the twelfth century. Nevertheless, her work in establishing the *Wisse* author's interest in the Benedictine-Cistercian controversy is invaluable.

51. Southern, *Western Society,* p. 244.

52. Gerard Sitwell, for example, in his introduction to Salu's translation, *Ancrene Riwle,* pp. xviii-xix, argues that large sections of the work do not seem to apply to anchoresses and are, in fact, "unsuitable" in a work addressed to them. These sections, as I argue below in chapter four, are central to the author's conception of the solitary life. The inclusiveness of the author's rule might explain why his work continued to be so popular among laymen throughout the Renaissance. Hope Emily Allen, "Wynkyn de Worde and a Second French Compilation from the 'Ancren Riwle' with a Description of the First," *Essays and Studies in Honor of Carleton Brown* (New York: New York University Press, 1940), pp. 187-189, and 216, notes that several manuscripts of the *Wisse* were owned by aristocratic married women. A Wycliffite version of the *Wisse* has been edited by J. Påhlsson, *The Recluse* (Lund: H. Ohlsson, 1911). For an interesting discussion of the Lollards' interest in the *Ancrene Wisse* see E. Colledge, "*The Recluse*: A Lollard Interpolated Version of the *Ancren Riwle*," *Review of English Studies,* 15 (1939), 1-15, and 129-145.

2. Self and Society

1. See, for example, Wilson, *Early Middle English Literature,* pp. 134-135; Hope Emily Allen, "On the Author of the *Ancren Riwle*," *PMLA,* 44 (1929), especially p. 657-661; and Chambers, "Recent Research upon the *Ancren Riwle*," p. 5.

2. Grayson, *Structure and Imagery in "Ancrene Wisse."*

3. Ibid., p. 13.

4. Gabriel le Bras, *Institutions ecclésiastiques de la Chrétienté médiévale;* Histoire de l'Eglise depuis les origines jusqu'à nos jours, vol. 12 (Paris: Bloud and Gay, 1959), 196–197. Cited also in Felperin, "Art of Perfection," p. 49, n. 41.

5. For the early history of the desert ideal, See Derwas Chitty, *The Desert a City* (Oxford: Blackwell, 1966), pp. 6–7; Thomas M. Gannon and George Traub, *The Desert and the City: An Interpretation of the History of Christian Spirituality* (London: Collier-MacMillan, 1969), pp. 17–50; and F. R. Hoare, ed. and trans., *The Western Fathers* (New York: Harper and Row, 1965), pp. xx–xxvii.

6. See Gannon and Traub, *The Desert and the City,* pp. 23–27.

7. Athanasius, *Vita S. Antonii, Patrologia Graeca,* 26, cols. 838–979. Translated in *Early Christian Biographies,* ed. and trans. Roy J. Deferrari (New York: Fathers of the Church, 1952), pp. 127–216. The influence of the *Life of St. Anthony* upon subsequent saints' lives is traced by Benjamin Kurtz, "From St. Anthony to St. Guthlac: A Study in Biography," *University of California Publications in Modern Philology,* 12 (1926), 103–146.

8. Bertram Colgrave, ed. and trans., *Two Lives of St. Cuthbert* (Cambridge: Cambridge University Press, 1940), pp. 112–113.

9. Ibid., pp. 96–97.

10. Ibid., p. 110.

11. For a concise analysis of the Church's optimism and efficient political strategy throughout the lay investiture controversy, see Gerd Tellenbach, *Church, State, and Christian Society at the Time of the Investiture Contest,* trans R. F. Bennett (1940; rpt. New York: Harper and Row, 1970), especially chapters 4 and 5.

12. Bennett D. Hill, *English Cistercian Monasteries and Their Patrons in the Twelfth Century* (Urbana, Ill.: University of Illinois Press, 1968), pp. 47, 53–54.

13. The Camaldolese monks, for example, called their northern Italian settlement a "desert." See Gannon and Traub, *The Desert and the City,* p. 73. The Carthusians referred to themselves as "poor men who dwell in the desert of the Chartreuse." See E. Margaret Thompson, *The Carthusian Order in England* (London: Society for Promoting Christian Knowledge, 1930), p. 12. Virtually every new religious order of the eleventh and twelfth centuries referred to its monastery as a desert-wilderness.

14. A. Squire, *Aelred of Rievaulx: A Study* (London: Society for Promoting Christian Knowledge, 1969), p. 32. See also Hill, *English Cistercian Monasteries,* p. 47, n. 11.

15. Hope Emily Allen, "On the Author of the *Ancren Riwle,*" p. 662, notes that Peter the Venerable "had a great friendship and close association with the Carthusians, whom he preferred to all other orders and he visited them every year." It was through the efforts of Peter the Venerable that Bernard of Clairvaux became interested in the Carthusians. See Thompson, *The Carthusian Order in England,* p. 18.

16. *The Letters of Peter the Venerable,* I, 28.

17. Epistle 250, *PL,* 182, col. 451. "Clamat ad vos mea monstruosa vita, mea aerumnosa conscientia. Ego enim quaedam chimaera mei saeculi, nec clericum gero, nec laicum. Nam monachi jamdudum exui conversationem, non habitum." A chimera is a mythical monster with the head of a lion, the body of a goat, and

the tail of a serpent. This self-portrait by Bernard is discussed by Squire, *Aelred of Rievaulx,* p. 23.

18. All references are to the 1959 Clarendon Press edition and translation and will be referred to in the text by page number only. The best recent study of the *Life* appears in Robert Hanning, *The Individual in Twelfth Century Romance* (New Haven: Yale University Press, 1977), pp. 35–50.

19. At least part of the difficulty Christina's biographer has in adjusting her life to the desert pattern might arise from the fact that the desert ideal, which was largely defined by heroic battles with devils and beasts, was difficult to adapt to women. For women, from the early martyrologies forward, the heroic combat was narrowly restricted to one area—the preservation of chastity. Under the best of circumstances women did not stand a great chance of achieving sanctity: Hugh of Flavigny, a chronicler of the early twelfth century, outlined the following order of precedence for entrance to heaven: "Peter, Paul, John the Baptist, the rest of the Apostles, holy hermits, perfect monks, good bishops, good priests, good laymen, women" (*Monumenta Germaniae historica, Scriptores,* VIII, 384; quoted and translated in Tellenbach, *Church, State, and Christian Society,* p. 52). The only sphere of activity in which women were allowed to excel, it seems, was the area of chastity. Philip of Navarre categorically asserts the double standard with reference to worldly "honor," but the same standard was applied to spiritual perfection: "Fames ont grant avantage d'une chose: legierement pueent garder lor honors, se eles vuelent estre tenues a bones, por une seule chose; mès a l'ome en covient plusors, se il vuet estre por bons tenuz ... Et la fame, se ele est prode fame de son cors, toutes ses autres taches sont covertes, et puet aler partot teste levée: et por ce ne covient mie tant d'ansaignemanz as filles comme au filz." See *Les quatres âges de l'homme: Traité moral de Phillipe de Navarre,* ed. Marcel de Fréville, Société des anciens textes francais, 26 (Paris: Firmin, Didot, 1888), p. 20. Such a narrow arena for combat required the hagiographer of female solitaries to work hard to achieve the same thrilling (as well as edifying) effects that he could easily relate in a male hero's epic battles with legions of devils. The hagiographer usually had to concentrate on *real* threats to the virgin's chastity—live men instead of devils—and thus was forced to provide many possibilities for human contact in what was supposedly the history of a solitary life. See, for example, *The Life of St. Pelagia the Harlot and The Life of St. Mary the Harlot, Vitae patrum,* I, PL, 73, cols. 663–690. As the titles imply, these lives are concerned primarily with chastity, or, more specifically, with the lack of it in the desert heroine's early life.

20. "[D]ivina disponente providencia contigit Autti ac Beatricem sumpta secum sua karissima filia Christina nostrum adire monasterium ac beati martiris Albani cuius inibi sacra venerantur ossa ... Perscrutans ergo puella sedulo visu locum. et considerans reverendam maturitatem inhabitancium monachorum. pronunciavit felices et consorcii eorum optavit fieri particeps" (p. 38). See Talbot, "Introduction," *The Life of Christina of Markyate,* pp. 15–16. Nunneries as class institutions for well-born unmarried ladies were a venerable tradition in England; furthermore, scholars have pointed out the political advisability of Anglo-Saxon women entering such institutions as a means of retaining some aristocratic status

in the francophile England of the period. See Talbot, "Introduction," *The Life of Christina of Markyate,* pp. 12-13, and Lina Eckenstein, *Woman under Monasticism* (Cambridge: Cambridge University Press, 1896), pp. 79-116, 207 ff.

21. At first Christina's family seems motivated by a typical middle-class desire to see their accomplished daughter well married, so that she will not dishonor her parents; see pp. 58, 66-68. But as the tale proceeds, Christina's parents become less interested in marriage and more determined to have their daughter deflowered by anyone as soon as possible. Christina's mother "iurabat quod non consideraret quis filiam suam corrumperet. si tantum aliquo casu corrumpi potuisset" (p. 72). See Hanning, *The Individual in Twelfth Century Romance,* p. 41.

22. There are a few exceptions. See for example, pp. 128-132.

23. See pp. 126, 138, and 150.

24. "In camino tamen paupertatis tribulabatur adhuc Christi virgo illarum egens rerum quarum egestas virtutes non minuit sed accumulat ... Cum vero secretorum ille conscius opportunum censuit ut illi et in hiis subveniret: hoc modo disposuit. Erat in confinio heremi ipsius persona quedam nobilis et potens ... abbas ... Galfridus" (pp. 132-134).

25. See pp. 161-171. One trip, on behalf of King Stephen, involves winning papal confirmation of Stephen's election as king, no easy task because Stephen's claim to the throne was at best dubious. Another trip, even more risky, was proposed by the English ecclesiastical hierarchy to urge Stephen's excommunication for imprisoning two unruly bishops. Concerning this latter journey to Rome, the biographer asks: "Quid [Geoffrey] ageret? Reniti non erat consilii. Negocium suscipere: gravis erat discriminis. Interminatus namque fuerat rex rerum omnium proscripcionem qui contra se romanum arriperent iter" (p. 166).

26. François Vandenbrouke, in *The Spirituality of the Middle Ages,* p. 277, notes that as many as 260 recluses lived in Rome in the early fourteenth century. See also Rotha Mary Clay, *The Hermits and Anchorites of England* (1914; rpt. Detroit: Singing Tree Press, 1968), pp. 203-263, for a tabulated list of anchorages in England during the High Middle Ages.

27. Squire, *Aelred of Rievaulx,* p. 32.

28. The Latin text has been edited by Charles Dumont in *La Vie de recluse et la prière pastorale.* All references are to this edition and will hereafter be given in the text as *DVE* plus page number. The first complete English translation has recently appeared by Mary Paul Macpherson, *Rule of Life for a Recluse.* All references are to this translation and will hereafter be given in the text as *LR* plus page number.

29. Squire, *Aelred of Rievaulx,* p. 32.

30. *De spirituali amicitia, PL,* 195, cols. 659-702.

31. Jean Leclercq, in Vandenbrouke, et al., *The Spirituality of the Middle Ages,* p. 207. See also Amédée Hallier, *The Monastic Theology of Aelred of Rievaulx,* trans. Columban Heaney (Spencer, Mass.: Cistercian Publications, 1969), p. 149.

32. *PL,* 22, cols. 453-454. Although Aelred does not share Jerome's enthusiasm for the solitary life, he does borrow frequently from Jerome's ascetic works. See Macpherson, *Rule of Life for a Recluse,* p. 44, n. 4.

33. See *DVE,* 44-56 and *LR,* 46-51.

34. Squire, *Aelred of Rievaulx,* p. 120.

35. See, for example, Dumont, "Introduction," *La Vie de recluse,* which is devoted almost entirely to the meditations.

36. "Ad Dei vero dilectionem duo pertinent, affectus mentis, et effectus operis. Et opus hoc in virtutum exercitatione, affectus in spiritualis gustus dulcedine. Exercitatio virtutum in certo vivendi modo, in ieiuniis, in vigiliis, in opere, in lectione, in oratione, in paupertate, et ceteris huiuismodi commendatur, affectus salutari meditatione nutritur. Itaque ut ille dulcis amor Iesu in tuo crescat affectu, triplici meditatione opus habes, de praeteritis scilicet, praesentibus et futuris" (*DVE,* 116).

37. See Clay, *The Hermits and Anchorites of England,* pp. 91–96, 193–198; and Edward Cutts, *Scenes and Characters of the Middle Ages* (1872; rpt. Detroit: Singing Tree Press, 1968), pp. 148–153.

38. See Bertram Colgrave, ed. and trans., *Felix's Life of St. Guthlac* (Cambridge: Cambridge University Press, 1956), pp. 92–94.

39. Cutts, *Scenes and Characters of the Middle Ages,* p. 120.

40. Francis Darwin, *The English Medieval Recluse* (London: Society for Promoting Christian Knowledge, 1944), p. 25.

41. Gaston Paris, ed., *La Vie de St. Alexis* (1872; rpt. Paris: Vieweg, 1887), pp. 151 ff.

42. This is but one of the many occasions on which the author looks forward to his extended discussion of confession in part V.

43. Grayson, *Structure and Imagery in "Ancrene Wisse,"* p. 11.

44. Ibid., pp. 11–12. I have supplied references to the Corpus text. Grayson uses Nero, but in these particular quotations the differences are negligible.

45. Ibid., p. 40.

46. The opening of part II is an adaptation of St. Bernard's *Steps of Humility,* chapter 10. See G. B. Burch, ed. and trans., *The Steps of Humility* (Notre Dame, Ind.: University of Notre Dame Press, 1963). The dynamism of the passage, however, and particularly the imagery of leaping, is the author's own. See R. Kaske, "Eve's Leaps in the *Ancrene Riwle,*" *Medium Aevum,* 29 (1960), 22–24. Kaske argues that Eve's leaps into sin and ultimately into hell are an ironic allusion to Christ's leaps to earth and to the cross, the latter idea a medieval development of Canticle of Canticles 2:8: "Vox dilecti mei; ecce iste venit, saliens in montibus, transiliens colles." This is a significant connection and one that the author of the *Ancrene Wisse* himself makes explicit in part VII (T193), but it is difficult to understand why Kaske calls the author's reference to Eve's leaps an example of "surface inconsequentiality" and "the limitations of pedagogic whimsy." Not only do Eve's leaps continue the imagery of leaping that the author established in the opening lines of part II, but also the imagery of leaping is, as I argue here, a vivid reminder of his argument that "much can come from little."

47. Grayson, *Structure and Imagery in "Ancrene Wisse,"* p. 40.

48. See *DVE,* 46 and *LR,* 47.

49. The author, following Bernard, joins the story of Eve with shorter versions of the stories of how Dinah and Bathsheba sinned, or caused others to sin, through looking (T32–33).

50. See, for example, H. Sweet, ed., *First Middle English Primer,* 2nd ed. (Ox-

ford: Clarendon Press, 1891), pp. 40-41; Richard Morris, ed., *Specimens of Early English*, pt. 1 (Oxford: Clarendon Press, 1898), p. 115; and A. S. Cook, ed., *A Literary Middle English Reader* (1915; rpt. Boston: Ginn and Co., 1943), pp. 275-276.

51. Wilson, *Early Middle English Literature*, pp. 132-133.

52. Felperin, "Art of Perfection," p. 29.

53. Beryl Smalley, *The Study of the Bible in the Middle Ages* (2nd ed., 1952; rpt. Notre Dame, Ind.: University of Notre Dame Press, 1964), p. 196. On the Victorine exegetical method see pp. 83-111.

54. *Benjamin Minor, PL*, 196, cols. 4-5. Clare Kirchberger, trans., *Richard of St. Victor: Selected Writings on Contemplation* (London: Faber and Faber, 1957), p. 66, cites the unusually large number of manuscripts in England and the early translation of the work into English.

55. Kirchberger, *Richard of St. Victor*, pp. 82-83.

56. Phyllis Hodgson, ed., *The Cloud of Unknowing and the Book of Privy Counsel*, Early English Text Society, 218 (London: Oxford University Press, 1944), pp. 24-26.

57. Gannon and Traub, *The Desert and the City*, p. 112.

58. Felperin, "Art of Perfection," p. 75.

59. Ibid., p. 34. Felperin notes that the anchoresses' "womanly preoccupation with affairs of the heart is acknowledged every step of the master's way, gently cultivated, elevated, but never denied. Surely it is not accidental nor simply traditional that the major theme running through all of the work . . . is a theme of love in all its earthly and familiar stages: courtship, betrothal, marriage and even motherhood."

60. See especially Gerard Sitwell's introduction to the Salu translation of the *Ancrene Wisse*, and Janet Grayson's *Structure and Imagery in "Ancrene Wisse."* Grayson, who points out in her introduction that the *Wisse* author's demonstration of love ends not in mysticism but in the romance of the Christ-knight, elsewhere in her study seems to assume that mysticism is the anchoresses' goal after all. For example, she argues that parts II and III of the work are "complementary exercises" that prepare the anchoress for the "mystical presence of the Bridegroom," pp. 56-57. The "end result" of following the *Wisse*, Grayson maintains, is "a mystical flight to the summit" of holiness, p. 81, n. 1.

61. See Chambers, "Recent Research upon the *Ancren Riwle*," 18-21; *Structure and Imagery in "Ancrene Wisse,"* especially pp. 148-150, 176-178; and especially Shepherd's introduction, notes, and appendix to *Ancrene Wisse: Parts Six and Seven*.

62. Jean Leclercq et al, eds., *Sermones super Cantica Canticorum, S. Bernardi Opera* (Rome: Cistercian Editions, 1957), I, sermon 20, 118.

63. Kilian Walsh, trans., *On the Song of Songs I, The Works of Bernard of Clairvaux* (Spencer, Mass.: Cistercian Publications, 1971), II, sermon 20, 152.

64. Bernard's theory concerning the movement from carnal to spiritual love is succinctly stated in *De Diligendo Deo*, ed. Jean Leclercq and H. M. Rochais, *S. Bernardi Opera*, III (Rome: Cistercian Editions, 1963). See also Etienne Gilson, *The Mystical Theology of St. Bernard*, trans. A. H. C. Downes (New York: Sheed and Ward, 1940), pp. 98 ff.

65. The author borrowed the classification of the elect from St. Bernard's sermon 7 for Lent (*PL,* 183, cols. 183-186), which Shepherd translates as an appendix to *Ancrene Wisse: Parts Six and Seven.* The *Ancrene Wisse* author, as always, borrows selectively, omitting all of St. Bernard's allusions to mystical flight as the attribute of the third and highest category of the elect. See Shepherd, p. lvii.

3. Self and the Sacrament of Confession

1. Sitwell, "Introduction," *The Ancrene Riwle,* trans. M. B. Salu, pp. xviii-xix. Sitwell does not clarify where "elsewhere" is, but we can, I think, safely assume that he refers to those sections of parts II and III that teach the anchoresses to be blind to the world and therefore "unspotted" by sin.

2. Ibid., "Translator's Note," p. xxv.

3. It is also unique as far as I can tell. No other writer of a religious rule for solitaries includes a consideration of confession.

4. Ibid., "Introduction," p. xix.

5. Paul Anciaux, *The Sacrament of Penance* (London: Challoner Publications, 1962), p. 110; see also Charles E. Curran, *Contemporary Problems in Moral Theology* (Notre Dame: Fides Publishers, 1970), pp. 5-6. On the history of the sacrament of penance see the following in addition to the more specific works cited elsewhere in this chapter: R. C. Mortimer, *The Origins of Private Penance in the Western Church* (Oxford: Clarendon Press, 1939); Bernhard Poschmann, *Penance and the Anointing of the Sick,* trans. Francis Courtney (New York: Herder, 1964); and O. D. Watkins, *A History of Penance* (London: Longmans, Green, 1920).

6. There were, of course, notable exceptions, the most famous of which is Augustine's moving description of his own state of mind at the moment of repentance in Book 8 of his *Confessions.*

7. *Liber de poenitentia, PL,* 1, col. 1241. Translated by Paul Palmer, *Sacraments and Forgiveness: History and Doctrinal Developments of Penance, Extreme Unction, and Indulgences, Sources of Christian Theology* (Westminster, Md.: The Newman Press, 1959), II, 23.

8. Tertullian does use the word "exomologesis" to mean confession, but it remains uncertain whether this refers to public penance or private confession. See Palmer, *Sacraments and Forgiveness,* pp. 25 ff. for the basic texts considered in this controversy, and pp. 382 ff. for Palmer's own conclusions.

9. Ibid., p. 79.

10. John T. McNeill, *A History of the Cure of Souls* (New York: Harper and Row, 1951), p. 133. After the twelfth century the indicative form "Absolvo te" became standard.

11. See Palmer, *Sacraments and Forgiveness,* pp. 126 ff. The early Celtic penitential system is examined by John T. McNeill, *The Celtic Penitentials and Their Influence on Continental Christianity* (Paris: Honoré Champion, 1932).

12. R. W. Southern, *Western Society,* p. 227.

13. See McNeill, *Cure of Souls,* pp. 119-121. Jean Charles Payen, in *Le Motif du repentir dans la littérature Française médiévale: Dès origines à 1230* (Geneva: Droz,

1967), p. 29, finds exceptions. Payen notes that tariffed penance is a better system than the earlier public penance because it is more adaptable to people's needs than the very formal solemn penance. Although this is certainly true, the fact remains that any steps the Celtic penitentials make in the direction of emphasizing sorrow for sin are small indeed and hardly enough to herald a new notion of penance, as Payen himself agrees. Evidence that I find much more interesting, though it too is scanty, supports at least some interest in the Celtic penitentials in the circumstances surrounding particular sins. See, for example, McNeill and Gamer, *Medieval Handbooks of Penance* (New York: Columbia University Press, 1938), pp. 323 ff. Thirteenth-century penitentials concentrate largely upon the circumstances that determine the gravity of a sin.

14. D. Wilkins, ed., *Concilia Magnae Britanniae et Hiberniae* (London, 1738), I, 366. Translated in Colin Morris, *The Discovery of the Individual*, p. 71.

15. Ibid., p. 71.

16. "Medieval Doctrine to the Lateran Council of 1215," in *Cambridge Medieval History,* ed. J. R. Tanner et al. (Cambridge: Cambridge University Press, 1929), VI, 659–660.

17. R. W. Southern, *St. Anselm and His Biographer* (Cambridge: Cambridge University Press, 1963), p. 101.

18. Payen, *Le Motif du repentir,* p. 34.

19. St. Benedict's prologue to his *Rule* is actually a call to conversion by which "you may return to Him from whom you had departed by the sloth of disobedience." Leonard Doyle, trans., *St. Benedict's Rule for Monasteries* (Collegeville, Minn.: St. John's Abbey Press, 1948), p. 1. The word "conversio" means literally a "turning."

20. Payen, *Le Motif du repentir,* pp. 33–36.

21. George Misch, *Geschichte der Autobiographie* (Frankfurt am Main: Schulte-Bulmke, 1959), III, pt. 2, 109, quoted in *Self and Society in Medieval France: The Memoirs of Guibert of Nogent,* trans. John Benton (New York: Harper and Row, 1970), p. 7.

22. My analysis of the conversion of Guibert's mother is an extension of Payen's suggestive remarks in *Le Motif du repentir,* p. 43.

23. *De vita sua, PL,* 156, cols. 863–864. Translated by Benton, *Self and Society,* p. 74.

24. *PL,* 156, col. 864. Translated by Benton, *Self and Society,* p. 74.

25. *PL,* 156, col. 864. Translated by Benton, *Self and Society,* pp. 75–76.

26. *PL,* 156, col. 865. Translated by Benton, *Self and Society,* p. 76.

27. See Payen, *Le Motif du repentir,* p. 43.

28. McNeill, *Cure of Souls,* pp. 124–127.

29. *Decretum,* Bk. 19, *PL,* 140, col. 949.

30. Payen treats these works extensively in *Le Motif du repentir.*

31. Joseph W. Yedlicka, *Expressions of the Linguistic Area of Repentance and Remorse in Old French* (Washington, D.C.: Catholic University Press, 1945), pp. 20, 34, 79, 384, points out the frequent recurrence of the language of "tariff-balancing" in popular French literature through the fifteenth century.

32. See St. Gregory's *Moralia on the Book of Job, PL,* 76, cols. 291-292; Benedicta Ward, *The Prayers and Meditations of St. Anselm* (Middlesex: Penguin, 1973), p. 55; and Payen, *Le Motif du repentir,* pp. 37 ff.

33. *Sermones super Cantica Canticorum,* ed. Jean Leclercq et al., I, 15.

34. *S. Anselmi: Opera Omnia,* ed. F. S. Schmitt (Edinburgh: Nelson, 1946), III, 9. Translated by Ward, *Prayers and Meditations,* pp. 98-99. See also Southern, *St. Anselm and his Biographer,* pp. 36-37, for discussion of the recipients of Anselm's prayers.

35. *Opera,* Schmitt, III, 3. Translated by Ward, *Prayers and Meditations,* p. 89. For a discussion of the significance and originality of Anselm's form of prayer, see Southern, *St. Anselm and His Biographer,* pp. 34-47.

36. See *De speculo caritatis, Aelredi Rievallensis: Opera Omnia,* ed. A. Hoste and C. H. Talbot (Turnhout: Corpus Christianorum, Continuatio mediaevalis, 1971), I, 91.

37. Southern, *St. Anselm and His Biographer,* pp. 95-98.

38. *Opera,* Schmitt, II, 42-133. The story of how Anselm came to write this extraordinary treatise and how reluctant he was to accept his own startling conclusions is interesting and provides ample evidence against those critics who assume that no orthodox Christian would take issue with, or even think critically about, St. Augustine's theology. The best introduction to St. Anselm, and certainly the liveliest, is that of R. W. Southern, *St. Anselm and His Biographer.*

39. *Ibid.,* pp. 100-101; see also pp. 93-97. The story has interesting parallels with the Christ-knight allegory in the *Ancrene Wisse* (T198-199). Both depend heavily upon feudal custom in trying to explain why God deserves our love. But it is important to note that in the *Wisse,* attention is focused not, as in Anselm, on the species Man, but on the individual lady on whose behalf the Christ-knight acts. For evidence of Anselm's primary interest in species in other works, see Morris, *The Discovery of the Individual,* pp. 64-65. It is also important to note that in the *Ancrene Wisse* the service is performed not to pay any debt but to win the lady's love. Thus the story, as told by the *Wisse* author, depends much more upon the Abelardian concept of the Incarnation than upon the Anselmian view.

40. *Expositio in "ad Romanos" PL,* 178, col. 836. Translated in Morris, *The Discovery of the Individual,* p. 144. Also quoted in Southern, *St. Anselm and His Biographer,* p. 96.

41. See D. E. Luscombe, *The School of Peter Abelard* (Cambridge: Cambridge University Press, 1969), pp. 274-275.

42. R. W. Southern, "From Epic to Romance," in *The Making of the Middle Ages,* pp. 219-257, provides ample evidence from both art and literature of this transformation of God's image.

43. Payen, *Le Motif du repentir,* p. 56.

44. *PL,* 40, cols. 1111-1130. A discussion of this treatise appears in Amédée Teetaert, *La Confession aux laïques dans l'Eglise Latine* (Paris: Gabalda, 1926), especially pp. 50-56.

45. *Ibid.,* pp. 45-84.

46. Teetaert's study traces the history of the practice in great detail. Payen, *Le*

Motif du repentir, p. 51, n. 152 notes that the Church had a good deal of difficulty eliminating the popular practice; as late as 1280 bishops were still excommunicating laymen illegitimately hearing confessions.

47. *PL*, 40, col. 1122. See Teetaert, *Confession aux laïques*, p. 52.

48. *PL*, 40, col. 1122.

49. Ibid. See Teetaert, *Confession aux laïques*, pp. 52 ff.

50. See Teetaert, *Confession aux laïques*, especially 248–251.

51. See Teetaert, *Confession aux laïques*, pp. 236–241, for an impressive list of theologians who followed Abelard's contritionist theory of confession. Theologians did part company with Abelard on his at least partial renunciation of the priest's power of the keys (the keys left by Christ to the apostles [Matthew 16:18], by which they could bind men to, or loose them from, their sins). But most thinkers, Hugh and Richard of St. Victor excepted, agreed with Abelard's emphasis on contrition in the sacrament of confession. For discussions of the difficulty in ascertaining Abelard's final stand on the issue of the power of the keys, see Luscombe, *The School of Peter Abelard*, pp. 140–141, and A. Victor Murray, *Abelard and St. Bernard: A Study in Twelfth-Century Modernism* (Manchester: Manchester University Press, 1967), pp. 68–69. Certainly in the *Scito te ipsum*, at least, Abelard is tentative and conciliatory on the subject. See *Peter Abelard's Ethics*, ed. and trans. D. E. Luscombe (Oxford: Clarendon Press, 1971), pp. 113–127, "Utrum generaliter ad omnes pertineat prelatos soluere et ligare."

52. See Luscombe, *Ethics*, p. 46, n. 1. Luscombe notes that Abelard was not alone and was probably not the first to claim the moral indifference of actions, "for some writers of the school of Anselm of Laon discussed the same view." On the ambiguity of the term "will," see Payen (*Le Motif du repentir*, p. 60), who points out that "will" can mean either desire or a natural tendency. For Abelard's discussion of will, see Luscombe, *Ethics*, pp. 6 ff. On Abelard's failure to avoid the same kind of ambiguity in his own terminology see Luscombe's notes, p. 8, n. 2; p. 25, n. 5; pp. 42–43, n. 2. For a general discussion of the word "will," see Robert Blomme, *La Doctrine du péché dans les écoles théologiques de la première moitié du XIIᵉ siècle* (Louvain: Publications Universitaires de Louvain, 1958), pp. 168 ff.

53. Luscombe, *Ethics*, p. 6–7.

54. Blomme, *La Doctrine du péché*, p. 115.

55. Luscombe, *Ethics*, pp. 14–15.

56. Ibid., pp. 88–89.

57. Ibid., p. 98, n. 2.

58. Ibid., p. 98.

59. See Ibid., pp. 98–101.

60. See Teetaert, *Confession aux laïques*, pp. 85–87. The more contrition is motivated by love of God rather than by fear of punishment, the more "perfect" it is. The notion of perfect contrition is another step in the direction of the monastic penitential sensibility, because it tends to eliminate the idea of punishment altogether from repentance. Toward the end of the twelfth century, the concept of "attrition," or imperfect contrition is invented, as the only kind of contrition most men are capable of. For the development of the term and its importance in the con-

fession controversy see Teetaert, pp. 258 ff., and Payen, *Le Motif du repentir,* pp. 81–83.

61. Teetaert, *Confession aux laïques,* pp. 236–241. Gratian is a possible exception. See Payen, *Le Motif du repentir,* pp. 70–71.

62. The term "contritionist" is Payen's. See *Le Motif du repentir,* chap. 2, "Le Contritionisme," pp. 54–75.

63. Robert Blomme sees Abelard's penitential theory as a direct criticism of the old harsh penitential system, but D. E. Luscombe disagrees, pointing to passages in the *Scito te ipsum* (notably pp. 104, 105, 108, 109) where Abelard seems to condone the harsh penances listed in some of the old manuals. See Luscombe, *Ethics,* pp. xxxii–xxxiii. Although I can agree that in these passages Abelard attempts to justify the harsh penances of the penitentials, his justification seems to me more a concession to an old tradition than a moral argument. Abelard makes the same careful concession in discussing the power of the keys, pp. 113 ff. Because in his scheme the levying of penance is useful but not necessary, the bulk of his theory could not help but draw attention away from external satisfaction and toward contrition itself as the greater part of satisfaction.

64. See Teetaert, *Confession aux laïques,* pp. 124–129, and Payen, *Le Motif du repentir,* pp. 66–70.

65. Teetaert, *Confession aux laïques,* p. 257. F. Broomfield, ed., *Thomae de Chobham: Summa confessorum* (Louvain: Editions Nauwelaerts, 1968), pp. xli ff., has an interesting discussion of the text of Canon Twenty-One.

66. Anciaux, *The Sacrament of Penance,* p. 110.

67. Broomfield, *Summa,* pp. xli ff. Broomfield notes that "from the tenth century onwards confession before each and every Communion was demanded with increasing emphasis. Hence, before 1215, there was a theoretical obligation to receive these sacraments three times a year." The emphasis is on the theoretical, of course, because in practice confession was very infrequent.

68. See Moorman, *The History of the Franciscan Order,* pp. 121–122, 363, 373–374.

69. Broomfield, *Summa,* p. xvii. For the range of possible subject matter and method in the *summae,* see p. xvii.

70. See *Summa,* Article Seven, "Que penitentia cui peccato sit iniungenda," especially pp. 344, 349, and 361.

71. Ibid., p. 345.

72. Ibid., p. 344. Broomfield notes that both Robert of Flamborough and Bartholomew of Exeter, from whose penitentials Thomas borrows extensively, impose a three-year penance for this sin.

73. Ibid., p. xv.

74. See Payen, *Le Motif du repentir,* pp. 566–567.

75. Broomfield, *Summa,* p. 45.

76. See Broomfield, *Summa,* pp. 45–61, 290–308, and in the section covering each sin.

77. Ibid., pp. 86–198, 5–13, 198–231.

78. Broomfield, *Summa,* p. xvi. D. W. Robertson, "A Note on the Classical Origin of 'Circumstances' in the Medieval Confessional," *Studies in Philology,* 43

(1946), 9, notes that the medieval source for the theory of circumstances was Cicero's *De inventione,* in which Cicero outlines for rhetoricians how the *narratio* "should be made more credible."

79. Payen, *Le Motif du repentir,* pp. 558 ff.

80. Ibid., p. 561.

81. See Broomfield, *Summa,* p. xv. For the history of the notion of conscience see Odon Lottin's massive study, *Psychologie et morale au XIIe et XIIIe siècles* (Louvain: Abbaye du Mont César, 1948), II, pt. 1, 103–417. See also M. D. Chenu's far less technical discussion, *L'Eveil de la conscience dans la civilisation médiévale* (Paris: Librairie J. Vrin, 1969). Closely related to both the confession controversy and the new interest in the notion of conscience is the widespread interest from the twelfth century forward in the Socratic dictum, "Know thyself." On the history and development of the notion see: Pierre Courcelle, *Connais-toi toi-même de Socrate à Saint Bernard,* 2 vols. (Paris: Etudes Augustiniennes, 1974–1975); J. A. W. Bennett, "*Nosce te ipsum:* Some Medieval Interpretations," in *J. R. R. Tolkien, Scholar and Storyteller: Essays in Memoriam,* ed. Mary Salu and Robert T. Farrell (Ithaca: Cornell University Press, 1979), pp. 138–158; and Joseph Wittig, " 'Piers Plowman' B, Passus ix–xii: Elements in the Design of the Inward Journey," *Traditio,* 28 (1972), 211–280.

82. Luscombe, *Ethics,* p. xv.

83. Payen, in *Le Motif du repentir,* pp. 569, n. 55, correctly notes that there are great differences between works like the *Ancrene Wisse,* written for laywomen, and confession manuals written for the clergy. But he implies that there are other confession manuals written for laymen, upon which the *Ancrene Wisse* author relies. He does not name those sources; furthermore, since the earliest confession manuals written for laymen that Payen discusses are all written considerably later that the *Ancrene Wisse,* one wonders what possible sources he could have in mind. He lists Jean de Journey's *Dîme de pénitence* written in 1288, as the first confession manual written for laymen (p. 558).

84. *Sentences, PL,* 192, col. 887. Translated by Palmer, *Sacraments and Forgiveness,* p. 195.

85. *Sentences, PL,* 192, col. 885. Translated by Palmer, *Sacraments and Forgiveness,* p. 194.

86. Actually the author's fluid use of the terms "inner" and "outer" might raise questions for any reader. Here is seems that the author no sooner mentions the most interior part of the sacrament of confession, a deep-felt shame for having sinned, than he reverses direction altogether, referring to the sacrament as "exterior penance."

87. Paul Anciaux, *La Théologie du sacrement de pénitence au XIIe siècle* (Louvain: Nauwelaerts, 1949), pp. 373–383. Peter Lombard, Peter Manducator, Simon of Tournai, and Stephen Langton all considered exterior penance as the "sign" of the sacrament.

88. See Broomfield, *Summa,* p. 13, and Anciaux, *Théologie du sacrement de pénitence,* pp. 364–373.

89. "Ah efter þe absolution, he schal þus segge" (T176).

90. See Grayson, *Structure and Imagery in "Ancrene Wisse,"* pp. 147–148.

4. Self-Awareness and Sin

1. J. H. Gray, "The Influence of Confessional Literature on the Composition of the 'Ancrene Riwle,' " Ph.D. diss., University of London, 1961), pp. 65, 85.

2. Ibid., pp. 64–65.

3. Ibid., p. 92.

4. See Butler, *Benedictine Monachism,* pp. 48–49, 62–63.

5. The relationship between the birds of part III and the beasts of part IV was brought to my attention by Joanne Kleidon, a graduate student at Columbia University in 1975.

6. Morton Bloomfield, *The Seven Deadly Sins* (1952; rpt. East Lansing: Michigan State University Press, 1967), chap. 2, "The Origin of the Seven Cardinal Sins," particularly pp. 148 ff.

7. See especially T126; S109, and T156; S135.

8. Siegfried Wenzel informs me that "tale" in this passage probably means "tale" or "story" rather than "number," as Salu translates, and refers to a tale about a desert father and the devil that appears in *Vitae patrum,* 665 (*PL,* 73, col. 1027).

9. See Hope Emily Allen, "Some Fourteenth Century Borrowings from 'Ancren Riwle.' " *Modern Language Review,* 18 (1923), 1–8.

10. *The Owl and the Nightingale,* ed. Eric G. Stanley (1960; rpt. New York: Barnes and Noble Imports, 1972), ll. 762–766.

> Oft spet wel a lute liste
> þar muche strengþe sholde miste:
> Mid lutle strengþe þurh ginne
> Castel an burӡ me mai iwinne.

11. See, for example, T106–107; S91, T117; S101, T126; S109, T139–142; S120–122.

Index

Abelard, Peter: *Scito te ipsum,* 2, 95–97, 101, 109, 111; *Expositio in "ad Romanos,"* 92

Aelred of Rievaulx: *De vita eremitica,* 37, 42–49, 50, 51, 58, 64, 66, 70–71, 148n12; *De speculo caritatis,* 91

Allen, Hope Emily, 9, 150n28, 152n42, 153n50

Anchorhold, 3, 7, 33–34, 51, 53–54, 59–65, 77

Ancren Riwle, 8

Ancrene Wisse author, 3, 9

Anselm, St.: *Orationes,* 90; *Cur Deus homo,* 91–93

Asceticism, 3–4, 18, 31, 32–34, 120–123, 133, 156n32; in *Life of Christina of Markyate,* 37, 39–41; in *De vita eremitica,* 37–38, 45–49, 70–71

Augustine, St., 1, 13–15, 159n6. *See also Regula Augustini*

Benedict, St., 8, 11–13, 22, 23, 24, 30, 45, 160n19

Benedictine-Cistercian quarrel, 12–13, 15, 28–29, 150n28, 153n50

Bernard of Clairvaux, 27, 36–37, 72, 73–74, 150n28, 157n46, n49, 159n65

Blomme, Robert, 95, 163n63

Bloomfield, Morton, 127

Brewer, Derek, 9, 152n41

Broomfield, F., 99, 163n65

Brunne, Robert, 101

Burchard of Worms, 89

Canons, 9, 13. *See also Regula Augustini*

Cat, anchoress's, 4–5, 65

Chambers, R. W., 146n10

The Chastising of God's Children, 134

Chastity, 72; in *De vita eremitica,* 45–46; in *Life of Christina of Markyate,* 155n19, 156n21

Chenu, M. D., 15, 17, 150n29

Christ, *see* God

Christ-knight allegory, 73, 77, 161n39

Christina of Markyate, Life of, 37, 38–42, 49, 50, 65, 152n46

"Circumstances" of sin, *see* Sin

Cistercians, 12–13, 14, 15, 18, 27, 28, 30, 31, 150n28, 153n50

The Cloud of Unknowing, 69

Compunction, 90–91

Confession, 2–3; in *Ancrene Wisse,* 7, 25–26, 61, 79–80, 101–119, 120–121, 124, 140–142; history of, 81–91; twelfth-century controversy over, 81, 93–98; as sacrament, 97–98; manuals, 99–102, 115, 159n13, 163n63; psychological benefits of, 110–114; devil's parody of, 133. *See also* Penance, canonical

Conscience, 3, 26–27, 100, 101, 141. *See also* Self-examination

Contrition, 113, 162n60

Contritionism, 94–98, 106–107, 110, 119, 162n60

Cur Deus homo, see St. Anselm

Dating of *Ancrene Wisse,* 3, 152n42, n43

David (King), 61–62, 123

Despair, 26–27, 125–126

De vera et falsa poenitentia, 94–95, 109

De vita eremitica, see Aelred of Rievaulx

Desert tradition, 34–36, 40, 43–46, 50–57, 64–65, 77. *See also* Solitary life

Devil, 131–140

Dickinson, J. C., 13
Dobson, E. J., 3, 9-11, 145n10,
    146n12, 148n9, 151n39, 152n44
Dumont, Charles, 147n2
Dymes, D. M. E., 146n10

Eremitic revival, 35-37, 53
Ethics, see Abelard, Scito te ipsum
Eve, 62-64

Felperin, Winifred, 148n4, 158n59
Francis, St., 17-18, 19, 21, 30, 31
Friars, 15, 17, 18, 28, 31, 32, 98-99,
    152n43

God, image of, 1-2, 33, 84-85, 91-93;
    in Ancrene Wisse, 50, 71-78,
    134-136; in De vita eremitica, 46-49
Gospel, 15-17, 21, 30-31
Gray, J. H., 120, 140
Grayson, Janet, 3, 57-59, 62, 145n7,
    148n11, 158n60
Gregorian Reform Movement, 35-36
Gregory, St., 84, 161n32
Guibert of Nogent, 85-88, 115

Handlyng Synne, 100-101
Hanning, Robert, 155n18
Haskins, Charles Homer, 1
Hugh of Flavigny, 155n19

Imagery, 32, 56, 57-59, 60-78, 111,
    126, 127
Incarnation theories, 84-85, 91-93,
    134, 135-136
Individuality, 1-2, 5-7; and religious
    rules, 15-18, 27, 31; in the solitary
    life, 3, 34; and confession, 81, 89,
    95-98, 100-101. See also Self-aware-
    ness, Self-examination
Inner-outer dichotomy, 5-7, 141-142,
    164n86; in religious rules, 20-23,
    31; in imagery, 32-33, 57-58; in De
    vita eremitica, 45-49; in the solitary
    life, 50, 54-78; in confession contro-
    versy, 110-111
Intention, 95-96, 101

Jerome, St., 44
Judith, 51, 54, 59, 64, 103-107

Kaske, Robert, 157n46
"Know Thyself," 164n81. See also Abe-
    lard, Scito te ipsum

Lateran, Fourth Council of, 81, 93, 98
Leclercq, Jean, 149n16
Legalism, 12-18, 27-30
Life of St. Alexis, 54
Life of St. Cuthbert, 35
Lombard, Peter, 97, 105-106
Love, 7, 19-21, 22-23, 31, 66-78; in
    De vita eremitica, 47-49
Luscombe, D. E., 96, 101, 163n63

Magoun, Francis, 147n4
McNabb, Vincent, 9, 148n9
Macpherson, Mary Paul, 147n2
Monastic values, 11-12, 14, 15, 30-31,
    33, 35, 43, 85, 89-90, 93-94,
    120-123, 141. See also Asceticism;
    St. Benedict; Chastity; Cistercians;
    Obedience
Morris, Colin, 83, 145n5
Morton, James, 8, 147n4
Mysticism, 73-78, 79

Obedience, 23-27, 30

Payen, Jean Charles, 85, 160n13,
    164n83
Pelican, as solitary, 55-56, 123
Penance, canonical, 82-83, 87, 88-89,
    99, 101, 109-110, 117-119. See also
    Confession
Peter of Blois, 153n50
Peter the Chanter (Verbum abbrevia-
    tum), 15-16, 19, 21, 26, 29, 30-31,
    101
Peter the Venerable, 36-37
Philip of Navarre, 155n19
Presumption, 26, 125-126

Regula Augustini, 9-11, 13-15, 18, 23,
    29, 30
Regula monasteriorum, see St. Benedict
Richard of St. Victor, 66-69, 71
Robert of Flamborough, 100
Robertson, D. W., 163n78
Romance, 1-2, 77

Rules, religious: in *Ancrene Wisse*, 6–7, 8–11, 18–31, 138–139; and antirules, 9, 13–15, 31; history of, 11–18. *See also Regula Augustini;* St. Benedict; Obedience

Saints' lives, 34–35, 54, 155n19. *See also* individual titles
Salu, M. B., 79, 120, 152n45, 153n47
Scito te ipsum, see Abelard
Self-awareness, 2–3, 5–6, 7, 23, 29–30, 119, 123–142. *See also* Individuality; Self-examination
Self-examination, 3, 7, 139–142; in early penitential practice, 83–84; in Guibert de Nogent's memoirs, 87–88. *See also* Conscience; Individuality; Self-awareness
Shepherd, Geoffrey, 145n7, 146n12, 150n30
Sin, 7, 120–140; inevitability of, 7, 50, 61, 78, 139; psychology of, 62–64, 113, 131–140; intention and, 95–96, 101; circumstances surrounding, 99–100, 116–117; versus temptation, 120, 140. *See also* Confession; Devil; Temptation
Sitwell, Gerard, 79–81, 101–102, 120, 153n52
Smalley, Beryl, 66
Solitary life, 3–6; homey details of, 4–5, 64–66, 71–78, 127–128, 134; in *Ancrene Wisse,* 32–34, 50–78; early history of, 34–37; in *Life of Christina of Markyate,* 37, 38–42, 49–50; in *De vita eremitica,* 37, 42–49, 49–50. *See also* Desert Tradition

Southern, R. W., 1–2, 12, 14, 91–92, 161n38, n42
Squire, Aelred, 45

Teetaert, Amédée, 161n44
Temptation, 69–71, 120, 123–126; as process, 131–133, 136–140; comforts against, 134–136. *See also* Devil; Sin
Tertullian, 81
Theology, 140; moral, 2, 100–101, 121–124, 141–142; of law, 15–16; rules of, 19–20; Victorine, 66; of the Incarnation, 84–85, 91–93; of confession, 93–98, 102–110, 114–119
Thomas of Chobham, 99–100
Thompson, A. Hamilton, 84
Twelfth-Century Renaissance, 1–3, 6–7

Ullmann, Walter, 27
Unity, 7, 79–80, 120

Vandenbrouke, François, 151n33
Verbum abbreviatum, see Peter the Chanter
Victorine theology, *see* Theology
de Vitry, Jacques (*Historia occidentalis*), 16–17, 30

Wenzel, Siegfried, 148n9, 165n8
Wilson, R. M., 65
Windows, *see* anchorhold
Women and chastity, 155n19
Worldly desires, 2, 5–6, 32–33, 49, 53–78, 114; in *Life of Christina of Markyate,* 40–42; in *De vita eremitica,* 47–49